Proceedings of the 2015 BALEAP Conference

EAP in a rapidly changing landscape: Issues, challenges and solutions

Edited by
Jenny Kemp

The global forum for
EAP professionals

Published by
Garnet Publishing Ltd.
8 Southern Court
South Street
Reading RG1 4QS, UK

ISBN: 978-1-78260-345-0

British Cataloguing-in-Publication Data
A catalogue record for this book is available at the
British Library.

Production
Project manager: Clare Chandler
Editorial team: Kate Kemp, Sarah MacDonald,
                       Jean McCutcheon
Design and layout: Sam Barden

Printed and bound
in Lebanon by International Press: interpress@int-press.com

Contents

Jenny Kemp

INTRODUCTION

In 2014, BALEAP officially adopted the strapline 'the global forum for EAP professionals', and the Leicester BALEAP 2015 conference was certainly a big step in the right direction, drawing over 300 delegates from more than a dozen countries, including China, Italy, Luxembourg, New Zealand, Russia, Sweden, Switzerland, Turkey and the United States. This volume reports on EAP contexts as geographically diverse as Bangladesh, Canada, Hong Kong and the UAE.

The theme of the 2015 conference was *EAP in a rapidly changing landscape: Issues, challenges and solutions*. This was an appropriate theme to capture at a conference, a dynamic event where you can have a snapshot of all that is going on in EAP at any one moment. There were 126 presentations, posters and workshops at the conference. This volume, published two years on, aims to represent that snapshot – but also to carry it forward into the world in which we find ourselves in 2017. But a conference is not just the themes that were decided in advance – it is also the themes

that emerge during presentations and discussions, such as the growth of English as a Medium of Instruction (EMI), the expansion of online learning and the value of reflection. This is one of the values of attending the conference, and of reading the papers collected in the proceedings.

The volume is divided into four sections: *Globalisation, acculturation, socialisation; Knowledge of ourselves and of our learners; Approaches to genre and discourse* and *Achieving specificity*. Though the papers all fall within these themes, it should be remembered that the headings are largely for convenience: just because a paper is not in Section III does not mean that it is not about discourse, for example; and arguably all the contributions increase our understanding of teachers and learners. For this reason, a thematic index can be found at www.baleap.org/resources that will enable you to find papers relevant to your interests and needs.

I have chosen Rebecca Hughes' plenary paper, *Navigation in a complex world,* to head the volume (and Section I) because she sketches a context for all our EAP practices.

She explains current trends, and gives us an idea of the direction in which the field is going and how EAP may look five to ten years from now. As BALEAP becomes more global, there are 'tectonic shifts' occurring in the EAP landscape (Hughes, p. 20). The impact of this globalising of EAP is, according to Hughes, that our students' needs are changing. Many started English at an earlier age and have access to wider resources than previously; increasing numbers have experience of EMI contexts. As a result, those coming to Britain may have higher general language abilities. They are also coming from a wider range of L1 backgrounds. Hughes suggests that what our students are aiming at has also altered. She draws our attention to the increasing number of multinational and multidisciplinary teams producing academic papers and argues that second-language writers are now aiming at a wider audience than in the past, and that we need to prepare students to join this much more complex conversation.

Hughes' paper opens the first section, *Globalisation, acculturation, socialisation,* and this theme is continued in the papers that follow. Irina Veleanu and Simon Gooch discuss the value of student reflection in relation to academic literacy, arguing that although acculturation is important, we should encourage students to establish their individual identity within an academic community. The next three papers describe the challenges and issues faced by courses which aim to prepare learners for the sorts of contexts that Hughes has described and propose potential solutions. Simon Gooch and Elaine Smith stress the need to develop student awareness of communities of practice and how they achieved this through a student conference on a general

pre-sessional course where students presented on discipline-specific topics. Blair Matthews then describes an online pre-sessional course which prepares students for studies in the UK by focusing on student life in a British city, as well as developing academic writing and critical responses to text. This section concludes with a paper by Julie Watson, who describes the success of another online course, this time designed to prepare students for their pre-sessional course by raising awareness of study skills through reflection, as well as developing language and skills.

Section II, *Knowledge of ourselves and of our learners,* will be of particular interest to teacher educators, TEAP Scheme participants and others who are eager to develop themselves professionally. The opening paper by Bee Bond emphasises the need for scholarly activity and recommends Exploratory Practice (EP) as a practical way for busy EAP professionals to engage with research. She uses the perennial puzzle of spelling to illustrate EP principles in practice. Maggie Heeney also focuses on the teacher, arguing that if they are to help their students, teachers need to be aware of the cognitive strategies they themselves employ when reading to write. Through cognitive modelling (think aloud) Heeney encourages the reader to consider their own teacher talk and whether they are a 'cognitive teacher'. With Dina Awad's paper, we turn our attention more specifically to the learner, in particular, to Arab learners in the UAE. She looks at task types and the types of cognitive knowledge that tasks tap into, which will be of interest to materials developers. Zoe Gazeley-Eke then focuses on extending students' academic skills by addressing the digital skills needs of her in-sessional students. She stresses the importance of learning technologies and gives us a vivid picture of how online collaborative software can be used in classes in an engaging way. Student engagement and motivation are also central to the final paper in this section: through the practical implementation of a Self-determination Theory framework, Mehtap Kocatepe addresses the issue of how to get students to do their homework. As with other papers in this section, her recommendations for future research may be of interest if you are looking for a research project.

One advantage of attending a conference is that many of the sessions get participants talking, enthusing and carrying the ideas forward into suggestions for practical application. One such talk at the 2015 conference was Steve Kirk's talk on *Waves of Reflection*. Legitimation Code Theory has been gaining ground in the social sciences, particularly since the publication of Maton's (2013, 2014) work on semantic waves and knowledge building. What Kirk does is to apply this model to an EAP context by looking at reflective writing in Anthropology. As he states, the model can be applied to other academic genres and no doubt you will consider its potential as you read his paper. Kirk has been placed at the start of Section III on *Approaches to genre and discourse*.

Continuing this section, we have two papers that compare an analysis of authentic discourse as captured in corpora with that found in published textbooks and materials. With student written reports as her example, Sheena Gardner looks at macrostructures, genre families and registers, while Katrien Deroey illustrates the issues by focusing on importance markers in lectures. Both papers make enlightening comparisons which will no doubt inform your teaching, testing and materials development. Olga Burakov

raises our awareness of the extent to which figurative language is used in academic text, particularly scientific text, and advocates teaching students to recognise and interpret its function. The last two papers in Section III concern how students respond to writing feedback. Jill Northcott, Pauline Gillies and David Caulton describe the benefits of writing feedback and share some guidelines on giving effective feedback. This is followed by Simon Smith and Christopher Smith's paper, which is centred on a collaboration between EAP specialists and content experts in order to help students write a literature review; indeed, the authorship of the paper – one is an EAP specialist, the other an engineer – is a sign of that collaboration. They share interesting findings concerning how their students responded to feedback.

The theme of Section IV is *Achieving specificity*. Illustrated with an example from his own EMI context in Hong Kong, Ken Hyland's plenary paper gives linguistic and discourse evidence to support the need for consideration of discipline specificity. He further justifies this approach through a description of how discourse communities vary in their approach to the notion of academic identity. David Donnarumma and Emma Blyth then discuss the theoretical underpinnings and design of an online in-sessional course for Law undergraduates, using student feedback to evaluate the success of the online content and interaction. This is followed by Anne Heaton, Andrew Preshous and Simon Smith, who provide an insight into how an in-sessional ESAP course can inform discipline-specific skills and language development in a general (EGAP) pre-sessional. The final paper in this section and the volume is, in fact, an amalgamation of two conference talks given independently by each author: Andrew Preshous and Jenny

Kemp each spoke on a similar theme, but looked at different disciplinary contexts. In this joint practical paper, the authors show how corpora can be used to develop materials which focus on discipline-specific vocabulary. They also advocate raising awareness of vocabulary knowledge through the use of concordances and suggest a methodology for readers to try.

To close this introduction, I would like to turn to the theme of the need for scholarship in EAP. You will notice that several authors refer to their eagerness to investigate and evaluate their own practices in order to improve. Bee Bond expresses this very succinctly:

> '… in order to fully meet the needs of students, it is vital for teachers to escape the sense of being on a seemingly endless EAP treadmill, and to re-engage with their teaching and their students in a scholarly manner.'
>
> (p. 65)

This lies at the very heart of what BALEAP is all about, and at the heart of the TEAP Scheme. The need for scholarship,

and for the promotion of scholarship, was one of the emergent themes from the conference, and was developed by the then Chair of BALEAP, Diane Schmitt, in her plenary at the Sheffield PIM in Autumn 2015. She argued that not only is it essential that theory informs practice, but practice must necessarily also inform theory, to complete the cycle. The contributors to the conference, and to this volume, have all made a step in the right direction. And so will you, by reading it, reflecting upon what you have read and then acting upon it.

TEAP RESOURCES

In order to encourage continuing professional development and scholarly activity, this volume is accompanied by tasks on the BALEAP website that will encourage readers to develop their knowledge and explore their own practices. The tasks can be found here: https://www.baleap.org/accreditation/individuals/teap-resources.

ACKNOWLEDGEMENTS

BALEAP would like to thank Philip Horspool and his Leicester team for their hard work in organising the conference. The success of the event was also due in no small part to the activity and enthusiasm of the presenters and delegates.

This volume would not have been possible without the commitment of Jean McCutcheon, the administrator and copy editor, and of the peer reviewers: Sue Argent, Sam Barclay, Bee Bond, Sarah Brewer, Ian Bruce, Maggie Charles, Edward de Chazal, Katrien Deroey, Charlene Dobson, Phil Durrant, Andy Gillet, Sandra Haywood, Mick Kavanagh, Steve Kirk, Martin Seviour, Hilary Nesi, Jayne Pearson, Steven Peters, Lisa Robinson, Diane Schmitt, Jenifer Spencer, Melinda Whong and John Wrigglesworth.

SECTION I
Globalisation, acculturation, socialisation

REBECCA HUGHES

NAVIGATION IN A COMPLEX WORLD: ENGLISH AS COMPASS OR MAP?

INTRODUCTION

I would like to open the first paper in this collection with some questions relating to students' needs and our assumptions about 21st-century international students. Which is the better-prepared candidate for study in the UK and a global career? Is it the bi- or often trilingual international student taught science from an early age in their home country in English, or the monolingual UK student who may never have left the shores of Britain or spoken to anyone from a very different culture? In this paper, I present a high-level overview to the practitioners and theorists of academic English teaching of what I consider the major changes that are shaping the needs and demands of international students and academics. These changes mean that our models of the international student and their needs will be required to develop in some quite new, and potentially exciting, directions.

Those who work with international students to support them in preparation for studies in the medium of English are helping them to navigate their paths to study in an increasingly complex, fast-changing and connected world. Academics are working across borders and publishing in multi-author teams in increasing numbers. Transnational education is booming and HESA (the Higher Education Standards Agency) statistics show that it was around 2011 that the numbers of international students undertaking a UK degree outside the British Isles started to outstrip those taking one on our shores, and these numbers continue to rise steeply. Many parts of the world where large numbers of students come from to study in the UK are themselves teaching content subjects in English from an early age as part of their state curriculum. Simultaneously, increasing numbers of international higher education institutions are starting to teach in the medium of English; taken together with increases in the teaching of English in primary and secondary schools, these phenomena have strengthened the language skills of young people dramatically in key markets for UK institutions and somewhat altered the balance of what teaching and learning is like 'home and abroad'. This paper asks what the role of those supporting students in their journey towards a successful completion of their degree might need to take into account in future, if we extrapolate from these trends and other demographic data. However, I begin this brief survey with a look at some of the most exciting academic achievements in 2014/15 that exemplify different types of scholarly collaboration. The nature of the academic activity behind these achievements is changing radically and rapidly, and the students we prepare are joining and are part of this changing landscape.

Academic teams are increasingly international, larger, and often interdisciplinary. They are also engaging with other major trends that are flowing from our online lives, such as the capacity for citizen science, and sharing of large data sets to create tailored solutions for individuals. These have included the landing of a probe on a comet by a pan-European scientific team (Klingelhoefer, Girones Lopez, Schmanke, Markovski, Brückner, d'Uston, Economu & Gellert, 2015); the halting of the spread of the Ebola virus in Africa by social scientists, scientists and public health officials understanding how burial practices were promoting the spread of the disease (Boscarino & Adams, 2015); the pushing back by four hundred thousand years the beginnings of symbolic representation of ideas (by a woman who had originally trained as a marine biologist) (Joordens, d'Errico, Wesselingh, Munro, De Vos, Wallinga, Ankjærgaard, Reimann, Wijbrans, Kuiper & Mücher, 2014); and the emergence of the amazing potential for personalised medicine in, for instance, the

area of targeted cures for cancer tailored to the individual body's responses to the treatment (Delamarre, Mellman & Yadav, 2015). This paper sets out in greater detail some of these major drivers that we see shaping English for Academic Purposes at large and changing the demands on students, academics and those who support them.

Against this backdrop, the paper is built around three main points that particularly influence the student 'journey' to effective communication in academic settings. These are that students worldwide are gaining access to better levels of English from earlier ages than ever before; that the nature of academic communities and practices is changing rapidly; and that we have increasing data to inform our curriculum and teaching from demographic and other sources.

STUDENTS ARE GAINING ACCESS TO BETTER LEVELS OF ENGLISH FROM EARLIER AGES

Students are increasingly coming to their academic studies from education systems that give them access to English either as a foreign language or as a medium of instruction from earlier ages and in greater numbers. We have seen the rise of the near-bilingual EU student as a norm in the latter half of the 20th century. Other systems are also adopting English as part of their core curriculum, as well as teaching other subjects through this medium. These changes in the educational systems of students' countries of origin are beginning to alter the nature of the students' educational journey and the academic English input that the students will require.

THE NATURE OF ACADEMIC PRACTICE IS CHANGING

The academic world is changing fast and these changes are shaping the landscape in which students and practitioners work. Science and scholarship are ever more rapidly 'going global'; ever larger teams of academics are working across international borders and English is their shared tool for communication. I opened with some examples of exciting large-scale scholarly activity and breakthroughs for the year 2014. Crucially, for those who help to prepare the next generation of academics, these academic teams will, on the whole, be communicating with one another in the medium of English and, increasingly, working in large, multi-language and multicultural teams. This is changing the nature of academic communication and the norms we teach to.

WE CAN USE DEMOGRAPHIC DATA TO INCREASE OUR PREPAREDNESS TO SUPPORT EXISTING AND NEW LEARNER TYPES

Headline figures for demographics and demand for higher education from a range of sources suggest that:

- by 2024, India, China, Indonesia and the US will be home to over 50% of the world's 18 to 22-year-old population. This is despite the fact that the Chinese tertiary-aged population is projected to fall by roughly 40 million people in the next decade;
- India, Indonesia, Brazil, Nigeria and China will dominate global higher education growth in the next decade;
- the highest growth in absolute terms in international students will come from

India, Nigeria and Malaysia (British Council, 2012).

In this paper, I reflect on these and other trends which are shaping, and changing, the student's journey from general English learner to proficient producer of student-level academic discourse and, in some cases, through to becoming a publishing academic. In Figure 1, I summarise the trends that EAP practice and theory have gone through as follows to help frame this discussion. During the 1980s, the dominant discourse around EAP was one of the learner as 'in deficit', and of the model or target they were aspiring to being relatively clear-cut. We assisted our students by conducting a needs analysis, and assumed that their knowledge could be 'topped up' to that of the target by giving them a toolkit of language examples, rhetorical patterns, signposting devices and explicit models to work from. These models were strongly influenced by discourse-analytical approaches to linguistics more generally, and, through time, have evolved into data-driven models such as the work of Doug Biber in academic corpus linguistics (Biber, 2006) or the Academic Word List (Coxhead, 2000). Alongside this approach in the later years of the 20th century, the notion of the student as a more independent, critical and active partner in the learning process began to emerge. This was influenced in part by the growth of critical linguistics as a sub-discipline. We began to think in terms of the contracts that we needed to set up between the learner/class and the teacher, and of encouraging the learner's active engagement with the decisions around the priorities for them, and how they would take responsibility for them. These were the underpinnings to the concept of 'agency', which became crucial in discussion of the development of the autonomy of the learner (Hyland, 2004). More recently, we have seen what might be termed the 'agency plus' model emerging (Nygaard, 2015; Hathaway, 2015), in which students and academics are continually negotiating how best to communicate ideas and new information in what is often English as a shared third language. English is continuing to grow rapidly as the world language for academia. Alongside this, students, their classmates and their teachers have unparalleled access to data, resources that can be individually tailored, social networks that can share new information within seconds, and other technological advances (particularly the access to excellent speaking and listening resources online and for free). Learners are now part of a globalised EAP community, or can be, and the barriers to engaging with this community and finding examples of how academic discourse is put together are now much lower than they were even a few years ago.

As an example of the changes to the resources and models that students and teachers can access, it is worth remembering that, when I started teaching in the mid-1980s, quite a bit of a teacher's time would be spent in a library looking for relevant material in a particular discipline, getting journals and other materials on loan, photocopying extracts from them (within fair copyright!) and cutting and pasting – that is to say, with scissors and glue – examples into hand-outs for a class. These constraints meant that the teacher almost inevitably controlled the resources that made their way into the classroom, and the student was the largely passive recipient of what had been chosen for them.

All the above leads me to suggest that 'Globalised EAP' positions the learner very differently from even a few years ago. They will need to navigate sophisticated and rapidly evolving intercultural behaviours and join an academic community of practice, rather than understand and reproduce static target discourses which can be easily mapped

1980–2000s – Target-led models		
Needs analysis and target functions and structures	Rhetorical patterns, signposting, explicit models	'Deficit' model

1990–noughties – Problematising the target		
Critical linguistics/ELF	Corpora, genres, wordlists, learning styles, autonomous learning	'Agency' model

Future trends		
Globalised EAP	Networked resources, personalised learning journeys, institutional support teams	'Agency-Plus' model

Figure 1 The evolving role of the EAP student and their resources

and presented to them. In this emerging landscape, the EAP practitioner also needs to rethink their core skills and knowledge. This may require a greater emphasis on team teaching with academic colleagues, in order to understand and then filter and translate the new ways of working and communicating that students are exposed to in their studies. In the rest of the paper, I expand on the areas introduced above.

TRENDS SHAPING THE STUDENT JOURNEY AND THE COMMUNITY OF ACADEMIC PRACTICE

ACCESS TO ENGLISH IN COUNTRIES OF ORIGIN

Access from an early age to English language teaching in the school curriculum is increasing worldwide. This is particularly the case in some of the parts of the world where large numbers of the UK's international students come from.

> In almost all countries of Asia, English has become a core course in primary schools … and is gradually being introduced into the curriculum earlier and earlier.
>
> (Kirkpatrick, 2011, p. 100)

Government level and other policy changes in our students' countries of origin have the effect, long term, of pushing up the fluency, accuracy and confidence of many learners when they arrive in pre-sessional programmes or in-sessional support classes. We have witnessed this change in young Chinese learners since the late 1990s, after the country began to open up in the previous decade, and then, later, the effects of the 'long dragon' programme to promote English teaching from the start of public schooling. This change for one country is part of a much wider trend. A 2011 survey of primary teachers of English

by the British Council in over 60 countries reported that, in around one third of these, there had been policy changes to lower the age at which English was taught. In some cases, this reduction in the age at which English became available in the curriculum was made in combination with making the teaching of English compulsory at Primary level (Rixon, 2013).

English is not only being taught much more widely as a core subject in new contexts, but is also being used increasingly as the medium of instruction for other subjects at school level and above. A pilot report for the British Council surveying 55 countries showed that, at all levels of the education system, the use of English as a medium of instruction (EMI) was legally allowed and was particularly prevalent in private schools and universities (Dearden, 2014). Figure 2 summarises the survey results from this report for primary through to university levels in these countries.

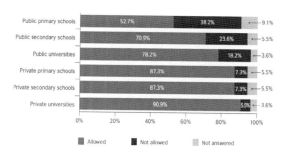

Figure 2 Percentage of educational establishments in 55 countries surveyed in which English is legally allowed as a medium of instruction

[Source: Reproduced courtesy of the British Council]

The EMI phenomenon is also increasing worldwide at tertiary level, as each year's OECD (Organisation for Economic Cooperation and Development) 'Education at a Glance' data testifies (see Figure 3).

Box C4.2. **OECD and partner countries offering tertiary education programmes in English (2012)**

Use of English in instruction	
All or nearly all programmes offered in English	Australia, Canada,[1] Ireland, New Zealand, the United Kingdom, the United States
Many programmes offered in English	Denmark, Finland, the Netherlands, Sweden
Some programmes offered in English	Belgium (Fl.),[2] the Czech Republic, France, Germany, Hungary, Iceland, Japan, Korea, Norway, Poland, Portugal, the Slovak Republic, Spain, Switzerland,[3] Turkey
No or nearly no programmes offered in English	Austria, Belgium (Fr.), Brazil, Chile, Greece, Israel, Italy, Luxembourg, Mexico,[3] the Russian Federation

Note: The extent to which a country offers a few or many programmes in English takes into account the size of the population in the country. Hence, France and Germany are classified among countries with comparatively few English programmes, although they have more English programmes than Sweden, in absolute terms.
1. In Canada, tertiary institutions are either French- (mostly Quebec) or English-speaking.
2. Master's programmes.
3. At the discretion of tertiary education institutions.
Source: OECD, compiled from brochures for prospective international students by OAD (Austria), CHES and NARIC (Czech Republic), Cirius (Denmark), CIMO (Finland), Campus France (France), DAAD (Germany), Campus Hungary (Hungary), University of Iceland (Iceland), JPSS (Japan), NIIED (Korea), NUFFIC (Netherlands), SIU (Norway), CRASP (Poland), Fundación Universidad.es (Spain), Swedish Institute (Sweden) and Middle-East Technical University (Turkey).

Figure 3 Summary of OECD and other countries where tertiary-level teaching is provided in English (OECD, 2014, p. 346)
[Source: Reproduced courtesy of OECD]

These trends imply we may see rises in general proficiency levels of many more students if all these types of intervention continue. We should also begin to think of the effects in receiving UK institutions of the impact of EMI contexts of teaching and learning. This may challenge the simple model of students moving from a 'home' L1 compulsory education setting to the UK setting. These changes, in turn, will require fresh thinking from the EAP community and I return to these issues in my final section.

GLOBALISED ACADEMIC ENGLISH AND WORK IN MULTICULTURAL TEAMS

In recent years, there has been a rise of internationally co-authored papers at a huge pace (Figure 4 shows this trend). The *Times Higher Education* in August 2015 noted 'on a recent paper by a team of researchers at the Large Hadron Collider, 24 of the 33 pages were devoted to listing authors' names' (THE, 2015). This article also suggests that the rise of papers with high numbers of authors is not confined to 'hard' science. Indeed, it states that there appears to have been a doubling in the mean number of authors in social science papers between 1980 and 2013. Undergraduates (including, we must assume, some international students) who assist with data processing can become named authors these days.

The interdisciplinary nature of some academic work is also leading to large and very disparate types of writing teams putting together academic texts. Another phenomenon shaping the landscape for EAP is the access to international audiences that non-Anglophone academics can gain through co-authorship (generally in the medium of English). Figure 4 shows some of the trends in this area. This, in turn, is driving some changes to the levels at which international researchers from other language backgrounds are cited. There has been a dramatic rise, in particular, of

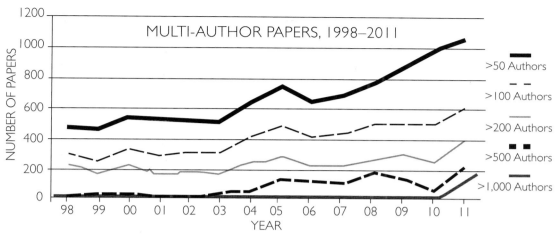

Figure 4 The rise of multi-authored papers (King, 2012)

[Source: Data from the Web of Science, courtesy of Clarivate Analytics (formerly the IP & Science business of Thomson Reuters)]

Table I British Council analysis of Scopus data extracted April 2015

Year	1980	1990	1996	2000	2005	2010	2013
English	64.8%	83.8%	88.2%	88.8%	87.1%	88.7%	91.6%
Chinese	0.3%	0.6%	1.3%	1.9%	4.4%	4.4%	3.7%
German	5.4%	3.7%	2.4%	2.3%	2.0%	1.4%	1.1%
French	3.5%	2.6%	1.7%	1.7%	1.6%	1.3%	1.0%
Spanish	0.9%	1.1%	0.9%	1.0%	0.9%	1.1%	1.1%
Japanese	2.2%	1.9%	1.7%	1.3%	1.1%	0.7%	0.5%

Note: Publications include journals, conference proceedings, book series, books and trade publications[1].

[Source: Reproduced courtesy of the British Council]

Chinese nationals' share of the world's citations since the start of this century. While the USA remains by far the highest producer of academic articles, as counted by citations and origin of authors, Chinese nationals overtook those from the UK around the year 2010 and continue to rise steeply. Table 1 shows some of the data.

Figure 4 and Table 1 show some of the high-level data shaping the landscape of academic communication, and the conclusion from these must be that bigger and more multinational teams are becoming more normal. We can similarly see that the dominance of English in academic publication continues apace (Table 1), with only Chinese language scholarly production showing a rise and several other languages remaining flat or dropping their share of academic publications worldwide.

These trends challenge our assumptions about the process and the practices of

---

[1] Note that years prior to 1996 are shaded, as Elsevier Scopus acknowledge that their methods and reach were different for this period. Data after 2013 has been omitted, as it could still be in the process of being updated.

academic writing. Taken together, they suggest the idea that we once may have had of a student on a journey from low-level learner of English to individual writer of academic texts – written in isolation or with one or two like-minded peers – is increasingly being challenged. As noted previously, the proficiency levels of learners may be increasingly on the rise. It also seems to be increasingly the case that, to succeed at the highest levels in academic text production, many academics (including Anglophone-background academics) will need to be able to communicate effectively with people from other language backgrounds to share information accurately and build and edit texts across large teams and across borders. The multilingual and multicultural backgrounds of students in the EAP classroom can perhaps, nowadays, therefore be seen as providing a microcosm of what academic normal life is like for many departments.

At the same time, the notion of English being a barrier to scientific participation and the 'foreign' learner or academic being in deficit is not clear cut. Indeed, my own interviews with international academics working in English as a second language suggest that they may be better able to communicate with one another and with students from multilingual backgrounds than Anglophone L1 background lecturers.

IMPLICATIONS FOR EAP PRACTICE AND INSTITUTIONAL POLICY

If EMI teachers slowly become more or additionally like language teachers then is it the case that EMI will gradually replace EFL as the main vehicle for furthering English

language proficiency? … What will be the role of language centres and preparatory year (pre-sessional) teachers and what status will they have in a rapidly developing EMI context?

(Dearden, 2014, p. 33)

There is evidence of an increase in access to English at an earlier age – at scale – by many young people in their education systems in those areas of the globe precisely where demand for tertiary-level qualifications is growing at its fastest. We can predict that this will, in time, drive up general proficiency and these students may begin to arrive for their UK degrees (if we think just of the UK context for the purposes of this paper) with greater confidence and general proficiency.

At the outset, in Figure 1, I outlined some changes that I have perceived over the years in the preconceptions that the EAP world holds about learners. This schema suggested that the clear-seeming path from an L2 'deficit' learner from an environment where English was alien, joining an homogeneous L1-user community, may not be the most helpful one to use in future planning of courses and support for students. As levels rise, and academics using English are themselves increasingly from diverse language backgrounds, ideas about how students joining the target community should be treated will need to shift. This is illustrated in Figure 5.

The first area to consider is that student 'baselines' may be very different from before. Students from existing markets such as Asia will have greater access to English from an earlier age and may have had previous experience of EMI. We can predict stronger speaking and listening skills for any motivated learner, whatever the compulsory education system provides as well, due to the increased access to authentic practice that the internet and language-learning apps have started to provide. They will be joined by students from new markets who may have higher proficiency and more diverse ranges of needs. Taking three possible growth 'markets' we may predict the arrival of:

- Nigerian students arriving with strong spoken English and fluent writing styles that resemble spoken genres;
- Indonesian or Vietnamese students whose needs resemble those of the earliest waves of Chinese students and who potentially present a reverse profile to the Nigerian students;
- Mexican and other Latin American students whose first language is closer to English, but who have limited access to advanced-level English tuition at the secondary level.

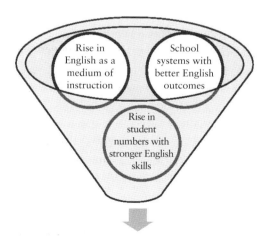

Figure 5 Indication of potential overall changes to student populations on pre-sessional courses

As an EAP community, we will need to reassess our expectations about what the balance of different incoming levels to UK courses at the pre-sessional level may be against these trends. Experienced EAP professionals are very aware of the types of distinctions between the three examples of learners' needs given above. There could be powerful benefits from a closer strategic union between the recruitment arms of universities and the EAP practitioners. The recruitment teams will be deciding where to put their global resources to attract new streams of students, and the EAP teams will know the risks and benefits in terms of probable linguistic barriers and strengths. This alliance could help universities provide a much more fine-grained level of preparation and support than is generally the case. Curriculum development for in-sessional programmes, for instance, could be tailored to the major cultural and linguistic backgrounds of a departmental intake, and pre-sessional courses could be planned bearing in mind the major countries that recruitment would be focusing on in the coming round. The EAP team will also be well placed to advise on the probable language strengths and weaknesses of new cohorts from different language backgrounds and the time, on average, to be set aside for language improvement pre-degree. The flip side of this is for the EAP community to remain alert to demographic and language policy changes and be in the position to give credible and timely advice when asked.

We rarely think holistically about the costs and benefits for students and academics of the language medium they work in. Nor do we often explore the links that can be made between recruiters and the support and preparation teams' knowledge and experience and how this might help the institution reduce costs and increase quality and, indeed, be maximally efficient. The reduction in language level required by a department increases the volume of students who can be recruited on degree programmes, and this trade-off is one well known and difficult to get right. A recent paper (Müller, 2015) analysed the effects on academic workload of taking in students with different IELTS levels, particularly in relation to difficulty of reading student writing, and concluded that some form of cost-benefit analysis would be beneficial since, the analysis suggests, significant increases in time spent on understanding students' meaning are evident as the scores move from 7.0 downwards. To turn this into actual institutional costs is difficult, but academics will, for instance, be unable to deal efficiently with written examination scripts and require more effort to read them as the number of errors increases. At IELTS 7.0, the number of errors per 1,000 words is similar to that of native speakers (around 35 per 1,000 words), and we can assume a similar level of effort is required to read this student's work, whereas, at 6.0, writers will be making over 200 errors per 1,000 words, with a distinct increase in effort required. For an academic with several tens of Masters dissertations to mark at a time and each a minimum of 10,000 words in length, the impact on efficiency and 'throughput' will be high. For a PhD student, the time spent by senior staff on proofreading, re-reading and remediation can be even higher – time that could be usefully put to research, creating new teaching materials, or to perhaps taking on further students within a reasonable workload. Seen from this perspective, Müller's recommendation that IELTS entry levels should be raised is worth a second look. The point here is that university policies for recruitment and those for academic workload (i.e., the different time and energy required for teaching,

assessment, high-quality curriculum development, student experience, feedback, and research) tend to be considered in silos, when they could usefully be looked at 'as a piece' in terms of costs, risks, benefits and income.

On a more radical note, some of the shifts noted above suggest that the distinction between the authoritative L1 user and the incoming student or academic is one that may be increasingly redundant. We need to keep in mind accuracy, clarity, range and depth of communication, but the Native Speaker/ Non-Native Speaker binary distinction, to my mind, is increasingly unhelpful in EAP for several reasons. We should remember, when thinking about academic communities of practice, models and norms, that UK academic staff are no longer (if they ever were) a homogeneous group of mainly British, native-speakers of English; over 30% of doctoral students come from outside the EU, and 72% of researchers in the UK were internationally mobile between 1996 and 2012 (British Council, 2012). Academic staff in UK universities are becoming less linguistically homogeneous, and the student mix in many departments is also very internationalised and, as a rough average, runs at 20% across the different types of institutions these days, and much higher in some popular subjects for international students, such as engineering and business.

SUMMING UP

To conclude, I have presented some evidence here that there are tectonic shifts happening in the academic environment and predict that these will strongly affect the EAP profession in future. I have suggested we will see the impact on incoming students to the UK of an increased access to good general levels of English in the coming years and the changes in the balance of student needs as new national groups enter the cohort mix. To meet these changes I would recommend that

- potential changes should be tracked by EAP practitioners by engaging with data on demographics and demand from new parts of the world (for example, via the British Council's Knowledge Centre (British Council, 2016);
- more analysis should be undertaken to understand the impact of rising EMI;
- we should be alert to what is happening across global academic communities working in international teams, and EAP should be engaging directly with the academic departments they work alongside.

It is possible to predict some of the changes to the study journey in terms of where our students are coming from and what they will be like by accessing these kinds of data, but I have also suggested that we can no longer write the map of their future environments quite as easily. This is, I think, a good thing, as the models we have sometimes used have placed the L2 learner too far in the 'deficit' side of the equation and have rather oversimplified the academic discourse and community that they were travelling towards.

We can, however, still provide students with the 'compass' points, and many of these remain as they always have been in a professional EAP curriculum:

- Good basic study skills, information capture, processing and synthesis, time management, unpacking the task and confidence building in relation to assessment requirements;
- Language improvement linked to real future academic disciplines and communities and delivered in ways that increase the independence and sense of agency of the learner;
- Self-reflection, clear communication, both orally and in writing, and ability to question others with skill, courtesy and precision;
- A sense of confidence and autonomy, and of our professional interest in them and their ability to succeed.

English language is a key part of the international infrastructure by which academic outcomes are achieved, and those who teach it at this rarefied level are part of this infrastructure. I suggest we all prepare for a future in which students are more demanding, more networked, and one where our role is to help them find their destination confidently, rather than draw them the map on a static landscape.

REFERENCES

Biber, D. (2006). *University language: A corpus-based study of spoken and written registers* (Vol. 23). John Benjamins Publishing Company.

Boscarino, J. A., & Adams, R. E. (2015). Assessing community reactions to Ebola virus disease and other disasters: Using social psychological research to enhance public health and disaster communications. *International Journal of Emergency Mental Health*, 17(1), 234.

British Council (2012). The shape of things to come: Higher education global trends and emerging opportunities 2020 [Report]. Retrieved July 13, 2013, from http://ihe.britishcouncil.org/news/shape-things-come-higher-education-global-trends-and-emerging-opportunities-to-2020

British Council (2016). The shape of global higher education [Report]. Retrieved May 9, from https://www.britishcouncil.org/education/ihe/knowledge-centre

Coxhead, A. (2000). A new academic word list. *TESOL Quarterly*, *34*(2), 213–238.

Dearden, J. (2014). English as a medium of instruction – a growing global phenomenon. British Council. Retrieved October 9, 2015, from http://www.britishcouncil.org/education/ihe/knowledge-centre/english-language-higher-education/report-english-medium-instruction

Delamarre, L., Mellman, I., & Yadav, M. (2015). Cancer immunotherapy. Neo approaches to cancer vaccines. *Science*, *348*(6236), 760–761.

Hathaway, J. (2015). Developing that voice: Locating academic writing tuition in the mainstream of higher education. *Teaching in Higher Education*, *20*(5), 506–517.

Hyland, K. (2004). *Disciplinary discourses: Social interactions in academic writing*. Michigan: University of Michigan Press.

Joordens, J. C., d'Errico, F., Wesselingh, F. P., Munro, S., De Vos, J., Wallinga, J., Ankjærgaard, C., Reimann, T., Wijbrans, J. R., Kuiper, K. F., & Mücher, H. J. (2015). Homo erectus at Trinil on Java used shells for tool production and engraving. *Nature*, *518*(7538), 228–231.

King, C. (2012). Multiauthor papers: Onward and upward. *ScienceWatch*, *23*, 1–2.

Kirkpatrick, A. (2011). English as a medium of instruction in Asian education (from primary to tertiary): Implications for local languages and local scholarship. *Applied Linguistics Review*, *2*, 99–120.

Klingelhoefer, G., Girones Lopez, J., Schmanke, D., Markovski, C., Brückner, J., d'Uston, C., Economu, T., & Gellert, R. (2015). The Alpha Particle X-Ray Spectrometer APXS on the Rosetta lander Philae to explore the surface of comet 67P/Churyumov-Gerasimenko. In *EGU General Assembly Conference Abstracts*, *17*.

Müller, A. (2015). The differences in error rate and type between IELTS writing bands and their impact on academic workload. *Higher Education Research & Development*, *34*(6), 1207–1219.

Nygaard, L. P. (2015). Publishing and perishing: An academic literacies framework for investigating research productivity. *Studies in Higher Education*, 1–14.

OECD. (2014). *Education at a Glance 2014: OECD Indicators*. OECD Publishing. Retrieved 28 August, 2016, from http://dx.doi.org/10.1787/eag-2014-en

Rixon, S. (2013). *British Council survey of policy and practice in primary English language teaching worldwide*. London: British Council.

THE. (2015). Is mass authorship destroying the credibility of papers? Retrieved September 26, 2015, from https://www.timeshighereducation.co.uk/news/mass-authorship-destroying-credibility-papers

Irina Veleanu and Simon Gooch

Encouraging mindful learning and academic self-development in EAP: Framing reflection as an integral part of a pre-sessional EAP curriculum

This paper looks at pre-sessional student experience with reflection; more specifically, it explores the impact which reflection work has had on students in terms of developing an understanding of their own learning and academic selfhood. Firstly, we undertake a brief exploration of the notion of reflection, as defined in relation to student learning. Then we look at the role of reflection in a pre-sessional curriculum informed by an academic literacies approach and briefly explain how reflection sits within a pre-sessional course we teach on. We argue that reflection (*reflectivity – reflexivity*) holds potential to help students with their academic self-development. In support of

this, we introduce a small-scale exploratory study which asked pre-sessional students to talk about any insights developed through their reflection work on the course. Based on an analysis of the data, we finally suggest a basic model of different levels of reflection which might be of interest to others wishing to use reflection as a component in similar or other EAP contexts.

Reflection as an integral part of an academic literacies approach in EAP

Attempting to capture the complex nature of reflection yields a wide array of definitions. Reflection is sometimes regarded as: a natural and intricate mix of cognitive and affective engagement, which can 'lead to new understandings and appreciation' (Boud, Keogh & Walker, 1985, p. 3); a phenomenon which arises at the interface between social and individual spheres (Brockbank & McGill, 2007); or a more introspective and, thus private, self-examination potentially leading to conceptual changes (Boyd & Fales, 1983). In a comprehensive review of different theoretical approaches informing reflection in the literature, Rogers (2001) notes several commonalities: most definitions seem to envisage reflection as both a cognitive and an affective process which requires active engagement on the part of the individual, is prompted by an event that challenges an individual's set ideas, involves examining one's responses and beliefs, and, finally, results in the emergence of new understandings that are integrated into one's experience.

Whether reflection is conceptualised as critical reflection (Mezirow & Associates, 1990), reflective thinking (Dewey, 1933), or metacognitive reflection (Fogarty, 1994) (see Rogers, 2001, for a comprehensive review), the literature on the whole tends to view it as having a beneficial role in learning by bringing added value to the learning process. However, of particular relevance to this paper is the potential role of reflection in helping international students on an EAP programme to develop an awareness of academic literacies.

An academic literacies approach to EAP seeks to take into account the underlying beliefs and values of how knowledge is constructed (*ontology* and *epistemology*) within an academic discipline, in helping to explain the organisation, practices and discourse of that community (Bruce, 2011, p. 25). This raises issues for prospective students and their roles as members of that community, such as the extent to which students adhere to or deviate from the community values and the establishment of identity within a new academic community. Such concerns range across both cultural and personal domains and can question quite fundamental beliefs and assumptions. In this opening section, we would like to suggest how reflection might be helpful for EAP students to explore some of these issues.

We see one of our key roles as EAP tutors as enabling international students to access knowledge, and to participate in, understand and master the discourse of their own discipline (i.e., 'acculturation' or the 'disciplinary socialisation' proposed by Lea and Street, 1998). Thus, understanding how knowledge is constructed, debated and communicated within individual disciplines, understanding the dynamic of these communities, and analysing the features of the various disciplinary written and oral discourses become central concerns for an EAP course. Students are then seen as undergoing a process of 'apprenticeship', as they become more fully integrated, over time, into the discourse practices of a new academic community (see Lillis & Scott, 2007).

However, becoming a member of an academic community does not only involve the process of apprenticeship, but also the establishment of an individual identity ('emancipation'). This echoes Street's advocacy for the plural form of literacies (2003), to help incorporate the unique interactions that take place between the host academic institution and the individual. Ivanič and Camps (2001, p. 7) also suggest a role for the individual with the observation that 'the possibilities of selfhood are never completely socially determined'. In other words, both apprenticeship and actual membership in an academic community must involve some negotiation between the disciplinary codes and the thinking individual.

Culturally determined epistemologies may also need some negotiation by the individual. For instance, many students arrive into their new academic environment with an already-emerging knowledge, and as Lea (2004) points out, this may generate conflicts of an epistemological nature. Ivanič and Camps (2001) also advocate the centrality of academic identity; it is fundamental for individuals to have the freedom and the resources to define their own authorial voices. This is perhaps where reflection can play a role for pre-sessional students; it can encourage and support students to explore their own emergent academic identity, by simply offering them thinking space to become increasingly aware of their potential cultural and ideological transitions.

In EAP, therefore, both reflectivity (mindful and observant engagement with environments, actors and disciplinary knowledge) and reflexivity (self-examination of assumptions, biases, values) can be legitimate aims for students' learning. On the one hand, an explicit analysis of one's own learning can lead to a heightened self-understanding of one's cognitive capabilities, emotive filters and motivational triggers, a process which can provide a good frame for deep learning in an academic context. On the other hand, the explicit and systematic analysis of one's epistemological and ontological orientations can have a powerful emancipatory role; such an analysis can

enable aspiring academics to start working on defining their disciplinary voice, and it can empower experienced scholars from other cultural and academic contexts on pre-sessional courses to (re)negotiate their academic identities. While remaining mindful of the constraints of short, high-stakes courses, both forms of reflection should therefore be encouraged, and the students' level of proficiency in English should not constitute a condition for access to reflective practice (ibid.).

All of the above indicates that reflection can be valuable in an academic context, and, therefore, we argue that it should be an integral part of an academic literacies curriculum, as it can add value to any pre-sessional EAP programme. More specifically, we argue that exposing students to notions such as voice, authorship, and membership, as well as supporting them to take notice of the ways in which they internalise these notions, can alert them to the importance of contouring their academic identity or the right to project their 'unique voice' (ibid.) in their respective disciplines.

INCORPORATING REFLECTION IN A PRE-SESSIONAL COURSE

Current trends in academia appear to encourage learners to complement the more implicit forms of thinking with reflection (a fully conscious, explicit and analytic way of thinking). For instance, learners are explicitly encouraged to think not only about *what*, but also about *how* they learn, i.e., to focus on the learning process itself. With regard to EAP, this is often focused on the language skills or language components of a course, with students being asked to reflect on, for example, their experiences over time in developing improved listening skills. However, by adopting a wider academic literacies approach to EAP, similar to that on our PEAP[1] (Pre-sessional EAP) courses, it is possible that the importance of reflection can be considerably extended. It could, for example, be used to create opportunities for students to make sense of their new academic environment, to define their role in a new learning community or to explore their reactions to the new educational setting, and help explain both their own and others' actions and decisions (see Appendix 1 for further areas). Enabling our students to reflect in a meaningful way in these areas might help them to come to a more nuanced understanding of the transient nature of their own beliefs and ideology, and of the relative nature of the bodies of knowledge within which they work. This can put them in a stronger position with regard to defining their academic voice and identity, and recognising and developing the linguistic and rhetorical resources they need to articulate their views and vision.

These dimensions of reflection are accommodated, to some extent, in a stand-alone reflection strand in each PEAP course. The data for this study was generated from student experiences on our PEAP 2 course (the second of four levels, which accepts students with an IELTS equivalent of 5.0). This has a number of sessions introducing students explicitly to the concept of reflection, culminating in the writing of a 1,000-word reflective text on key areas of their experience on the course such as 'community', 'language learning' and the research project they undertake.

METHODOLOGY

The main focus of this exploratory piece of research was to find out more about students' perception of the reflection work undertaken as part of the PEAP 2 course. Since our main aim was to capture student voices and allow the respondents to help determine the data, we set up two focus groups with a flexible guide for discussion (see Appendix 3). Each focus group consisted of six volunteer students of mixed nationalities and disciplines (from a total cohort of 52), and lasted for an average of 45 minutes. The discussions focused on the students' experiences of reflective practices on the course, and students were encouraged to talk freely about these. The discussions were transcribed, and we undertook a thematic analysis of the data which reflects both individual agendas and issues arising through group interaction.

Clearly, there are certain limitations – the use of one research tool, the self-elected sample, and the small scale of the study. However, we tried to ensure inter-researcher reliability and time triangulation, which involved both researchers analysing the data and negotiating the findings over different points in time.

DATA ANALYSIS: THE IMPACT OF REFLECTION ON THE STUDENT LEARNING EXPERIENCE

The data suggests a number of areas where reflection may be helping build awareness, relating to the students' own environment both present and past, their reactions to these and a deeper understanding of

---

[1] The idea of an academic literacies-oriented pre-sessional curriculum was initiated in CELE, the University of Nottingham, by Dr Julie King and Dr Alex Ding, and has since been developed by a number of others.

themselves. We present them below divided into subthemes, each of which we exemplify.

UNDERSTANDING OTHERS' AND ONE'S OWN ENVIRONMENTS

The comments below suggest that reflection has helped individual students to become more aware of the cultural environment within which any individual exists, at a number of different levels, including values underpinning educational systems and ways of communicating knowledge.

Differences in educational systems

1) I know how I can improve … impact on my country's educational system … I have some ideas … before I was asking why in the UK they have high-quality education … I think I know now … they teach us how we can think in critical ways … before I didn't know this but now I touched this and I participate and it's truth from me and I know what it is and I can explain now 'cos I touched it … very important because how we think is how you live.[1]

Different ways of approaching and communicating knowledge

2) … [when undertaking research] we use to come from bigger circle to inside but in English I think they are more specific on centre.

Reconsidering ways of approaching knowledge in own discipline

3) I get involved I think about consequences all the time and how things are related … I can link with Law … I expand my mind when I work with laws and codes I always think only of what is in front of me but now I think about how I can separate things and find links and find things that are behind the surface.

Culturally-bound understandings of appropriacy and acceptability

4) I am from Eastern countries and in our countries you don't say what you think openly … I write something and I know that it's not just me reading that … someone else will read about so it's like I open my mind I open my heart for somebody and it's very difficult to open yourself … in my culture … you open your mind your heart if you are familiar if this person is familiar for you.

The value of cultural diversity

5) I used to be pessimistic but now I can trust myself … and I start to see things in positive ways so I think this is significant benefit … like when you are wearing black glasses you see everything in black but if you are wearing coloured glasses you see everything in these colours like cultural differences … I start now to see them as the soul of our life … in the past I used to reject other cultures … you need to change your ways to looking at things.

The observations quoted above appear to be generated through the desire to make sense of the host academic culture and show some critical engagement with this. Extracts 1 and 4 emphasise a desire to uncover the values that lie at the core of the speaker's previous and current learning environments; more specifically, what exactly it is that makes such a difference to one's learning experience in two educational systems. The second one makes reference to different scholarly approaches encouraged in two academic contexts, i.e., the value of generating papers demonstrating extensive coverage of a field, versus papers with a sharp focus of investigation. Extract 3

---

[1] Consent was obtained from the participants in this study to use the data generated in the focus group interviews for research purposes, dissemination in conferences and publication.

signals an awakening to the relativity of knowledge even when one works with authoritative bodies of knowledge (e.g., Law), while Extract 5 illustrates a transition from rejecting to embracing diversity.

EXPLORING ONE'S OWN ACTIONS AND REACTIONS

Reflection also appears to help students to become more observant about how their own learning unfolds, the thinking processes involved and the strategies that seem to work for them.

Recognising elements of higher-order thinking in one's reasoning

6) … you think in your thinking so you think in deep you analyse things you link cause with reasons you as a person you see issued with different points of view so you do a very deep thinking process not just … you can't just simply say 'I think' and that's it.

Identifying flaws in one's thinking

7) … sometimes people confused between critical thinking and judgment … maybe I tried to judged … my job is related with people … and one of the requirements of my job is don't judge people so now I if I think about something or somebody I think in a critical way I never judge …

Perceiving reflection as a self-regulating tool

8a) … for example, if your room [is in] some kind of chaos, all stuff lying on the floor, and you put all stuff on the wrong places and you understand that all your plan, all your things, you put in right things and you can look inside and find exactly what kind of feelings you have to, some kind of situation … it's like to reduce the chaos from your head …

8b) … when you write down your reflective thoughts you see the structure of your mind.

Becoming more observant about one's subjective–objective engagement

9) I found that I need to put my feelings on a side to start analyse the situation … to be objective and that's the hardest thing, how you are describing your feelings by putting your feelings outside … you move outside so you look from outside at you … So thinking from the outside I think it's what's changing me.

Engaging with suggested frameworks of reflection

10) I have difficulty with learning that process [cycle diagram – see Appendix 2] how to describe analyse you have to give each process the meaning … it was useful for me 'cos [initially] I described and analysed and then I go back to describe which is difficult but once I followed all the steps [in the cycle diagram] I felt my writing was getting better.

11) Like if you are in a xxx situation, like you are following the circle … and trying to follow it and we wanna put each part, or each problem, or each sentence … but the sentences [are] coming mixed together it's not coming like that …

Focusing on meaning making

12) I wrote before about other people but about yourself it's very difficult also the language makes it a bit difficult so you have to be very careful what words you choose to describe your experiences and reflect on them.

These extracts indicate that reflection offers fertile ground for enriched cognitive engagement; the students seem to scrutinise their own thinking to get a sense of the depth of their engagement with the content at hand, while also trying to pinpoint flaws in their own reasoning (Extracts 6 and 7). The students' responses also indicate a tendency to work on a metacognitive level, as they appear to use both written and dialogic reflection as a tool to manage trains of thought or to enhance clarity of vision (Extracts 8a and 8b). Extract 9 notes a perceived desirability towards disciplining one's subjective approach in favour of an unemotional and impartial self-evaluation. Some of these comments from students bring to the fore the highly individualised nature of learning. Unsurprisingly, reflection opportunities (with regard to tasks and tools) resonate differently with each individual: one student finds analytic frames helpful for putting structure into her own thoughts (Extract 10), while another student finds following analytic frames somewhat restrictive and prefers to allow the content and nature of their own individual reflection to generate an analytic frame (Extract 11). Finally, opening up one's written reflections seems to incentivise some students to depict their emotions and thoughts with precision, a process during which they indicate they may need to pay greater attention to conveying nuanced meaning and projecting voice (Extract 12).

THE SELF

At the deepest level, reflection seems to give students a glimpse of shifts in their own ideology and this can enable them to explore the principles upon which their behaviour is based.

Noticing elements of emergent self-reliance

13) For me the reflective essay give me more confidence because it give me a chance to reflect what I need to do, separately without assist from others.

Self-discovery – a way to learn about oneself

14) ... you see yourself in a mirror, who's I am, what I'm going to do, what I've done ... what I've done, what I'm going to do, that's it ... it's like you will be honest with yourself, if you are not honest with yourself, you will never be honest with anybody else.

A gateway to freedom of thought and opinion

15) ... for me, the reflective it's help me to thinking about something I couldn't talk to anybody else, something like having two different nationalities, different religions, so I can talk about this.

Self-awareness of changing perspectives

16) ... going past the time your mind is changing, your views for everything ... it's like when you see the last pictures of you but it's in the light.

These final quotes suggest students' enhanced interest in their own making as academics – from glimpses of emergent self-reliance to introspections on one's truthfulness, and in Extract 16, a realisation of the transient nature of ideology itself.

FRAMEWORK FOR CONCEPTUALISING REFLECTION

The main categories which emerged from the data presented above suggest that reflection may be of value at different levels, equating to an inward journey of self-discovery. The underlying idea of the framework proposed here ('journeying inwardly') resonates, to a certain extent, with Weiner's attribution theory, according to which, humans are naturally inclined to strive to understand their environments by looking for causality relationships, a process through which they come to learn more about themselves (Weiner, 1985). The students in this study seem to have taken notice of new elements and events arising from their interactions with the host academic environment. They have tried to make sense of these by comparing contexts and by looking for underlying causes. In this process of construing explanations, students seemed to be attempting to grasp the significance of these events in relation to their own self. In brief, the students in this study appear to have gained insights into 'Others' and one's own environments', 'One's own

actions and reactions' and 'The self' (see Figure 1 below).

CONCLUSION

In agreement with others (Poole, Jones & Whitfield, 2013; Granville & Dison, 2005), this study argues that explicit exposure to reflection can help students with their academic self-development in several areas. More specifically, we regard reflection as a key component of an academic literacies approach in an EAP context. It can do so by helping engender a balance between enabling students to better understand the cultural aspects of entering disciplinary academic communities, whilst, at the same time, helping them explore their own beliefs and assumptions, which may be required to empower them to make individualised contributions in their fields. The findings presented here indicate that reflection can engender an active interest in the values

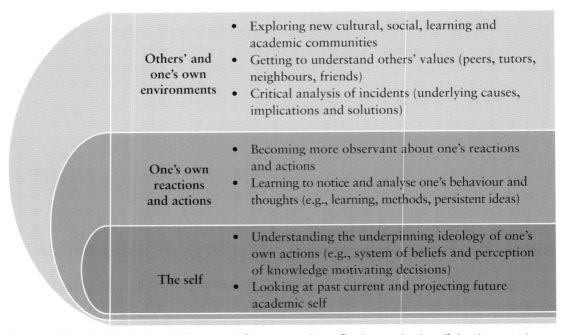

Others' and one's own environments	• Exploring new cultural, social, learning and academic communities • Getting to understand others' values (peers, tutors, neighbours, friends) • Critical analysis of incidents (underlying causes, implications and solutions)
One's own reactions and actions	• Becoming more observant about one's reactions and actions • Learning to notice and analyse one's behaviour and thoughts (e.g., learning, methods, persistent ideas)
The self	• Understanding the underpinning ideology of one's own actions (e.g., system of beliefs and perception of knowledge motivating decisions) • Looking at past current and projecting future academic self

Figure 1 Levels of reflection: A framework for encouraging reflective academic self-development in an EAP presessional curriculum

underpinning one's academic environments; it can enhance metacognitive awareness (Yusuff, 2015), stimulate self-regulation (Masui & Corte, 2005 on reflection and attribution), and, finally, reflection can play a fundamental role in explorations of one's roots and academic identity.

The simple model we have introduced here based on these findings could be used to structure reflection across different levels of an EAP programme, for example, moving from observations of learning environments to reflection on self. More usefully, perhaps, this might take the form of a more integrated approach, whereby students reflect on an event or area, and the levels in this model can be more or less foregrounded at any given point. Finally, these levels can simply be used to provide a frame to determine the depth of reflection occurring, which could potentially inform descriptors if assessment is an option.

A network of case studies across contexts would be needed to establish the value of reflection, and to explore ways of constructing and facilitating reflective work most appropriate for academic purposes. However, this small-scale research does suggest that reflection, as embodied and experienced in our PEAP 2 course, can have beneficial impacts on students.

REFERENCES

Boud, D., Keogh, R., & Walker, D. (Eds.) (1985). *Reflection: Turning experience into learning.* London: Kogan-Page.

Boyd, E. M., & Fales, A. W. (1983). Reflective learning: Key to learning from experience. *Journal of Humanistic Psychology, 23*(2), 99–117.

Brockbank, A., & McGill, I. (2007). *Facilitating reflective learning in Higher Education.* Maidenhead: Open University Press.

Bruce, I. (2011). *Theory and concepts of English for Academic Purposes.* Basingstoke: Palgrave Macmillan.

Dewey, J. (1933). *How we think: A restatement of the relation of reflective thinking to the educative process.* Boston: D. C. Heath.

Fogarty, R. (1994). *Teach for metacognitive reflection.* Arlington Heights, IL: IRI/SkyLight Training and Publishing.

Gibbs, G. (1988). *Learning by doing: A guide to teaching and learning methods.* Oxford: Further Education Unit, Oxford Polytechnic.

Granville, S., & Dison, L. (2005). Thinking about thinking: Integrating self-reflection into an academic literacy course. *Journal of English for Academic Purposes, 4*(2), 99–118.

Ivanič, R., & Camps, D. (2001). I am how I sound: Voice as self-representation in L2 writing. *Journal of Second Language Writing, 10*, 3–33.

Lea, M. (2004). Academic literacies: A pedagogy for course design. *Studies in Higher Education, 29*(6), 739–756.

Lea, M., & Street, B. (1998). Student writing and faculty feedback in Higher Education: An Academic Literacies approach. *Studies in Higher Education, 23*(2), 157–172.

Lillis, T., & Scott, M. (2007). Defining academic literacies research: Issues of epistemology, ideology and strategy. *Journal of Applied Linguistics*, 4(1), 5–32.

Masui, C., & Corte, E. D. (2005). Learning to reflect and to attribute constructively as basic components of self-regulated learning. *British Journal of Educational Psychology*, 75(3), 351–372.

Mezirow, J., & Associates. (1990). *Fostering critical reflection in adulthood: A guide to transformative and emancipatory learning*. San Francisco: Jossey-Bass.

Poole, G., Jones, L., & Whitfield, M. (2013). Helping students reflect: Lessons from Cognitive Psychology. *Advances in Health Sciences Education*, 18(4), 817–824. doi:10.1007/s10459-012-9373-0

Rogers, R. R. (2001). Reflection in Higher Education: A concept analysis. *Innovative Higher Education*, 26(1), 37–57. doi:10.1023/A:1010986404527

Street, B. (2003). The implications of the new literacy studies for education. In S. Goodman, T. Lillis, J. Maybin, & N. Mercer (Eds.), *Language, literacy and education: A reader* (pp. 77–88). Stoke on Trent: Trentham Books.

Weiner, B. (1985). An attribution theory of achievement motivation and emotion. *Psychological Review*, 92, 548–573.

Yusuff, K. B. (2015). Does self-reflection and peer-assessment improve Saudi pharmacy students' academic performance and metacognitive skills? *Saudi Pharmaceutical Journal*, 23, 266–275. doi:10.1016/j.jsps.2014.11.018

APPENDIX 1

THE CORE PRINCIPLES AND AIMS INFORMING THE REFLECTION STRAND IN OUR **PEAP** COURSES (ACROSS ALL 4 LEVELS)

Developing learner independence

Helping students to take charge of and make informed decisions about their own learning by:

- reflecting on topics of academic interest from a multidisciplinary perspective
- finding out more about their own learning style and tailoring effective strategies for learning language and developing research skills
- learning to make/question conventions and decisions.

Developing academic identity

- Helping students to develop and maintain a positive academic self-concept through our work and interactions with them.
- Helping students to become increasingly aware of one's multifaceted identity (e.g., roles within various communities, past and prospective self).
- Showing students respect as academics, but also as individuals, with individual needs and goals.

Developing awareness of multiple modes and models of reflection

- Written and oral reflection (mode)
- Independent and collaborative reflection (mode)
- Problem-solving-oriented reflection (purpose → models)
- Ideology searching reflection (purpose → models)

APPENDIX 2

FRAMEWORK SUGGESTED TO PEAP 2 STUDENTS FOR THEIR REFLECTIVE WRITING

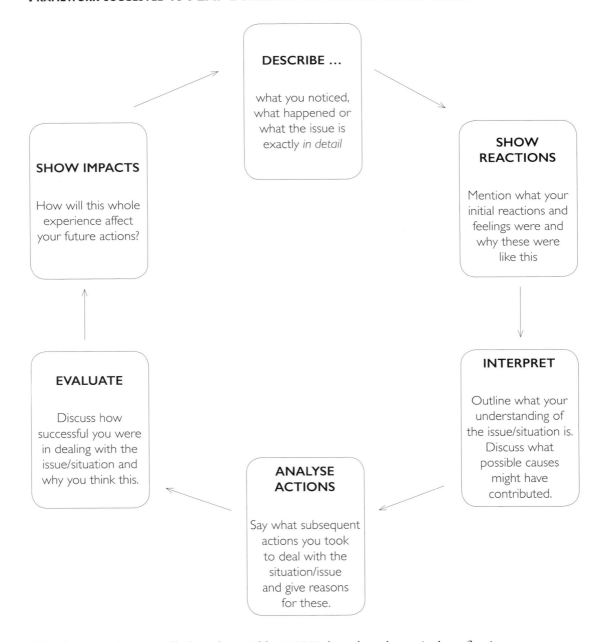

DESCRIBE ...

what you noticed,
what happened or
what the issue is
exactly *in detail*

SHOW IMPACTS

How will this whole
experience affect
your future actions?

SHOW REACTIONS

Mention what your
initial reactions and
feelings were and
why these were
like this

EVALUATE

Discuss how
successful you were
in dealing with the
issue/situation and
why you think this.

INTERPRET

Outline what your
understanding of
the issue/situation is.
Discuss what
possible causes
might have
contributed.

ANALYSE ACTIONS

Say what subsequent
actions you took
to deal with the
situation/issue
and give reasons
for these.

This framework is initially based on Gibbs (1988), but altered to suit the reflection assessment task set for our students. It was made clear to the students that this is not a framework which suggests how reflection itself should occur – we acknowledge reflection is a highly individualised exercise; this is simply meant to provide some structure for the students' reflective essays and is intended to support, rather than dictate, student reflective writing.

APPENDIX 3

INTERVIEW GUIDE

Q1: How familiar were you with reflective work/writing before you started this course?

Q2: Has this been a useful learning experience for you at this point in your academic work?

Q3: What did you find difficult about engaging in reflective work?

Q4: Tell me a bit about aspects you found enjoyable or interesting?

Q5: In what way did reflective work impact on your learning here?

Q6: Can you notice any difference in the way you think about things now after this experience with reflection? Are there any ideas or beliefs that may have been challenged as a result of your reflective engagement with what you do and how you learn?

Q7: We are tempted to think we know ourselves ... but what new things did you learn about yourselves as individuals, academics, learners (only if you are happy to share)?

Q8: If you were to create a definition of reflection, what would reflection be for you?

Simon Gooch and Elaine Smith

Perspectives on presenting: Using a student conference to help develop academic literacies

Introduction

Providing an authentic and worthwhile framework for the development and assessment of spoken academic discourse on pre-sessional EAP courses can be problematic and is probably most often carried out through a series of student 'academic presentations'. These typically result in desultory audience participation and high tutor input in the question phase. There may be a number of possible reasons for this, including lack of task authenticity in terms of audience/purpose, poor integration of the presentation element with other aspects of the course, and little attention paid to the wider discourse practices of the different disciplines which students will be entering.

In this paper, we explore an approach to developing academic presentation skills in a general pre-sessional EAP course, based on our experiences of organising

and participating in a pre-sessional student conference which is fully integrated with other aspects of the course, i.e., writing, criticality and reflection. The course tries to develop students' 'academic literacy', defined here loosely as the linguistic, cognitive, conceptual and skill resources for analysing, constructing and communicating knowledge in a specific subject area (Warren, 2003). The conference presentations reflect this by acting as a vehicle for exploiting differences and similarities between disciplines, rather than simply as a demonstration of generic presentation skills. We argue that these features help to provide a more authentic and academically purposeful experience for students.

First, we show how the conference fits into the wider course structure and explain the key components in the module. We then discuss the conference experience in relation to some of the theoretical underpinnings of the course, in particular, the notions of academic literacy (or literacies) and communities of practice (the development of shared goals and sociocultural practices of groups such as discipline-specific academics through interaction, see Wenger, 1998). Finally, we give examples of some of the insights students say they have gained through the conference and a post-conference 'perspective paper', which asks students to reflect on how presenters from different disciplines have responded to the conference theme.

THE COURSE FRAMEWORK

Pre-sessional English for Academic Purposes Level 3 (PEAP 3) is a ten-week pre-sessional EAP course, aimed mainly at prospective postgraduate students. Students typically enter at IELTS 5.5 (or equivalent) and progress to a further ten-week course (PEAP 4) before exiting the pre-sessional programme. Student numbers on PEAP 3 vary from term to term, but typically range from about 20 to 60.

Figure 1 gives an overview of the course and the links between key components in the oral/presentation strand. These run alongside accompanying reflective and written paper strands (not shown, for clarity). The initial impetus for the whole module starts with a general conference theme which can be easily exploited by a number of different disciplines – past themes include, for example, 'Time', 'Risk', 'The Mind' and 'Creativity'. Students are asked to identify an issue related to both the theme and their own discipline for a secondary research report, which also forms the basis of their conference presentation (see Appendix 1 for examples of student presentation titles linked to the theme of 'Time').

Sessions throughout the module focus on developing awareness and understanding of different areas relating to their presentation within the conference context. The various text, genre and wider discourse practices associated with conferences culminate in students writing an appropriate title, biodata and abstract for their own presentation, and these are collected in a conference programme which is used on the day (see Appendix 2 for extracts from a conference programme). They also decide on the overall title of the conference. Ongoing sessions throughout the course focus on helping students to develop specific practical presentation skills, both in developing their own presentation skills and also in evaluating both their own, and peers' work in this area.

There is also a 'communities of practice' (CoP) strand, which aims to raise awareness about the notion of CoP and how it might be applied to academic communities and disciplinary practices. For example, based loosely on an introductory CoP text (Wenger, 2006), students work (as far as possible) in similar discipline groups on a short joint presentation, which tries to highlight the specific community practices of their discipline and associated professional areas, in order to explore how these are different from other disciplines. Later, on the day of the conference itself, a plenary speaker from a department within the University speaks on the theme of the conference in relation to their own discipline and practice.

Following the conference, students are asked to write a 1,000-word 'perspective paper' to help reflect on how their perspective of the conference theme has been changed by attending presentations from different disciplines (see Figure 1 on page 39 for further details).

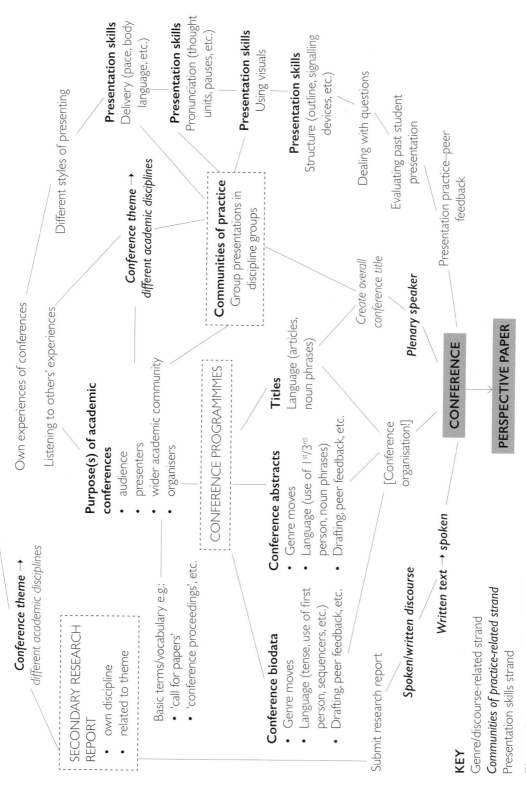

Figure 1 An overview of the PEAP 3 course

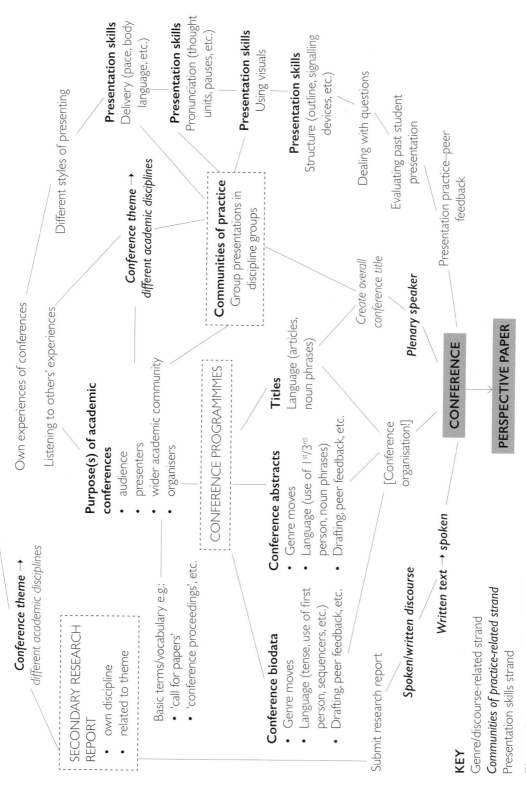

Figure 1 An overview of the PEAP 3 course

RELATING THEORY TO PRACTICE

Here we briefly explore some of the theories that underpin the course and explain how placing student presentations in a conference context might support these.

ACADEMIC LITERACY

The conference presentations need to be seen in the context of the whole course and its focus on raising awareness of wider discourse practices and academic literacy, rather than just as a vehicle for assessing language skills. Braine (2002) argues that academic literacy includes not only areas such as 'knowledge of one's chosen field of study' and 'research skills', but also social practices, specifically the adaptation to the 'academic and social culture of [students'] host environments' (p. 60). This can have implications for EAP practitioners and course designers with, for example, McKay (1996, p. 440) suggesting that 'collaborative literacy practices' need to be fostered in the classroom. Alexander, Argent and Spencer add a further discipline-specific dimension to this by suggesting that, when developing an EAP course, it is essential that not only do the texts used on a course 'reflect text types that students will meet', but that they also take into consideration 'the purposes for which they will read them' (2008, p. 121). They suggest that students need to develop an awareness of the social practices in which academic texts are situated and that this can be achieved by encouraging them to respond to texts in ways which focus on an evaluation of their purpose and significance within that specific academic community (ibid. 2008, p. 122). This is developed yet further by Bruce, who argues that to fully understand these practices, the underlying ontological and epistemological principles 'in relation to disciplinary knowledge and its particular characteristics' (2011, p. 26) may also need to be explored.

Not only are students required to present in the conference on a subject related to their own discipline, but they are encouraged to find out how others from different disciplines respond to the same conference theme. This can help make them more aware of the discourse associated with their own discipline, but also see how other disciplines respond in contrasting ways, due in part to their different underlying disciplinary perspectives.

COMMUNITY OF PRACTICE

The conference can also be seen in the light of a 'communities of practice' approach (CoP) as helping to develop the idea of academic community in an active and participatory manner. Lave and Wenger (1991) suggest that learning within a CoP is acquired by its novice members from the whole community through interactive participation in its practices ('situated learning' and 'legitimate peripheral participation' p. 93). This seems very relevant to our students' conference experience on a number of levels.

Firstly, as a typical academic community event, the conference gives students a way to conceptualise their future department as a community in general (in terms of common 'academic' practices, discourse and speech). In addition, it may make them aware that, as yet, they may be novices in handling these and that further efforts may be required for community membership. This is not to ignore the fact that the majority of students on our pre-sessional courses are postgraduates, and have been active members of academic communities in their own countries. However, practices in these communities may be fundamentally different from those in the UK, and the conference, therefore, serves as a vehicle to help bring students from diverse academic backgrounds into a common shared set of academic community practices appropriate to the UK. Arguably, this would not be the case with a set of stand-alone assessed student presentations.

Furthermore, regardless of the community status in their home countries, or their peripheral standing (for a short time) in the UK, students are part of a genuine CoP at CELE[1]. Although this is a multidisciplinary rather than a specific subject community, they are part of a community formed by 'people who engage in a process of collective learning in a shared domain of human endeavour' (Wenger-Trayner & Wenger-Trayner, 2015, p. 1). The conference is an event which brings this community together and the conference theme helps to establish a 'shared domain'. Within this, an individual's conference presentation makes an important contribution to the 'collective learning' of the community as a whole.

TASK AUTHENTICITY

A third area which the conference seeks to address is providing students with an authentic context, purpose and audience for their academic presentation. The event is organised to resemble an academic conference as closely as possible. Students have already been provided with a conference programme made up of their collected abstracts and biodata. After an opening plenary (see above) participants are free to choose which presentations to attend. Tea, coffee and biscuits are provided in one of the breaks.

Since students share the results of their secondary research paper in an academic conference setting, this provides an authentic context which accurately reflects the way this kind of knowledge would be used in academic life (Herrington, 2011). The purpose of the presentation can also be seen to be beyond just simply providing a text or performance for assessment, or even as a final outcome of the course; it has a wider, arguably more authentic purpose, which is to feed into the collective knowledge of the community. It therefore has a genuine, and academic, communicative purpose (Guariento & Morley, 2001). Audience authenticity is enhanced by allowing students from other PEAP levels to attend, further reinforcing the community aspect. Although two tutors are part of the audience for assessment purposes, the audience otherwise has actively chosen to attend an individual presentation. This should lead to higher levels of audience engagement, another key criterion for task authenticity (Guariento & Morley, 2001). In addition, audience members have a clear motivation to ask questions, because responses potentially feed into the requirements of the subsequent perspective paper.

Admittedly, the perspective paper could be considered to be non-authentic in this context (academic conference participants are highly unlikely to have to write one!). However, it does help provide a quite specific purpose and focus for students in

---

[1] Centre for English Language Education, University of Nottingham.

each presentation they attend, as well as a general framework for reflection on their own disciplinary practices in contrast to other disciplines, concepts they will need to engage with in their future academic lives.

OUTCOMES

THE CONFERENCE

There is a genuine community feel on the day of the conference and students are often very supportive of each other. The mood is of anticipation and excitement along with nerves, but lacks the sense of dread (on the parts of both students and tutors) often apparent in assessment situations. Despite knowing that they are being assessed, the students seem to feel the community aspect of the experience[2]:

> *I think the whole idea of presentation at conference is new for me I think. I think the CoP helped me a lot with communicating with people and trying to ask if I don't know something and also makes you feel much more confident with it because if you find the people like you, the same experience, you will be much relaxed and I think when I give my presentation in the first I was a little scared but also confident because I know I'm still learning and it's okay to make mistakes.*
>
> Student

The community feel is a continuation of the supportive environment that students have built in their classes, and can lead to students being pleasantly surprised by the reactions to their presentations and the discussions that follow:

> *I was surprised but maybe my topic is interesting but I felt like in a community. Also*

> *when I did practice before for the conference, I did some preparation with the group, some friends, so it's like practising in a community.*
>
> Student

Another noticeable effect is that the presentation Q&A sessions are much more student driven, with assessing tutors rarely needing to contribute. As one tutor commented:

> *There's a nice sense of, as a tutor, not having to ask a question in order for there to be a Q&A, but rather asking because you are genuinely interested, or want to know more, or want to clarify your understanding. I like that that bit isn't assessed, it makes it feel more natural and real and takes the pressure off a bit.*
>
> Tutor

A cursory analysis of videoed presentations suggests that many of the audience are indeed motivated by the subsequent assessed perspective paper to challenge, seek clarification and question inconsistencies from presenters. Furthermore, the presence of students from different PEAP courses in the audience can lead to students being questioned by students from their own disciplines who, despite having a lower level of English, may well be experts in the same academic field. From an assessing tutor:

> *I remember one presentation where an audience member from PEAP 2 challenged something that the student presenter had said in a question and it turned into a full on discussion involving everyone in the room. Luckily it was the last presentation of the day, because I'm sure we must have gone on well after time.*
>
> Tutor

---

[2] Comments from students were gathered during a reflective session the week after a conference. Tutor comments come from conversations with tutors about their thoughts on the conference experience.

Students also learn from the experience of being on the receiving end of questions:

> *At the last part when the audience ask the question to me, some of them ask me interesting questions that make me think maybe next time is a good way to improve my presentation, it's like I got some advice from others.*

THE PERSPECTIVE PAPER

As mentioned previously, the perspective paper is completed after students have attended the conference and consists of a short introduction and an analysis of at least three presentations in relation to their own. The first short annotated extract in Appendix 3 shows some of the typical genre moves students are encouraged to include in order to help fulfil this purpose. In this case, the student (from an Engineering discipline) has made a link between the long-term costs of fast food and the long-term costs of using fossil fuels and has suggested that long-term costs be included in any future calculations of engineering developments.

Extract 2, shows a student developing understanding of her own perspective (International Law) through comparison with a medical perspective. Aside from the direct benefits of the often quite insightful and creative links students make between their own and other disciplines, it seems to us that there are some wider academically authentic thought processes and associated language use involved here, i.e., making connections, summarising information, developing citation skills, offering logical explanations, thinking of possible consequences and drawing legitimate conclusions. By focusing on finding similarities between their own and other disciplines, it is also possible that students

are building awareness that academic work in general may have wider underlying concerns which may not always be apparent from their own disciplinary perspectives. As one student commented:

> *So I attend a presentation of pharmacy and it was about the best time to take medicine, so I was surprised because even medicine has best time like my presentation is about the best age to learn a second language and in pharmacy there is a best time to take a medicine so it was fantastic and I was surprised.*

CONCLUSION

Despite obvious time and organisational demands, organising academic oral presentations as part of a student conference has, in our experience, brought considerable benefits. It has improved the commitment, enthusiasm and interaction of participants, created a closer feeling of community, and has appeared to bring about improvements in the quality of student academic presentations, especially in the Q&A phase. However, deeper analysis of videoed presentations and perspective papers, together with further feedback information from both students and tutors will be required to confirm this.

In attempting to help explain these benefits, we have suggested that this may be due to a number of possible factors. Firstly, the proper integration of the presentations into the course as a whole – the conference is not an event merely tacked on to the end of the module to assess student presentation skills and oral work; it is, as we have tried to show, the culmination and ultimate goal of a series of interconnecting syllabus strands that are developed over the course of the module from the very first session. Secondly, the conference provides a clear authentic purpose for an academic presentation which is already based on the student's own previous research, in terms of task, setting and audience. Thirdly, the conference and subsequent perspective paper allow students opportunities to reflect on how different disciplines respond to a common theme and, therefore, help clarify the key concerns of their own discipline.

Although there are still areas for further development (for example, encouraging students to have more of a stake in the conference event itself by helping to organise more aspects of it) and more comprehensive evaluation of outcomes, this module and conference have proved to have many positive aspects for us. We hope other institutions can apply some of these ideas and experiences to their own situation with similarly positive results.

REFERENCES

Alexander, O., Argent, S., & Spencer, J. (2008). *EAP Essentials*. Reading: Garnet Publishing Ltd.

Braine, G. (2002). Academic literacy and the nonnative speaker graduate student. *Journal of English for Academic Purposes, 1*, 59–68.

Bruce, I. (2011). *Theory and concepts of English for Academic Purposes*. Basingstoke: Palgrave Macmillan.

Guariento, W., & Morley, J. (2001). Text and task authenticity in the EFL Classroom. *ELT Journal, 55*(4), 347–353.

Herrington, J. (2011). *Authentic Learning 1 – Authentic Contexts/Authentic Learning 2 – Authentic Tasks*. Retrieved 22 December, 2015, from https://www.youtube.com/watch?v=QB_EarRcoFU

Lave, J., & Wenger, E. (1991). *Situated learning: Legitimate peripheral participation*. Cambridge: Cambridge University Press.

McKay, S. L (1996). Literacy and literacies. In S. L. McKay & N. H. Hornberger (Eds.), *Sociolinguistics and language teaching*. New York: NY Cambridge University Press.

Warren, D. (2003). Developing academic literacy: A discipline-based approach. *Investigations in university teaching and learning, 1*(1), 46–51.

Wenger, E. (1998). *Communities of practice: Learning, meaning and identity*. Cambridge: Cambridge University Press.

Wenger, E. (2006) *Communities of practice: A brief introduction*. Retrieved August 31, 2015, from http://wenger-trayner.com/introduction-to-communities-of-practice/

Wenger-Trayner, E., & Wenger-Trayner, B. (2015). *Introduction to communities of practice: A brief overview of the concept and its uses*. Retrieved August 31, 2015, from http://wenger-trayner.com/introduction-to-communities-of-practice/

APPENDIX I

STUDENT PRESENTATION TITLES BASED ON THE THEME OF 'TIME'

- A cure for Ebola: The race against time
- When is the optimal age to learn a second language: Childhood and adulthood?
- Wind Farms: Back to the Future
- Early intervention to prevent childhood disability
- The role of technology to save time in Education
- An Evaluation of the Effect of Transit Time on Concrete Properties
- The effect of aging on the knee osteoarthritis joint over time
- Forensic entomology: The use of insects for death-time estimation
- Two Benefits of Using Time Management for Reducing Stress in the Workplace
- How can we predict the fatigue life of composite materials?
- The effect of population aging on raising the retirement age and its consequences
- The impact of robots on the labour force over time

APPENDIX 2

EXTRACTS FROM A PEAP 3 CONFERENCE PROGRAMME

Extract 1: Conference timetable
Time: Its Role across Different Disciplines

9:00–9:20	Introduction to Conference with Thomas Chesney (The Business School)
9:30–11:10	Presentations
11:10–11.35	Coffee
11:40–12:55	Presentations
12:55–13:40	Lunch
13:45–15:25	Presentations
15:25–15:35	Break
15:40–16:55	Presentations

Extract 2: Presentations timetable

Time	Name	Title of Presentation
09:30	Student M	An Evaluation of the Effect of Transit Time on Concrete Properties
09:55	Student H	Social media applications: How they affect your business
10:20	Student W	Cervical Cancer: Changes in Treatment and Prevention Over Time
10:45	Student S	The effect of aging on the knee osteoarthritis joint over time
BREAK 11:10–11:35		

Extract 3: Bio-data and abstracts

Name & Biodata	Title & Abstract
Student M I graduated from the University of Babylon in 2008 with a Bachelor's degree in Civil Engineering. I then completed a Master's degree in 2011 focusing on Road and Transportation at the above University. I took up a position as an assistant lecturer at the Almustaqbal University in 2012.	**An Evaluation of the Effect of Transit Time on Concrete Properties** This session will discuss and share fears and knowledge to help minimise the effects of delay in the transit time of ready-mixed concrete. When delay occurs in this period, it will lead to a reduction in the workability of the fresh concrete. Consequently, the jobsite team would take the decision to reject this batch of concrete, but, on the other hand, the concrete has good properties except workability. This decision will lead to a loss of money, time and good materials. Therefore, the aim of this presentation is to evaluate and discuss different types of admixtures, such as retardant and superplasticizer, which may help to increase transit time without any effect on both the properties of freshly-mixed as well as hardened concrete. Also, it will show how these admixtures can be used in real life to improve concrete properties and extend transit time.
Student Y Y is a civil servant in the government of Kazakhstan. He graduated from the South Kazakhstan State University in 2002. He has been working as a civil servant since 2004. He will be pursuing a Master's degree in Public Policy at the University of Nottingham.	**The Role of Nuclear Weapons in International Relationships** This presentation shows two different views about the role of nuclear weapons. First, it seems that most of the countries believe that international security can be provided without nuclear weapons and the second view shows that some countries cannot imagine their security without nuclear weapons. In this study was an attempt to research the negative consequences of nuclear weapons and some problems of nuclear disarmament, also their influence on international security. The first section of this presentation will reveal general information about the role of nuclear weapons as a political instrument of intimidation in the 20th century. Then, in the next part, will be shown the evaluation of the problem of the nuclear disarmament and its impact on international security. The final part will discuss the reasons of renounced nuclear weapons in Kazakhstan.

APPENDIX 3

EXTRACTS FROM STUDENT PERSPECTIVE PAPER

Extract 1

In the Animal Nutrition presentation, *The impacts of Fast Food: Health and the Economy*, Moftah (2015) reported that fast food consumption become as a main part in everyday life. He also explained that the large proportion of people who often consume the different types of fast food believe that they are saving money and time. However, the consumption of fast food has a negative influence on the health such as Obesity and diabetes (ibid). Consequently, the cost of consuming fast food in long term is expensive because governments will lose a huge amount of money to treat the future results of fast food. For example, in the USA, they are spending 51 million to treat different diseases which are caused by obesity and diabetes (ibid). As a similar link, I presented that in the middle of the 19th century, fossil fuels had been used massively in many countries. Because they seem at the first moment cheaper than any kind of renewable energy like, wind farm. However, they have a harmful effect on our health and the environment because they produce high amount of pollution. Therefore, we will lose a huge value of money to treat all those problems which are caused by using fossil fuels instead of using wind farms as an example of renewable energy. Thus, we have to look at the future results of any development before calculating its capital cost.

> Clear, appropriate reference to the presentation attended.

> A brief summary of the presentation attended (based on notes made on the day).

> An explicit link made to their own presentation.

> An explanation of how the link works.

> A further brief exploration/discussion of any insight gained and its possible implications.

Extract 2

The second presentation was linked to biology. Cervical Cancer: Changes in Treatment and Prevention Over Time (Wang, 2015) focused on cervical cancer is an important public health problem worldwide, and it is one of the main cancers suffered by women. Wang also explained the two changes in treatment and prevention of cervical cancer over time. Finally, Wang also discussed the problems and challenges of help women all over the world, particularly in developing countries. On the other hand, in my research, I indicated that UNHCR has been helped women health by have equality rights access to health centres; also provision of healthy materials improves health. Nevertheless, those were only basic public health protection. The complicated health problem protection still a big issue not solved yet. Thus, the common point for both of our research was the change and challenge of seeking the women health protection over time. According to Wang's presentation, there was not enough attention to women about prevention in cervical cancer. Particularly in developing countries, because the high cost and advanced medical treatment can be a huge challenge for those countries. That helped me understand why it was difficult for UNHCR help women health when the health problems became more complicate. In this presentation, I realized that to seeking the health protection for refugee women can not be finish by UNHCR alone, but also need the scientist to find a new treatment that is low cost for developing countries in the future.

> Finding a common point of comparison, the link.

> Development of own perspective through making connections with the perspective of another discipline.

BLAIR MATTHEWS

DESIGNING AND DELIVERING PRE-SESSIONAL ONLINE

INTRODUCTION

This article details the development of an online pre-sessional course at the University of Bristol aimed at postgraduate international students who have met the language requirements for their Master's degree, yet still have a need for the academic socialisation, cultural learning and academic literacy development provided in pre-sessional courses. In order to address these needs, we designed a three-week pre-sessional online course which was delivered to students before they arrived in the UK. The online course provided an introduction to student life and life in Bristol alongside two academic strands, which developed academic writing and critical responses to reading and listening texts (mirroring the face-to-face pre-sessional course). The course featured a series of online self-study tasks, videos, reading texts and discussion, with the aim of familiarising students with their departments, the university and the city.

CONTEXT

The Centre for English Language and Foundation Studies (CELFS) offers in-sessional, pre-sessional and foundation courses to international students at the University of Bristol. Ten-week and six-week pre-sessional courses are offered to all postgraduate students with conditional offers based on their language scores. These courses are intensive full-time courses which develop not only the language skills of students, but also academic and cultural literacy of participants.

The pre-sessional online course offered an abridged version of the pre-sessional courses to students who had been given unconditional offers for postgraduate study (https://bristolcelfs.blogs.ilrt.org/). The online course was piloted in January 2014, and then offered again to August 2014's intake of Master's students. About 30 students signed up to participate in the second offering, with 16 completing the course. The course was not compulsory or assessed.

RATIONALE

International students are confronted with a new academic and cultural context, and they find a need to adopt new behaviours, mindsets, expectations and communication styles (Hotta & Ting-Toomey, 2013). In response, universities often provide pre-sessional courses with the aim of presenting international students with opportunities to gain familiarity with postgraduate study in the UK. However, students who have achieved the necessary language requirements for direct entry to university are not usually required to do a face-to-face pre-sessional course, and, therefore, do not receive the opportunities for academic skills development or acculturation that such courses provide. The pre-sessional online course aimed to bridge this gap.

Adaptation can be viewed as a process of cultural learning, whereby participants develop the knowledge, skills and strategies to participate effectively on their Master's degree course. As such, the design of the online course was informed by a social constructivist view of learning. Social constructivism refers to a set of beliefs which emphasises the collaborative nature of learning (Vygotsky, 1978). Learning, therefore, is best explained as a product of social interaction, where those who know are able to pass on information and ideas about activities, practices, values and behaviours to those who don't know.

The implications of a social constructivist perspective on learning design is that learning requires instruction and a platform for social interaction. Therefore, a series of interactive self-study tasks were designed on academic skills, and a platform for discussion was provided where participants could engage with each other and with a teacher. During the design process, we referred to Kuhlthau's (1994; 2005) concept of a zone of intervention (based on Vygotsky's (1978) zone of proximal development) to inform the delivery of the course. Kuhlthau (2005) defines a zone of intervention as 'that area in which users can do with advice and assistance what he or she cannot do alone or can only do with great difficulty'. We identified a need for a strong tutor presence during the course, and the tutor aimed to respond to as many student posts as possible. At the same time, we strongly encouraged students to interact with each other.

DESIGNING THE TASKS

The project began with the development of a set of tasks consisting of small 'getting to know you' activities, which revolved around introducing the university, the city of Bristol and the students' departments. For the second and third weeks, we designed tasks for two learning strands which are offered to our face-to-face students: *Academic Writing* and *Text Response* (a critical response reading and listening module). Each task was designed using the software Wimba Create, a package which allows designers to combine a series of learning tasks into webpages. Wimba allowed us to combine video, audio, text and quizzes into a series of reuseable learning objects (RLOs) which students could use for online self-study. These tasks were woven together to create a longer sequence of tasks which built up from lower-order to higher-order skills (Krathwohl, 2002), which mirrored the structure of the face-to-face course. For example, the academic writing strand began with tasks on sentence-level structures in order to elicit the production of features of academic discourse (Hyland, 2009), and gradually built up to a paragraph level and, eventually, a textual level of analysis. In a similar way, the text response module began with listening and reading skills in the beginning, before graduating to a slightly more advanced summary writing and synthesis tasks over the two weeks.

Each task was made up of between five and seven pages, and used video (some in the form of online lectures we made using the screen capture software, Camtasia, others using authentic lectures made by the University of Bristol), authentic reading texts (principally PDF files), text and quizzes to check comprehension and provide immediate feedback to students. Each task related to the development of a particular skill, and were designed to take students about an hour to complete (including the discussion task).

Discussion tasks were set at the end of each RLO, where participants were invited to discuss, reflect or produce a piece of work for comment. This related to Kulthau's zone of intervention, as it gave the tutor an opportunity to review and check participants' understanding. It also acted as a record of work and progress over the period and provided a space for tutor and peer feedback.

DISTRIBUTED LEARNING

We had a number of requirements for our learning platform. First, the course needed to be accessible in different countries. Some platforms are banned in certain countries (e.g., China or Iran), and there was a need to find something that was useable all over the world. Second, the platform needed to be able to host discussion threads. Third, we wanted the course to be useable across

a number of devices (mobile phones, tablets, PCs and laptops). This meant that the university virtual learning environment (Blackboard) was not practical. Finally, the platform needed to be supported by the University of Bristol.

Wordpress, the platform that was chosen, is a free, open-source software widely used for designing websites. The main advantage of using Wordpress was that it provided full control over the design and functionality of the website. As a result, users, content and access could be managed on one platform, and the design of the website could be altered so it was mobile responsive, meaning that the website was able to detect the size of the screen it is being displayed on and reconfigure itself to fit that screen. This was hugely advantageous, because it allowed us to facilitate student participation in a number of different ways, so as to create the widest possible range of opportunities for social interaction. Students could use their mobile phones, laptops, tablets or PCs to participate.

The tasks were hosted on the University of Bristol web server, and embedded into Wordpress, which we also hosted on our server. Tasks were presented in reverse chronological order (that is, the most recent post at the top of the page). Two tasks a day (one for academic writing and one for text response) were released on a timer (17:00 GMT every day) from Monday to Thursday, with Friday designated a catch-up day for students and tutors. Participants were encouraged by tutors to complete the tasks, participate in the forum and respond to other students' comments throughout the course.

CHALLENGES

Participants of the pre-sessional online came from all over the world. This created a number of challenges, since it meant social interaction had to be managed across different time zones. Students' responses to a particular task often took place over an extended period of time. This resulted in a time lag for teacher and student responses to comments, particularly for students who were going slowly through the course. For example, if a student in China responded to a student in Mexico's post, their conversation might take place over two or more days after the original post was written. This was not a major problem, but it did impact the uptake of the later tasks. Students were often more interested in maintaining conversations with others than doing the tasks.

Another issue was that most of the students were going on to do different courses at university, ranging from engineering to education, and therefore were unlikely to come across each other at university. While one of our aims was to encourage the development of social networks, it was difficult to maintain this aspect of the course.

EVALUATION

Feedback was gathered by way of an online survey and by student feedback on the Wordpress site. We received survey feedback from a small sample (n = 16) so this did not really allow us to evaluate the success (or not) of the course in any reasonably objective way. It is very difficult to gather good data on the development of short courses since, obviously, sample sizes are small. However, the feedback did pose a number of interesting questions.

About 50% of students maintained active participation throughout the three weeks. We were happy with this response, as it is common for online courses that do not have a required assessment to have high non-completion rates. Moreover, students were expected to do the course at a particularly busy time, preparing to come to the UK (some students travelled to the UK during the course), so we were delighted with the level of engagement they showed.

Students also gave us some specific feedback on some tasks, positively evaluating the academic tasks:

> *I liked each task, they were all selected appropriately. I found as useful all links which led me to related website where I could simply practice more.*

Some students offered criticisms on tasks, particularly language tasks.

> *Grammar stuff, it is very important, but so hard to understand through exercices [sic].*

Of course, it is difficult to design online language tasks that fit the particular needs of all students, particularly for advanced students who we do not know. There are features of academic grammar (such as the use of noun phrases or the passive voice), which even advanced users of English still need help with. However, we found that, in general, the language tasks were not as positively evaluated as academic skills tasks (such as note-taking).

Nevertheless, students were particularly enthusiastic about the interactive nature of the course design:

It was a good idea of yours to place Everybodys [sic] comments there because this gave me an overall picture of my personal presentation compared with the rest.

Interaction offered participants opportunities to learn from each other, to practise their English, to benchmark themselves against other students; and it also provided a record of work. The level of engagement from students was encouraging. However, with a non-completion rate of nearly 50%, there is still a need to explore ways of keeping as many students as possible engaged in the course.

One response to this could be to shift emphasis away from self-study tasks towards a task-based approach, initiated through discussion tasks, where students could produce their own content on which tutors and peers could comment. This would require a redesign of tasks away from quizzes, and towards more authentic reading and listening, with the scaffolded input in the discussion forums. It is a lot to ask even highly-motivated students to do two hours of self-study a day over two or three weeks. Moreover, while the structure of the course from lower- to higher-order skills did provide a useful framework for course design, it sometimes felt that students were being rushed through tasks. We can question how much students can reasonably be pushed through these skills in a three-week time frame. Since there were no assessments (formative or summative), there was no way for us to know what students were doing in their own time, or how effective these tasks were for student learning. By requiring students to produce content, evidence of learning could be better captured in a short time.

CONCLUSION

This paper has described the design of the pre-sessional online course at the University of Bristol. Online course design has become a topical area due to the increased availability and sophistication of software, making online courses more affordable and accessible as a means of distributed learning. There are a vast number of choices of software, platforms and combinations of tasks. Using learning frameworks to underpin the design of the course helped us structure the course in a way that was manageable and useful for participants. We have continued to offer the online pre-sessional course to students at the University of Bristol. We also hope to develop the course into the future, improving task design and course design in response to feedback.

REFERENCES

Hotta, J., & Ting-Toomey, S. (2013). Intercultural adjustment and friendship dialectics in international students: A qualitative study. *International Journal of Intercultural Relations, 37*(5), 550–566.

Hyland, K. (2009). *Academic discourse: English in a global context.* London: Continuum International Publishing Group.

Krathwohl, D. R. (2002). A revision of Bloom's taxonomy: An overview. *Theory into Practice, 41*(4), 212–218.

Kuhlthau, C. C. (1994). Students and the information search process: Zones of intervention for librarians. *Advances in Librarianship, 18,* 57–72.

Kuhlthau, C. C. (2005). *CITE Seminar: Information Literacy and Pre-service Programs.* Hong Kong, China, 7 July 2005.

Vygotsky, L. (1978). *Mind in society.* London: Harvard University Press.

Wimba Inc. (2009). *Wimba Create* [Course content software]. Retrieved May 11, 2016, from http://www.wimba.com/products/wimba_create/

Julie Watson

Evaluating an online course to improve students' academic readiness for UK pre-sessional study: A pilot study

Introduction

The degree of academic readiness of many international students for an intensive pre-sessional course in EAP and then a one-year Masters programme has always been a matter of concern. Most students begin a short or longer pre-sessional course with an IELTS score that reflects the need for further progress to fulfil the entry criteria for their main programme of study. Moreover, the assessment of student performance on pre-sessional courses, especially to decide whether students have achieved a sufficient level of improvement and readiness for intensive Masters-level study, is widely acknowledged to be challenging (e.g., Banerjee & Wall, 2006). Pre-sessional programme designers, recognising this, attempt to ensure courses include comprehensive EAP skills development, sufficient familiarisation with the practices and conventions of UK academic culture, development of independent study skills, as well as socialisation and general acculturation. However, the time available is always the constraining factor. Extending pre-sessional study time to allow students to begin academically acculturating may help address typical problems experienced by students.

With this aim, the University of Southampton has developed an online Prepare for Pre-sessional course that can be bolted onto a taught pre-sessional course to form a longer hybrid option. It is delivered as a five-week tutored and assessed online course before students arrive for ten or eleven weeks' further study. The focus of the course is on developing students' academic reading and writing skills, vocabulary, grammar and study skills awareness. Prepare for Pre-sessional is a generic course for students of mixed disciplines, which is modelled on Pre-sessional Boarding Pass, a similar discipline-specific online course for Business students delivered since 2011 to international applicants. This paper will outline Prepare for Pre-sessional, its learning design and development. It will provide an evaluation of the pilot course conducted in the summer of 2014.

THE DESIGN AND DEVELOPMENT OF PREPARE FOR PRE-SESSIONAL

The overall course objective is to help students develop a basic understanding of the process of preparing and producing a short 500–700-word academic written assignment, supported by evidence from appropriately-referenced sources. Using provided source reading material, students work towards the production of such a piece of writing by the end of the course. They are guided in the development of reading and critical thinking skills, as well as production of written assignment drafts as weekly sub-assignments. There is also a focus on reviewing and using writing conventions and grammar and vocabulary appropriately for academic purposes. The course aims to facilitate general academic acculturation and allow students to begin learning pre-departure, without the additional pressure of needing to adapt to life in a new and unfamiliar environment at the same time.

ONLINE COURSE DESIGN

A dialogic approach to online learning was adopted for Prepare for Pre-sessional. The course elements (see Fig. 1) are underpinned by the key role of the online tutor, who scaffolds and reinforces students' learning by linking and expanding concepts presented and developed through interactive core content designed as activity-based learning objects. Tutor-guided discussion tasks also prepare students for the weekly assignments. Asynchronous forums and synchronous text chat sessions, and more recently, voice chat sessions are the main channels for tutor–student interaction. Students receive weekly tutor feedback on their individual reading and writing assignments by email and can self-assess their weekly learning in grammar and vocabulary development. Automated quizzes for self-assessment provide instant feedback and also return students to appropriate learning content for review in case of wrong answers.

This design model for online learning seeks to take into account four aspects identified in Laurillard's Conversational Framework for teacher–student interaction, which are highlighted as important when including technologies in the learning process (Laurillard, 2002), namely: discussion, adaptation, interaction and reflection. The design also includes essential elements of the online tutor's role adapted from Salmon (2011), such as initiating course orientation and socialisation. For example, at the start of week 1, the tutor leads the use of the Social Wall as an ice-breaking activity and scaffolds the course orientation through the forum and a scheduled chat session. The four aspects derived from Laurillard's framework are built in through the tutor's role, especially in facilitating discussion, group interaction, and development (adaptation) of students' understanding of key concepts. Also, at the micro level of the learning objects, activities are designed to promote reflection, with feedback to support adaptation of understanding. Tutors play a central role in this iterative process for online learning. Figure 1 shows how course elements are linked together to support the process of learning.

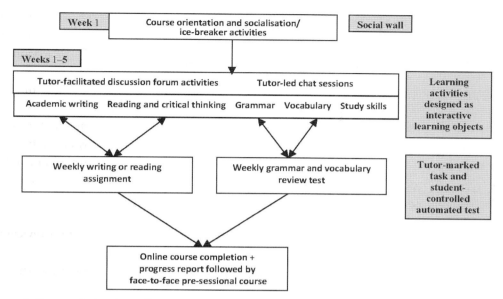

Figure I Course design for online pre-sessional course

COURSE DEVELOPMENT

As a basis for the development of Prepare for Pre-sessional, the course structure and core delivery tools from Pre-sessional Boarding Pass, the pre-existing discipline-specific course, were adopted. The Prepare for Pre-sessional entry level is the same as for those taking Pre-sessional Boarding Pass. An overall IELTS score of 5.5 or 6.0 is required. In both cases, the courses are aimed at those with a weaker profile in core skills of reading and/or writing. The evaluation of Pre-sessional Boarding Pass (Watson & White, 2012) had established its value and led to it being permanently integrated with the university's face-to-face pre-sessional course. Moreover, by reusing the overall course structure and only repurposing content where necessary, considerable time was saved in the development process for Prepare for Pre-sessional. However, to provide a variety of academic subject areas and representative writing conventions

for a mixed-discipline student cohort, new examples needed to be identified for a proportion of the learning object content, and new reading and writing assignments had to be created. These were drawn from a range of authentic texts, which authors gave permission to use and/or modify. The writing assignments were modelled on the discipline-specific ones, but modified so that the context was more accessible to a mixed student cohort.

As shown in Figure 1, a short socialisation and orientation stage precedes the five-week course. Students use an embedded Web 2 technology, a Social Wall created with a Linoit curation tool (Infoteria, 2016), to post introductions with photos, which helps to initiate socialisation. Platform-orientation activities are provided in the form of learning objects. The study pattern for each week then combines the use of the independent learning content overarched by tutor-led chat sessions (text- and voice-based) and forum-based discussion activities on topics with a social or general culture focus, as well as on academic themes, an automated self-assessment test and a reading or writing assignment linked to the learning content and academic discussion.

Pilot study

Course participants

A pilot course was delivered in May/June 2014 with a small cohort of students registered for an 11-week Pre-sessional Course. Its primary aim was to evaluate the usefulness of the online course. The response of student participants and their pre-sessional teachers was sought. The pilot also allowed the consistency of the new learning content and assessment tasks to be trialled with students, in context.

Students who had already met the entry requirements (5.5 or 6.0 IELTS) and been accepted for the 11-week taught pre-sessional course were identified. A random sample of 50 were contacted by email and offered a place on the pilot course as a free option. Twenty-one students with mixed IELTS profiles elected to take the course in order to improve their readiness for study on the pre-sessional course and were duly enrolled and sent course access details in mid-May in time for the start of the pilot course. These students represented eight nationalities and were from South Asia (China, Japan, Macao), Middle Eastern countries (Saudi Arabia, Libya, Palestine) and South America (Colombia). Nearly all students undertook the online course whilst still in their home country.

Course evaluation

Qualitative and quantitative data were gathered for the course evaluation. An end-of-course online questionnaire was sent to all students. Semi-structured interviews were conducted with student respondents post-arrival and with a small number of teachers who received students into their classes on the 11-week pre-sessional course. Student activity and resource usage were tracked through the course platform (Moodle).

Unsurprisingly, the level of engagement varied widely amongst participants. This was a non-mandatory online course and platform tracking showed that two students failed to enter the course, while 19 students began the course and participated to varying levels (see Table 1). For the evaluation, a level commensurate with satisfactory/sufficient course participation was established. Approximately half of the cohort (10/21) met this level through use of at least 40% of the learning resources, active participation (posting) in discussion forums or through other communication tools, and/or submission of one or more weekly assignments and self-assessments. The individual participation profiles of these ten students occupy the top part of Table 1. All performed a minimum of 100 course actions overall and displayed fairly evenly distributed activity within the course. Interestingly, these students later proved to be those with higher entry levels, suggesting that they may have been more motivated learners.

Qualitative data were collected from student questionnaires and post-arrival interviews were also conducted with respondents. Only four of the most engaged students (A, F, R, D) responded to the questionnaire. However, this data supported the perception of the usefulness of the course

Table 1 Overview of 19 student profiles of engagement on pilot course

Students' level of engagement	Number of 'course actions' performed	Active (posting) engagement through communication tools (DF = forum; C = chat sessions; or SW = social wall)	Number of submissions (/5) of weekly assignments (A) and weekly automated tests (T)	% use of learning resources
Student A	994	DF, C, SW	3A 3T	100%
Student F	608	DF, C	5A 5T	95%
Student R	589	DF, C, SW	4A 5T	90%
Student L	123	DF	1A 4T	70%
Student Z	571	DF, C, SW	5A 5T	90%
Student LH	471	DF	2A 3T	65%
Student D	491	DF, C	3A 5T	60%
Student K	238	C, SW	2A	60%
Student DZ	135	DF, SW	-	40%
Student YL	180	DF	1A 1T	40%
Student DB	84	C	-	6%
Student KY	67	-	-	32%
Student MK	67	DF, SW	-	32%
Student FL	56	C	-	9%
Student XYZ	22	-	-	2%
Student YX	19	-	-	-
Student WX	8	-	-	-
Student XL	6	-	-	-
Student YXX	4	-	-	-

amongst those who had engaged with it, since all responded 'Excellent' or 'Very Good' to 'How would you rate the Prepare for Pre-sessional course overall?' All rated themselves 'Pleased' or 'Satisfied' with their own progress on the course. They confirmed, in a post-arrival interview, that their level of course satisfaction was high, one noting that it gave 'a chance to start with academic skills before the pre-sessional course … especially in writing'. They particularly commented on tutor contact: 'The best part is chatting, I have chatting with teacher (to) explain what is my wrong or what is my mistake.' The tutor's assignment feedback was also appreciated, one student noting that it 'showed where is my weak, where is my strength, I like this course'. Another student sent feedback which reflected the typical issue of competing summer priorities for students: 'I would like to have participated more in the course but was busy. When I was participating the course, I was having a job'.

Although all 21 enrolled students had been sent the questionnaire, given the intensive and pressurised nature of the follow-on pre-sessional course and the students' busyness at such time, it was decided not to pursue non-respondents. The evaluation of the course based on the actions of the ten most-participating students and limited data from the post-course response pointed to a fairly satisfactory result. The course had been well-received and engaged with by at least half of the cohort who had initially signed up to do it on an optional basis, and the piloting of the new assessment tasks had yielded no issues in terms of their validity. Only a few revisions were subsequently made in the light of unclear assignment instructions.

In addition, as part of the course evaluation, five pre-sessional class tutors (each receiving one of the most engaged student participants) agreed to be interviewed after the students had arrived in the UK. Most were unaware that their student had done the five-week online course. However, they were unsurprised to learn this, since the student had already shown signs of prior relevant learning and/ or higher levels of confidence:

> *I was not aware about (Student A)'s participation in the online course until about three weeks ago, when she mentioned it to me. What is mostly apparent is that she quickly recognises what I am teaching; she tends to grasp the point before the other students. In these situations it is apparent that she has prior knowledge of the topics I introduce to the class.*

> *Right from the beginning – the very first writing task they do on the first day – (Student F) had proper structure, her paragraphs were organised and she had some logic. So her essay structure and her paragraph structure was immediately visibly better than everybody else's.*

CONCLUSION

Although the pilot study of the Prepare for Pre-sessional online course was limited in scale, the course evaluation was broadly encouraging. Judging from student respondents and tutor comments concerning classroom competence level and confidence, some students' readiness for their pre-sessional course and UK academic culture have improved. In addition, students who reflected a higher level to begin with appeared to be the most motivated learners. The link between motivation, entry level and progress is an area to be investigated in future research. The extension of a pre-sessional course to include a pre-arrival online component also needs further research to determine how to maximise such potential benefits most effectively for all students who are required to take it.

There is, undoubtedly, a challenge in persuading international students at a distance to take and commit to an optional online pre-sessional course. Even if it is free, many are distracted by other more pressing practical issues prior to departure. However, if such a course is fully integrated as a mandatory and recognised part of students' pre-sessional requirement, it could offer significant benefits in the pre-arrival preparation of international students. A final outcome of the evaluation of this in-house online pre-sessional course was to pave the way for the creation of a bolt-on addition for any institutional pre-sessional course. This has now been realised through the provision of a customised platform and ready-to-go course for use by other institutions with their own tutors and students. With proof of concept established, the next stage will now be to undertake more research into measuring the benefits and make this offering available more widely.

ACKNOWLEDGEMENTS

In the successful development and delivery of our online pre-sessional programmes, I am grateful for the technical expertise of Andrew Davey, who customised the course platform and tools to meet the learning design and who manages the platform for each iteration of an online course. I would also like to thank Charlotte Everitt, online tutor and online course coordinator, who oversees the 100+ international students annually taking such courses as part of their pre-sessional programme. She also trains and manages the online tutors.

REFERENCES

Banerjee, J., & Wall, D. (2006). Assessing and reporting performances on pre-sessional EAP courses: Developing a final assessment checklist and investigating its validity. *Journal of English for Academic Purposes (JEAP)*, 5(1), 50–69.

Infoteria. (2016, February 9). Linoit. Retrieved from en.linoit.com

Laurillard, D. (2002). *Rethinking university teaching: A conversational framework for the effective use of learning technologies* (2nd ed.). London: Routledge Falmer.

Salmon, G. (2011). *E-moderating: The key to teaching and learning online* (3rd ed.). London: Routledge Falmer.

Watson, J., & White, S. (2012). Designing and delivering an e-pre-sessional course in EAP for the 21st century international student. In L. Bradley, & S. Thouësny (Eds.), *CALL: Using, learning, knowing, EUROCALL Conference, Gothenburg, Sweden, 22–25 August 2012, Proceedings* (pp. 314–319). http://dx.doi.org/10.14705/rpnet.2012.9781908416032

SECTION II

Knowledge of ourselves and of our learners

Bee Bond

The E(A)P of spelling: Using Exploratory Practice to (re)engage teachers and students

There is an intensity to life in the EAP classroom. The outcomes of our work are frequently high-stakes (Alexander, Argent & Spencer, 2008, p. 18), and there is little downtime for teachers away from the classroom. With increasing focus in higher education (HE) on 'internationalisation', and the commensurate increase in numbers of international students, it can at times feel like we are working, as Hadley (2015) coins it, in a 'Student Processing Unit'. Whilst much has been written about the (often opposing) demands or needs of receiving departments, sponsors and students as stakeholders (Alexander et al., 2008; Bruce, 2011; Hyland, 2006), there seems to be less focus on the needs of teachers within the EAP classroom. Yet, I would argue that, in order to fully meet the needs of students, it is vital for teachers to escape the sense of being on a seemingly endless EAP treadmill,

and to re-engage with their teaching and their students in a scholarly manner. This paper suggests that Exploratory Practice is one approach to teaching, scholarship or research which allows this re-engagement to take place, and can lead to development and greater understanding for both students and teachers.

Exploratory Practice (EP) (Allwright, 2003; Allwright & Hanks, 2009; Hanks 2015a; Hanks, 2015b) positions itself under the general umbrella of practitioner research. However, it can also be seen as a pedagogical approach or as a form of scholarship, where theoretical understanding and practice of teaching and learning intertwine. Generally, it can be seen as a stance or perspective:

> It signals, above all, an ethical commitment to understand and to recognise others as valuable contributors, not only to knowledge, but also as

contributors to understandings of educational activities and contexts for the benefit of all.

(Ding, 2012, p. 315).

Central to understanding EP is the concept of 'puzzling' (Allwright & Hanks, 2009). Rather than, as in other forms of practitioner research, conceptualising a problem and working towards an answer or a solution with a suggested change for the better, EP practitioners develop a puzzle (most commonly framed through 'I wonder why ...') and work, simply, towards a better understanding of classroom life. Exploratory Practice, therefore, works towards clarity, but not necessarily change.

Exploratory Practice has no specific methodology attached to it, but follows seven principles (for the full list, see Allwright & Hanks, 2009, pp. 149–153); all are based around reflexive working practices, collaboration, co-operation, mutual development, and are contextually embedded within classroom life. The first one, 'Put quality of life first' (ibid.), seems key if the issues around workload and working patterns are to be addressed. Importantly, there is also a focus on working *with* students (unlike the more teacher-as-agent focused Action Research). Exploratory Practice views students as 'developing practitioners' and places the student at the centre of classroom life and interaction, basing its approach on five propositions (captured within one sentence):

Learners are both unique individuals (1) and social beings (2) who are capable of taking learning seriously (3), of taking independent decisions (4), and of developing as practitioners of learning (5).

(Allwright & Hanks, 2009, p. 15; numbers added)

Deconstructing this sentence within an EAP environment, few would argue with the basic principles. Yet, how often do we hear staffroom generalisations around 'Japanese students not being able to ...' or 'all Arabic speakers are ...', thus creating a homogeneous group, rather than seeing the individual? Moreover, there are clear sociocultural difficulties around concepts of independence and the choices students make in their learning. There is a tension in the EAP classroom between the demands of the Academy, the EAP teacher acting as intermediary and the student, who often arrives expecting and, therefore, wanting (needing) 'language' – for example, help with spelling or decontextualised grammar. Frequently, EAP ignores this 'want', thus ignoring the student voice, both in our teaching and our scholarship. Despite a general argument for a move away from the deficit model, in terms of language, and towards the less tangible 'skill' of independent learning, we continue to argue that students do not know what they want, and need 'teaching' to be independent. The constraints of our working lives, of the treadmill of pre-sessional teaching, lead us to generalise and stop seeing our students as individual, social, independent and serious learners capable of making their own choices. Exploratory Practice, conversely, offers an opportunity to re-evaluate, to view our work from a different perspective, and puts students at the heart of scholarship and pedagogy, allowing the teacher and students to become mutually involved in co-creating a shared understanding of classroom life.

In order to exemplify how Exploratory Practice can be used within an EAP context, I provide a case study based on my own experience. The narrative provides the stages of teacher development and re-engagement through EP, rather than a clear 'methodology'. Although a personal journey and context specific, the practicalities involved and the process can be applied to other contexts, people and puzzles.

THE CONTEXT

I was feeling dissatisfied with my teaching. I felt stale, ineffective, slightly bored and in need of a challenge. However, I did not feel I had much time to do anything other than the work in which I was already engaged (see Hanks, 2013, p. 161 for the original expression of this state of being). I was, at the time, teaching on a pre-sessional programme designed specifically for undergraduate or pre-Foundation students. The programme had a clear academic focus, but was constrained by the need to teach IELTS and by students focusing largely on achieving their desired score in this exam. As pre-undergraduates, they had no previous experience of academic contexts, so were generally unclear of their own academic purposes. The specific group I was working with were highly homogeneous. All of the students were male, aged 18–21 and Arabic L1 speakers; the majority were sponsored by one of two different oil companies. With reference to Exploratory Practice's five propositions about learners, I was struggling to perceive my students in these terms – other than as social beings in the sense that I felt their social life outside the classroom was negatively interfering with their learning. Collectively, there was a general sense of frustration within our classroom. I felt ineffective, and that the students were not taking their learning seriously;

the students felt they were not learning. I decided to engage in Exploratory Practice in the vague hope that it would improve the quality of this classroom life.

THE PUZZLE

Although ultimately quite a simple question, the development of the puzzle took effort and thought. I began with a sense of frustration: 'Do I have any impact at all?' However, this question suggests a search for an answer, and desire for improvement from a negative position, rather than Exploratory Practice's notion of puzzling for understanding. Through a number of conversations with Judith Hanks[1] and some thought, taking into consideration the suggestion that '... learners will be involved not as objects of research, but as fellow participants and therefore as co-researchers' (Allwright, 2003, p. 129), I began to ask myself what might be puzzling my students about their learning. The answer, for almost all of them, seemed to be spelling.

I had already tried to 'solve the problem' of spelling with my students through, for example, providing spelling tests, word lists to learn and error correction, but to little effect. Therefore, I could either abandon the issue in despair or attempt a different approach. Rather than asking myself what I could do to help them, I could ask 'why'. Thus, the Action Research style question of 'How do you best teach spelling (in an EAP setting) to Arabic L1 speakers?' became an EP puzzle: 'I wonder why Arabic-speaking students in my class don't seem to be able to spell?' Here, I was no longer questioning my teaching methods or competency, but working with my students to understand.

---

[1] My puzzle became part of Judith Hanks' PhD (2013), and is described in detail in Hanks (2015b). I am Bella.

REACHING AN UNDERSTANDING

Once the puzzle was formulated, I went back to my classroom. I shared my puzzle with my students, and received an immediate and enthusiastic response. There was no clear plan or approach, but a desire to involve my students and to share our (lack of) understanding. Once we had discussed our thoughts, and immediately begun to develop some understanding based around Arabic vowel use, we continued our normal, planned work within our usual syllabus. However, the puzzle remained with me.

Over a few weeks, I continued to investigate. This involved visiting my children's primary school, where teachers were providing training to parents on how to support their children with the heavily phonics-based teaching of reading and writing. I spoke to my own work colleagues, in particular, one colleague who had, unbeknown to me, also recently developed an interest in the same puzzle. Together, we developed a short, simple questionnaire to find out what other teachers understood about the teaching and learning of spelling. I also read literature on spelling, but what I found suggested methods for how to teach spelling, but not why it was a particular problem for Arabic speakers[2]. Every time I discovered something new, or considered a different approach, I shared it with my group of students.

Spelling did not dominate our time together in class, but became the occasional focus of discussion and sometimes teaching. We tried mnemonics, which were rejected as 'more English to learn'. Ultimately, sounding out words, listening carefully to the vowels, was the most popular approach. Previously,

my students had argued that English spelling was difficult because there was no connection between pronunciation and spelling. The realisation that, at least most of the time, there was a connection, and that they already knew many of the consonant clusters or vowel combinations used to show this connection was key. Through this realisation came a more profound understanding. I had told them that spelling and pronunciation were connected earlier on in our journey; they had not believed me. In order to learn, my students needed to discover and understand something for themselves; I needed to allow them to do this. As Freire (1973) suggests, learning can only take place if it is owned and framed by the person who is supposed to be doing the learning.

Whilst my students continued to make spelling mistakes (in fact, I could not necessarily claim they became 'better' at spelling at all) they understood why they made the mistakes they did. This understanding removed some of the sense of frustration and gave them a more balanced view of a problem which, for some, had become a barrier to all other learning. By taking my students' expressed need to 'learn spelling' seriously, rather than dismissing it as less important than the more obviously EAP-focused skills and language I had been teaching them, other opportunities were opened up to us. It was through sharing my puzzle with my students and allowing them to question my approaches to teaching, to critique the materials I used to support them, that the 'academic purpose' previously lacking in my group developed.

---

[2] Since I began working on this puzzle in 2010, I have found this addressed elsewhere; see Kavanagh (2013), for example.

Therefore, the outcome of this puzzle was ultimately not connected to the teaching of spelling, but to an increased understanding of and respect for each other. My students' cultural norms of a teacher–student relationship began to break down as they realised that their knowledge and understanding of their first language and their learning were as key to the puzzle as my own understandings and knowledge as a teacher. This realisation has previously been highlighted as a key positive outcome of EP:

> When students see their teacher's questions and puzzles, they see a humanised professional. When students can understand a teacher better, they see a chance to open up their inner selves as well. As teachers and students gain possibilities for constructing mutual understandings about the classroom environment, practitioners – students and teachers – show growth in their intellectual and critical perspectives.
>
> (The Rio de Janeiro EP Group in Allwright & Hanks, 2009, p. 226)

I would argue that it is this outcome that makes EP also an EAP pedagogy.

Yet, EP is more than a pedagogy; it is a scholarly approach to teaching and an attitudinal stance around what education should involve. Whilst Borg (2010; 2011) has posed questions around why practitioners do not do research, Hanks (2013, p. 249) has suggested that they are doing 'interesting and worthwhile work, but that the current definitions of research fail to incorporate such a possibility'. This follows the argument of Freeman that

> (w)hen pursued in a disciplined manner, teaching itself becomes a form of research. It is a matter of balancing and assembling different points of view, each of which knows – or can know – aspects of the story of teaching and learning.
>
> (1996, p. 112)

Exploratory Practice is, at least, a way in to scholarly teaching, the scholarship of teaching and, ultimately, classroom-based research.

It is vital that, as EAP teachers, we not only guide our students to understand the academic context they are preparing to join, but we also reflect and are part of it. Doing this with a heavy teaching load and little or no dedicated time for scholarship or research is problematic. Exploratory Practice allows a way in that it is not overly time-consuming and does not remove focus from praxis; rather, it re-enforces and enhances classroom life. Tangible outcomes from EP are not necessary, expected or certain. It is probable that some puzzles will wilt and fade quickly; others will lead to deep reflection, but of a very personal nature. However, puzzling can also lead to a sharing of understanding with colleagues, the development of classroom materials, conference papers and articles. It allows 'emancipatory development', where a teacher 'critically questions why they do what they do' (Kreber & Cranton, 2000, p. 484), and explores these questions with their students, co-constructing a better understanding. Approaching practice through scholarly exploration encourages (re-)engagement, but does so as a manageable, continuous enterprise where quality of life is at the forefront, thus meeting the social and academic needs of both students and teachers.

REFERENCES

Alexander, O., Argent, S., & Spencer, J. (2008). *EAP essentials: A teacher's guide to principles and practice*. Reading: Garnet Publishing Ltd.

Allwright, D. (2003). Exploratory Practice: Rethinking practitioner research in language teaching. *Language Teaching Research, 7*(2), 113–141.

Allwright, D., & Hanks, J. (2009). *The developing language learner: An introduction to Exploratory Practice*. Basingstoke: Palgrave Macmillan.

Borg, S. (2010). Language teacher research engagement. [State-of-the-art article]. *Language Teaching, 43*(4), 391–429.

Borg, S. (2011). Language teacher education. In J. Simpson (Ed.), *The Routledge Handbook of Applied Linguistics* (pp. 215–228). Abingdon: Routledge.

Bruce, I. (2011). *Theory and concepts of English for academic purposes*. London: Palgrave Macmillan.

Ding, A. (2012). *Deconstructing and reconstructing teacher autonomy: A case study of teacher–learners' autonomy on a TESOL MA course* (Unpublished PhD thesis). University of Nottingham.

Freeman, D. (1996). Redefining the relationship between research and what teachers know. In K.M. Bailey, & D. Nunan (Eds.), *Voices from the language classroom* (pp. 88–115). Cambridge: Cambridge University Press.

Freire, P. (1973). *Education for critical consciousness*. New York: Seabury Press.

Hadley, G. (2015). English for academic purposes in neoliberal universities: A critical grounded theory. *Educational Linguistics, 22*. doi: 10.1007/978-3-319-10449-2

Hanks, J. (2013). *Exploratory Practice in English for Academic Purposes: Puzzling over principles and practices* (Unpublished PhD thesis). University of Leeds.

Hanks, J. (2015a). 'Education is not just teaching': Learner thoughts on exploratory practice. *ELT Journal, 69*(2), 117–128.

Hanks, J. (2015b). Language teachers making sense of exploratory practice. *Language Teaching Research, 19*(5), 612–633.

Hyland, K. (2006). *English for academic purposes: An advanced resource book*. Abingdon: Routledge.

Kavanagh, A. (2013). Arabic-L1 speakers' difficulties with reading in English. In M. Kavanagh & L. Robinson (Eds.) *The Janus moment in EAP: Revisiting the past and building the future. Proceedings of the 2013 BALEAP conference* (pp. 133–140). Reading: Garnet Publishing Ltd.

Kreber, C., & Cranton, P. (2000). Exploring the scholarship of teaching. *The Journal of Higher Education, 71*(4), 476–495.

Maggie Heeney

Cognitive modelling: Think aloud as an expert while teaching

Introduction

While university EAP courses aim to improve academic writing skills, English language learners may still be considered poor writers by mainstream standards (Hirvela & Du, 2013). Summarising, paraphrasing and critically synthesising readings are main skills required to write research papers, which challenges language learners (Grabe & Zhang, 2013). Their work may result in unintentional plagiarism, possibly due to weak language or vocabulary knowledge (Li & Casanave, 2012) or poor reading expertise when synthesising (Hirvela & Du, 2013). To overcome these challenges, Hirvela (2004) suggests learners cannot be skilled writers without being skilled readers. One skill informs the other, as the learner strategically constructs meaning from and with texts; accordingly, EAP writing teachers need to integrate these skills. This suggests that explicitly teaching reading-to-write strategies may guide learners to improved academic literacy (Hirvela, 2004; Grabe & Zhang, 2013).

As an EAP writing instructor and teacher educator, my interest is how teachers implement strategy instruction into reading-to-write classrooms. This case study, described in detail in Heeney (2015), illustrates how strategy instruction occurred within a university EAP reading-to-write course and how the students perceived the impact of this instruction on their writing. The findings are discussed and teaching implications for both experienced and novice teachers are given.

Literature review

This section reviews cognitive strategies, strategic teaching, teacher modelling and strategy implementation in an integrated reading-to-write classroom.

WHAT ARE COGNITIVE STRATEGIES?

Cognitive strategies describe what learners do when problem-solving a task. Dörnyei and Scott (1997) describe this as having awareness of the problem, 'intentionality' to solve it and awareness of strategies that potentially solve it. Similarly, it could be said that teachers follow the same cognitive process when instructing: having an awareness of learners' problems, intentionally beginning to teach problem-solving strategies and then being aware of the strategies' success.

OPPORTUNISTIC STRATEGY TEACHING

A literature review involving longitudinal observational studies of strategy instruction revealed a paucity of studies conducted in L2 literacy classrooms. However, one study by Pressley, Allington, Wharton-McDonald, Collins Block and Mandel Morrow (2001) detailed how reading-to-write strategy instruction occurred in elementary Grade 1 L1 classrooms. By investigating what five experienced teachers essentially do in the classroom, the researchers created a model of how strategy training actually happened. They found that teachers deliberately scaffolded learning and heightened task awareness in order to teach appropriate strategies. Importantly, the researchers determined that 'teaching was opportunistic and driven by the needs of the students' (ibid. p. 64). The researchers' main conclusions were 'experience matters' (ibid. p. 220). They found commonalities whereby teachers learn from their students' needs, successes and failures and change their approach accordingly, thereby building expertise. Although the study was conducted in L1 classrooms, it may be possible to apply these methods to other teaching contexts,

regardless of students' ages and language of instruction.

Hirvela (2004) called for L2 teachers to be opportunistic and to deliberately integrate reading and writing strategies. Hirvela suggests teachers actively scaffold learning by teaching reading-to-write strategies by 'mining' the texts. 'Mining' is a highly directed, explicit strategy training using texts to point learners towards understanding the choices a writer makes: identifying main ideas and support, learning cohesive devices, developing lexical knowledge, providing content input, and building rhetorical knowledge.

THINK-ALOUD COGNITIVE MODELLING

Strategic teachers are generally self-aware, being able to think aloud and talk about their own thought processes (Wilson & Bai, 2010). Teacher talk should play an important role in teaching strategies. Roehler and Cantlon (1997) defined L1 teacher talk as a think-aloud process engaging the learners in rhetorical questioning: 'I was wondering … Let's think … Maybe we could be thinking about …' (ibid. p. 21), whilst the teacher demonstrated the steps of the strategy.

Cumming (1995) used the term 'cognitive modelling' to describe teacher talk in L2 writing classrooms. Cognitive modelling entails the teacher verbalising by thinking aloud and practising cognitive strategies needed to perform a task. Cognitive modelling scaffolds strategies to student learning, as learners see the strategy being expertly modelled and hear the teachers' thinking processes; furthermore, the social aspect of using think-aloud rhetorical questioning while modelling a task promotes learning (Cumming, 1995; Roehler & Cantlon, 1997).

READING AND WRITING STRATEGIES

Reading and writing are interdependent skills, and the strategies that experts use are similar in both. These include, but are not limited to, activating prior knowledge, monitoring comprehension (reading) or monitoring production (writing), using lexical strategies, and critically analysing text (Grabe & Kaplan, 1996; Grabe, 2009). Readers tend to use strategies pre-, during, and post-reading, while writers also use strategies pre-writing, during and post-drafting. Expert readers employ effective strategies unconsciously and are able to move back and forth in a text and not lose comprehension (Pressley & Harris, 2006). Skilled writers spend time planning and revising at the discourse level and edit at any stage (Chenoweth & Hayes, 2001).

As experts, teachers need to have an awareness of their own use of reading and writing strategies and should be able to articulate them by thinking aloud. Zhang (2008) developed a set of principles and procedures for strategy instruction that emphasised defining the strategy, explaining why, how, when and where it should be used, and, finally, evaluating its success (See Appendix). While Zhang's study focused on reading strategies, the connections between reading and writing are strong in both teaching and learning contexts. Thus, these principles have importance, as they may prove effective in teaching the two skills together.

METHODS

This case study took place in a Canadian EAP reading-to-write university credit course with 25 undergraduate students. The course was 10 weeks long for 5.5 hours a week. I observed 45 teaching hours of the experienced instructor, Sophia (a pseudonym). Extensive notes were taken of all teacher talk related to instruction. In order to gauge the impact of the instruction, six focal students completed retrospective stimulated-recall think-aloud protocols after writing in-class assignments. They read their essays aloud for approximately 10–12 minutes and described their thinking process when writing. These recalls were audio-recorded, transcribed and analysed for connections to the teacher data. Other data-collection strategies included teacher interviews, focal student interviews and two class surveys.

The extensive teacher and student speech episodes were categorised into five thematic categories (See Table 1), based on descriptions of expert reading and writing strategies (Grabe, 2009; Grabe & Kaplan, 1996; Pressley & Afflerbach, 1995). Each category included several strategic activities, all of which needed to be teachable and preferably observable, suggesting that they could be modelled. Each strategy needed to be able to be articulated by learners during stimulated recalls.

RESULTS

Analysis of the teacher talk revealed 195 teaching episodes across the taxonomy's five categories. However, the intensity of the teacher talk within the cognitive episodes varied. Accordingly, a method of coding that delineated these variations was needed, and three types of episodes for teaching were developed.

Table 1 Taxonomy of reading-to-write cognitive strategies for teaching and learning

Categories	Reading-to-write strategies
Teacher discusses/ demonstrates/evaluates:	*Student refers to/demonstrates/focuses on:*
Ideas and information	1.1 Activating previous topic knowledge before reading/writing
	1.2 Raising awareness of reading for topic information to inform writing topics
	1.3 Raising awareness of thinking critically about/beyond content in texts to build ideas for writing
Language below sentence level (vocabulary)	2.1 Building comprehension/use of collocations/synonyms
	2.2 Building awareness of academic vocabulary
Language below sentence level (sentence grammar)	3.1 Awareness of parallelism
	3.2 Awareness of subordination/coordination
	3.3 Awareness of the form/use of passive
	3.4 Awareness of other grammar/punctuation
Discourse: Language use above the single clause	4.1 Awareness of organisation in reading texts/writing essays
	4.2 Awareness of genre in reading/writing
	4.3 Awareness of paragraphing/cohesion
Regulation of reading and writing task processing	5.1 Awareness of planning reading/writing tasks
	5.2 Awareness of the importance of audience in reading texts/writing tasks
	5.3 Awareness of revising/editing texts for grammar/ sentence errors
	5.4 Summarising/paraphrasing for comprehension/for an academic writing task
	5.5 Awareness of how to connect/assess ideas in readings for synthesis in writing tasks

EPISODES OF RAISING AWARENESS (ERA)

Episodes of Raising Awareness tended to be teacher centred with little student engagement. Modelling and think-aloud were at a minimum. In the following example, the words in bold highlight that Sophia drew attention to the strategies of building vocabulary and generating ideas:

> **I can't stress** enough the importance of vocabulary … **You need** to have a bank

account of synonyms for paraphrasing … **See how** that blank page is getting full … **Think about what** you know. **Think about** the language and ideas.

Here, Sophia is telling students what to do, but not giving the rationale for why building vocabulary or using previous knowledge to generate ideas is important.

EPISODES OF STRATEGY EXPLANATION (ESE)

In these episodes, Sophia not only used awareness-raising activities, but also engaged learners in her thinking with some think-aloud, rhetorical questioning and modelling. Frequently, she wrote on the board or used student-generated work. The following shows how she explained synthesis:

> *What does* **synthesise mean**? **Group** *the ideas.* **Look for** *connections* … **Every time** *you read,* **analyse each** *reading and* **then connect** … **Think about** *the theme and ideas.* **How do** *we do this?* **Take notes** *on your readings to* **make connections** *and* **this will inform your writing**.

The bolded phrases highlight how Sophia pointed out what the strategy is, why it is important, when to do it, where to use, how to use it and how to evaluate it (Zhang, 2008). Her use of questions with 'we', 'I' and 'you' socially involve and engage the learners; however, she did not explicitly demonstrate specific strategies for synthesising texts.

EPISODES OF COGNITIVE MODELLING (ECMs)

In these episodes, Sophia intentionally took students through the process through explicit awareness-raising activities that expertly demonstrated the importance of strategic behaviours. Unlike the example ESE, in the following ECM, Sophia engages in a form of teacher talk where she thinks aloud to bring the process of 'how' and 'why' to life in the manner of an expert. Here, Sophia writes on the board as she speaks about building collocations for an upcoming essay on branding.

> *The collocations would be 'brand' as an adjective + noun* … **Let's write this down** … **When I do this**, *I put the word 'brand' first. I* **can't say** *loyalty of brand.* **Why?** *Well, it sounds like the brand is loyal*. **But what is loyal?** *Yeah. The consumer is loyal to the brand.* **That is why** *I have to say brand loyalty* … **Let me think.** *Brand awareness! Brand identity!* **Look how I** *am building vocabulary!* **I need to remember** *these words when writing.*

Sophia is explicit in her modelling and explains what collocations are, why they are important, when they are used. She shows how and where to use them, and evaluates them as being correct or not. As the expert, she explains that 'brand loyalty' is the correct choice over 'loyalty of brand'. Specifically, she engages in rhetorical questioning as she thinks through other collocations with the word 'brand'. Students are involved in the process through her questioning and her writing the words on the board. Her meta-language has words such as 'Let's …', 'Let me think', 'Look …' and 'I need,' all of which give learners the opportunity to share in her expert thoughts. There is a difference between telling students *what* (ERA), explaining and showing students *how* (ESE), and *modelling* extensively and *thinking aloud* about how to expertly do the task (ECM).

Of the 195 teacher episodes, 47% were ERAs, 24% were ESEs, and 29% were ECMs. Accordingly, 53% of episodes focused on explicitly modelling strategies and engaging the students, rather than just telling them about strategies.

EPISODES OF COGNITIVE LEARNING (ECL)

Analysis of focal-student-stimulated-recall data into ECLs revealed that the 346 episodes converged thematically with the teacher data (See Table 2).

Table 2 Frequency of teacher and focal student cognitive episodes compared

Category	Teacher (ERA, ESE, ECM)			Focal students (ECL)		
Assignment	Contrast	Paraphrase	Argument	Contrast	Paraphrase	Argument
Ideas	18	2	6	38	0	21
Vocabulary	19	13	13	28	37	13
Sentence grammar	28	26	7	8	28	4
Discourse	7	1	18	5	10	45
Regulation	9	22	6	12	72	25

The findings indicate that teaching situations where Sophia had the highest number of ESE and ECMs were reflected in the ECLs of the focal students' stimulated recalls. During the recalls, focal students frequently referred specifically to Sophia or to specific classroom activities that had engaged cognitive strategies. For example, a student commented about paraphrasing, 'I thought about it first … switched the order a bit. There are two paragraphs. I did the second one first … I used the method Sophia teached us. Changing sentence structure, using synonyms'.

Interviews revealed that both the teacher and the students perceived the integration of reading and writing through cognitive teaching as being successful. Student comments included 'I like how Sophia showed the good and bad paraphrases,' and 'I see how professionals think about the topic and then put ideas together. It helped me write.'

DISCUSSION

Sophia could be considered an expert teacher, suggesting that she understood students'

needs (Pressley et al., 2001). She had vast pedagogical knowledge and was able to model concepts in an expert manner by mining the text for grammar, vocabulary and content. Sophia's ESEs and ECMs were explicit. By nature, she is an outward thinker; thus, it is likely that cognitive teaching comes naturally to her, which may not be so for another instructor. Sophia's explicit modelling and constant provision of rationale related to the 'when, where and why' of strategies, combined with her approach of engaging the learners in the 'how' by performing the task, and evaluating its success, is consistent with Zhang's (2008) principles and procedures in strategy instruction.

The findings of this study carry implications even for seasoned teachers, suggesting they can benefit from reflection on and self-evaluation of their teaching practices. Such an evaluative and reflective process can include an assessment of their meta-language. In her ESEs and ECMs, Sophia frequently used phrases such as 'Notice how …', 'I have to think about how …' and 'I need to think why'. This approach, as Roehler and Cantlon (1997) suggest, allows students into the teacher's head, which, in turn, increases students' active engagement in the problem-solving or teaching process. Ultimately, the results indicate that teachers can develop their own set of cognitive actions, self-regulate and evaluate the success of teaching the task in the same way that learners cognitively plan and assess a task.

This study also carries implications for ESL and EAP teacher education. Becoming a cognitive teacher is a learned skill (Pressley et al., 2001). In my experience, novice teachers frequently depend on teacher-centred approaches with little modelling. Integrating think-aloud strategies into

pre-service education could prove beneficial. Student teachers should be encouraged to practise these think-aloud strategies with extensive practice demonstrations.

In conclusion, although this research is limited to the behaviour of one EAP class and teacher, and to the researcher's interpretation, the findings suggest this is a useful technique for teaching reading-into-writing strategies. Furthermore, future studies of the influence of teachers' expert 'think-aloud' on learner development in any discipline may give further insights into student success when applying learning to a task.

REFERENCES

Chenoweth, N., & Hayes, J. (2001). Fluency in writing: Generating text in L1 and L2. *Written Communication, 18*(1), 80–98.

Cumming, A. (1995). Fostering writing expertise in ESL Composition. In D. Belcher & G. Braine (Eds.), *Academic writing in a second language: Essays on research and pedagogy* (pp. 3–22). Norwood, N.J.: Ablex.

Dörnyei, Z., & Scott, M. (1997). Communication strategies in a second language: Definitions and taxonomies. *Language Learning, 47*, 173–210.

Grabe, W. (2009). *Reading in a second language: Moving from theory to practice.* New York, NY: Cambridge University Press.

Grabe, W., & Kaplan, R. (1996). *Theory and practice of writing.* Harlow, U.K.: Addison Wesley Longman.

Grabe, W., & Zhang, C. (2013). Reading and writing together: A critical component of English for academic purposes teaching and learning. *TESOL Journal, 4*(1), 9–24.

Heeney, M. (2015). *Cognitive modelling: A case study of reading-to-write strategy instruction and the development of second language writing expertise in a university English for academic purposes writing course* (Doctoral dissertation). Retrieved from ProQuest Dissertation and Theses database: http://www.proquest.com/products-services/pqdtglobal.html

Hirvela, A. (2004). *Connecting reading and writing in second language writing instruction.* Ann Arbor: University of Michigan Press.

Hirvela, A., & Du, Q. (2013). "Why am I paraphrasing?": Undergraduate ESL writers' engagement with source-based academic writing and reading. *Journal of English for Academic Purposes, 12*(2), 87–98.

Li, Y., & Casanave, C. P. (2012). Two first-year students' strategies for writing from sources: Patchwriting or plagiarism? *Journal of Second Language Writing, 21*(2), 165–180.

Pressley, M., & Afflerbach, P. (1995). *Verbal protocols of reading: The nature of constructively responsive reading.* New Jersey: Lawrence Erlbaum Associates.

Pressley, M., Allington, R., Wharton-McDonald, R., Collins Block, C., & Mandel Morrow, L. (2001). *Learning to read: Lessons from exemplary first-grade classrooms.* New York: The Guildford Press.

Pressley, M., & Harris, K. R. (2006). Cognitive strategies instruction: From basic research to classroom instruction. In P. A. Alexander & P. H. Winne (Eds.), *Handbook of educational psychology* (2nd ed.) (pp. 265–286). Mahwah: Erlbaum.

Roehler, L., & Cantlon, D. (1997). Scaffolding: A powerful tool in social constructivist classrooms. In K. Hogan and M. Pressley (Eds.), *Scaffolding student learning: Instructional approaches and issues* (pp. 6–41). University of Michigan: Brookbine Books.

Wilson, N., & Bai, H. (2010). The relationships and impact of teachers' metacognitive knowledge and pedagogical understandings of metacognition. *Metacogntion Learning, 5*(3), 269–288.

Zhang, L. (2008). Constructivist pedagogy in strategic reading instruction: Exploring pathways to learner development in the English as a second language ESL classroom. *Instructional Science, 36*, 89–116.

APPENDIX

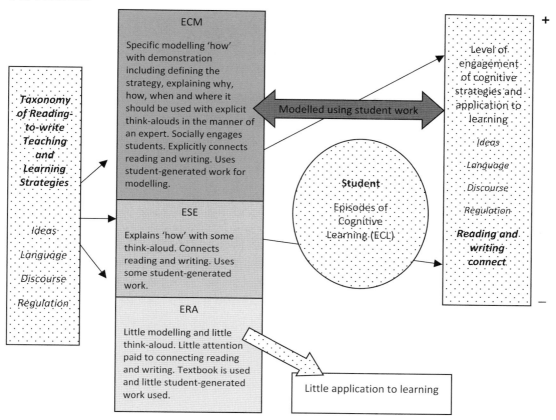

Figure I Teacher modelling: The framework of teaching and learning strategies (based on Zhang, 2008)

ECM = Episode of Cognitive Modelling; ESE = Episode of Strategy Explanation; ERA = Episodes of Raising Awareness; ECL = Episodes of Cognitive Learning

Dina Awad

Cognitive theory and task-based competence

Introduction

The role of cognitive knowledge is essential in second language learning (VanPatten, 1994) and it is therefore necessary to take it into consideration in both task design and assessing achievement. However, the influence of factors such as the type of knowledge has not been sufficiently discussed in EAP contexts. This paper aims to draw educators' attention to the relationship between cognitive features and task type on one hand, and the effect this relationship might have on students' level of achievement on the other. Raising awareness of this particular issue could possibly contribute towards more incorporation of cognitive aspects in EAP programmes, in order to arrive at a better-informed assessment of students' competence.

Cognitive theory

Driven from research in psychology in the seventies (e.g., Rosch & Lloyd, 1978),

cognitive theory was concerned with particular functions of areas in the brain that determine which kind of information people know and how it is processed and stored, accessed and monitored.

This theory filtered into language research through the works of Chafe (1973), Fillmore (1976) and Lakoff (1981, cited in Lakoff (1987)), and most influentially, Langacker (1987). Cognitive elements in second language learning were first discussed by Schmidt (1992) and began to gain popularity in the following years. The research was further developed by Swain and Lapkin (1995) who proposed that knowledge of language can be generally divided into two types: conscious and subconscious.

Competence, aptitude and achievement in language acquisition are closely related to knowledge types. Conscious knowledge, on the one hand, means that students are aware of the grammar, structure and spelling rules that govern the second language use. Thus, this type is also known as declarative.

Since learners have been informed through formal educational settings by teachers and textbooks, it is also known as 'learned linguistic knowledge', referring to the information about a set of rules that are a result of prescriptive instructions (Sorace, 1985; Sajavaara, 1986). Some of the language produced by students in formal educational settings can be the outcome of deliberately planned and analysed form that is closely monitored by both learners and educators. In this type of knowledge, learners employ meta-language, such as parts of speech, to control production.

The second type is known as subconscious knowledge. Acquired through exposure, meaningful input and interaction, the language-learning process in this case parallels that of the first language. It is evident in the capacity to produce grammatical utterances and to judge whether an expression is correct or incorrect, without being aware of the set of rules governing language elements. This type of knowledge, also known as procedural knowledge, reflects implicit information that filters into the long-term memory over a period of time. Micro procedures such as guessing, recognition, hypothesis formation, testing and confirmation are involved. Thus, subconscious L2 knowledge undergoes continuous changes during various interlanguage stages until it becomes entirely automated.

It is worth mentioning that the two types are not mutually exclusive, because learning is a complex process that involves multiple and simultaneous cognitive activities. Some researchers, e.g., Krashen (1981) and Hulstijn (2002), believe that interface is not possible and that the two types are categorically separate, since they are stored in different parts of the brain (cf. Paradis, 1994). Others,

including DeKeyser (1998), hold that *partial* interface is likely. Finally, most language educators see that there is a substantial degree of interface between the two types, as shift is possible from one type to the other. Wallach and Lebiere (2003) propose a combined learning system consisting of a permanent procedural memory functioning simultaneously with a declarative memory. In practice, many language educators believe that explicit information about the language can lead to implicit knowledge and, ultimately, target-like usage through sufficient exposure (Birdsong, 1989; Birdsong & Molis, 2001) or practice.

TASK TYPE AND L2 COMPETENCE

In EAP, practice might be limited to classroom settings through tasks. These may vary in terms of the knowledge required to process learners' information. Researchers refer to task-induced L2 variation to identify the extent to which task type can affect the way learners produce the target language (Bialystok, 1982; Tarone & Parish, 1988; Krashen, 1981). It has been found that task type could drive production to the extent that one group would project incompatible, and sometimes contrastive, error maps if tasks were of different focus.

Different tasks tap into different types of knowledge. The common view is that form-focused tasks generally reflect explicit analysed knowledge, whereas more spontaneous, communicative tasks involve L2 learners' implicit knowledge (Muranoi 2000, Ellis 2005, *inter alia*).

Researchers have measured and compared learners' implicit and explicit knowledge by eliciting data from different tasks. It was found that competence varies according to the knowledge related to each task type (Trenkic, 2000; Ellis, 2009; Zhang, 2015). Although most tasks include elements of both, some tasks are more reflective of one type of knowledge rather than the other. For example, form-focused tasks explore declarative knowledge *about* the language, while free-production tasks elicit more subconscious knowledge *of* the language (Ellis, 2005; Roehr, 2005). The first type is reflected mostly in situations where students are following instructions, correcting word forms and verb tenses with accuracy as a goal, including cloze tests and grammaticality judgement tests in controlled settings. The second type is more prevalent in tasks that are primarily meaning-oriented, e.g., discussions, oral narration and describing pictures, as well as free composition. Generally, the latter includes explaining ideas in less formal conditions of group work, reflective writing, role playing and storytelling. Therefore, it seems that spontaneous, communicative and interactive production better reflects implicit, automated knowledge (Krashen, 1981; Paradis, 1994). However, overlap of both types of knowledge is possible in contextualised tasks with direct instructions, although most of these have accuracy, rather than communicating meaning, as a goal.

THE PRESENT STUDY

In order to examine the relation between L2 knowledge and task type, three tasks with different cognitive requirements were devised: a free composition test (T1), a blanks test (T2) and a grammaticality judgement test (GJT, T3). In all tests, students' use of the English articles was examined.

In the writing task, students were asked to describe their home towns in essays of 350–500 words. There was no indication to

article use in the prompts. The blanks test (T2) comprised six short stories with the articles removed, resulting in 270 blanks. Learners were instructed to fill in the blanks with one of four options (*a, an, the,* Ø). The final test, GJT, comprised 40 sentences which participants were to judge as either correct or incorrect.

The three tests vary in awareness levels, control degrees, focus and presence/absence of contextualisation, representing a full range from one extreme to the other. For example, learners were unaware of the purpose of the writing test, whereas noun phrases (NP) with articles were underlined in T3. Maximum production was expected in T1 with the least control in the instructions, while the GJT (T3) was the most controlled with minimum freedom to produce language and no context. Focus in the three tasks is scaled from full attention to communicating meaning (in T1) to full attention to form (T3). The blanks task (T2), however, possessed some degrees of both types. Table 1 below illustrates the scale of testing elements in the three tasks.

Table 1 Range of task type variation

Free writing (T1)	Blanks (T2)	GJT (T3)
Meaning		Accuracy
Contextualised		Decontextualised
Least controlled		Most controlled
Production: Maximum		Minimum
Unaware of purpose		Aware

Data collected from all three tests was entered as separate noun phrases; each was described by the criteria that determine article use, namely definiteness, countability and number. The same NPs were categorised into either correct or incorrect. The latter was further subdivided by error type: overuse, omission and replacement.

Eighty students enrolled in in-sessional EAP programmes in the United Arab Emirates University took the Quick Oxford Placement Test to roughly determine their English proficiency levels (PL). Based on the test scores, participants were divided into three groups: Elementary (G1), Intermediate (G2) and Advanced (G3). In order to increase the gaps between groups and further clarify the responses, lower intermediate scores were included in G2 while the higher end of intermediate scores were placed into G3. Borderline scores were excluded, leaving 20 students in each group.

It is worth mentioning that only a few results were selected as examples for this paper, due to limitations of scope.

RESULTS

Participants of the same PL produced significantly diverse results across the three tests.

Figure 1 (below) demonstrates the differences in accuracy rates of the weaker group (G1) in marking indefinite plural and uncountable nouns across tasks.

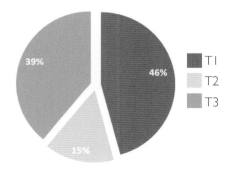

Figure 1 Correct zero marking by Group 1

Similar to the results of G1, the strongest group (G3) achieved higher accuracy rates on plural and uncountable indefinites in the task with least attention to form (T1), while significantly lower rates were observed in the blanks task (T2). Table 2 further illustrates the significant cross-task difference.

On the other hand, with a feature that is not present in the learners' L1[1], in this case the indefinite article, higher accuracy rates are expected in tests that reflect explicit knowledge, in this case, T2 and T3. The figures shown in Table 3 confirm that this expectation was correct.

In examining errors, overuse rates indicate that all participants supplied the indefinite article more frequently in task 2 than 1, while exceedingly higher error rates were observed in task 3. Similar results were recorded on the overuse of the definite article, as shown in Table 4.

In contrast, the highest omission rates were recorded when learners were not prompted to supply articles (T1), while the lowest omission rates were recorded in the task which required higher levels of consciousness (T2) (see Table 5). This resonates with previous studies (Hawkins et al.; Liu & Gleason, 2002), where oversupply was more evident in blank-filling tests than in other test formats.

Table 3 demonstrates how the indefinite article was better supplied when participants' attention was driven to form (T2, T3) rather than meaning, while it was more challenging to automatically supply a linguistic feature unavailable in the L1 without being explicitly prompted to do so (T1).

---

[1] There is no obligatory marking of singular indefinite nouns in Modern Standard Arabic.

Table 2 Cross-task difference in correct indefinite plural and uncountable nouns

	T1 %	T1 v T2	T2 %	T2 v T3	T3 %
G1	81.00	p<0.0001	26.81	p<0.0001	69.17
G2	85.22	p<0.0001	56.35	p<0.0001	73.68
G3	90.70	p<0.0001	63.67	p<0.0001	89.71

Table 3 Correct marking of singular indefinites across tasks

	T1 %	T1 v T2	T2 %	T2 v T3	T3 %	T1 v T3
G1	60.38	p=0.1419	67.83	p=0.4584	66.67	p=0.8729
G2	74.14	p=0.0702	81.85	p<0.0001	91.23	p<0.0001
G3	89.06	p=0.3812	85.46	p<0.0001	100.00	p=0.0050

Table 4 Overuse of the indefinite article across tasks

	T1 %	T1 v T2	T2 %	T2 v T3	T3 %	T1 v T3
G1	2.15	p<0.0001	27.02	p<0.0001	57.33	p<0.0001
G2	2.32	p<0.0001	14.73	p=0.0015	47.37	p<0.0001
G3	2.33	p=0.0014	6.29	p<0.0001	37.65	p<0.0001

Table 5 Omission of the indefinite article across tasks

	T1 %	T1 v T2	T2 %	T2 v T3	T3 %	T1 v T3
G1	39.62	p<0.0001	11.30	p<0.0001	37.78	p=0.7915
G2	25.86	p<0.0001	4.46	p=0.0443	16.67	p=0.0030
G3	10.94	p=0.0442	2.99	p=0.0129	10.78	p=0.9754

Table 6 Replacement errors across tasks (*the-for-a*)

	T1 %	T1 v T2	T2 %	T2 v T3	T3 %
G1	4.72	p<0.0001	24.78	p=0.3724	31.11
G2	3.45	p<0.0001	17.39	p=0.7450	14.04
G3	3.13	p<0.0001	15.08	p=0.9085	15.69

Finally, with regards to replacement errors, the lowest rates were recorded in T1, as learners did not automatically replace one form with the other. Thus, the error rates in the writing task were significantly lower than those observed in T2 and T3, which, in turn, were not considerably different from one another (see the percentages in Table 6). This was true for all PL groups.

DISCUSSION

From the results, it is noticeable that divergent accuracy and error patterns emerge across tasks, regardless of achievement rates by proficiency level. Participants seem to have performed differently, depending on the task focus and their level of awareness of its purpose and the linguistic features they were expected to provide. Results also suggest that, despite higher accuracy rates in form-focused tasks, more overuse and replacement errors have been observed than in meaning-based and content-driven tasks that reflect more implicit knowledge of the second language. Hence, there is significant inconsistency of outcomes across tasks with dissimilar cognitive requirements. Therefore, dependence on the results of one task type could be deceptive of learners' actual proficiency level. For example, the high accuracy rates of *a/n* observed in task 3 can

be misleading because they are not matched by the considerably lower rates in task 1, where answers are derived from learners' store of implicit knowledge. Similar findings were reported in other studies that examined task variation (Foster & Skehan, 1996) and knowledge type (Zhang, 2015). It is also noticeable that the implicit/explicit element was influential in deciding patterns of L2 development (see also Awad, 2014).

IMPLICATIONS FOR EAP

In teaching, raising students' awareness of L2 forms, structures and rules does not necessarily yield more target-like production. Instead, better language learning *can* be achieved by strengthening implicit mental processes that draw on learners' knowledge of the world through meaningful interaction in the L2 (Ortega, 2007). Since both conscious and subconscious systems function co-operatively to better learn a given task (Willingham, 1998; Ullman, 2005), it becomes essential to take both equally into consideration while designing materials and tests for EAP programmes. With planned deployment of all types of knowledge, educators can obtain data that is more reflective of students' overall understanding and actual ability within a more comprehensive framework of L2 competence.

REFERENCES

Awad, D. (2014). Diverse acquisition patterns. *The Linguistics Journal*, 8(1), 2–28.

Bialystok, E. (1982). On the relationship between knowing and using linguistic forms. *Applied Linguistics*, 3, 181–206.

Birdsong, D. (1989). *Metalinguistic performance and interlinguistic competence*. Berlin: Springer.

Birdsong, D., & Molis, M. (2001). On the evidence for maturational constraints in second language acquisition. *Journal of Memory and Language, 44*(2), 235–249.

Chafe, W.L. (1973). Language and memory. *Language, 49*(2), 261–281.

DeKeyser, R. (1998). Beyond focus on form: Cognitive perspectives on learning and practicing second language grammar. In C. Doughty, & J. Williams (Eds.), *Focus on form in classroom second language acquisition* (pp. 42–63). Cambridge, UK: Cambridge University Press.

Ellis, R. (2005). Measuring implicit and explicit knowledge of a second language: A psychometric study. *Studies in Second Language Acquisition, 27*(2), 141–172. doi:10.1017/S0272263105050096

Ellis, R. (2009). Measuring the implicit and explicit knowledge of a second language. In D. Singleton (Ed.), *Implicit and explicit knowledge in second language learning, testing and teaching* (pp. 27–31). Bristol: Multilingual Matters.

Fillmore, C. (1976). Frame semantics and the nature of language. *Annals of the New York Academy of Sciences: Conference on the origin and development of language and speech, 280*, 20–32.

Foster, P., & Skehan, P. (1996). The influence of planning and task type on second language performance. *Studies in Second Language Acquisition, 18*, 299–323.

Hawkins, R., Al-Eid, S., Almahboob, I., Athanasopoulos, P., Chaengchenkit, R., Hu, J., Rezai, M., Jaensch, C., Jeon, Y., Jiang, A., Leung, I., Matsunaga, K., Ortega, M., Sarko, G., Snape, N., & Velasco-Zarate, K. (2006). *Non-target-like article use in English: Implications for current UG-based theories of SLA*. University of Essex.

Hulstijn, J. H. (2002). What does the impact of frequency tell us about the language acquisition device? *Studies in Second Language Acquisition, 24*, 269–273. doi:10.1017/S0272263102002115

Krashen, S. D. (1981). *Second language acquisition and second language learning*. New Jersey: Prentice Hall International.

Lakoff, G. (1987). *Women, fire, and dangerous things. What categories reveal about the mind*. Chicago: University of Chicago Press.

Langacker, R. (1987). *Foundations of cognitive grammar, (1): Theoretical prerequisites*. Stanford: Stanford University Press.

Liu, D., & Gleason, J. I. (2002). Acquisition of the article *the* by nonnative speakers of English: An analysis of four nongeneric uses. *Studies in Second Language Acquisition, 24*, 1–26.

Muranoi, H. (2000). Focus on form through interaction enhancement. *Language Learning, 50*(4), 617–673.

Ortega, L. (2007). Meaningful L2 practice in foreign language classrooms: A cognitive-interactionist SLA perspective. In R. M. DeKeyser (Ed.), *Practice in a second language: Perspectives from applied linguistics and cognitive psychology* (pp. 180–207). New York: Cambridge University Press.

Paradis, M. (1994). Neurolinguistic aspects of implicit and explicit memory: Implications for bilingualism and SLA. In N. Ellis (Ed.), *Implicit and explicit learning of languages* (pp. 393–419). San Diego, CA: Academic Press.

Roehr, K. (2005). *Metalinguistic knowledge in second language learning: An emergenist perspective* (Unpublished PhD Thesis). Lancaster University, UK.

Rosch, E., & Lloyd, B. B. (1978). *Cognition and categorisation.* Hillsdale, NJ: Lawrence Erbaulm Association Inc.

Sajavaara, K. (1986). Transfer and second language speech processing. In E. Kellerman & M. Sharwood-Smith (Eds.), *Cross-linguistic influence in second language acquisition* (pp. 66–79). Oxford, UK: Pergamon Press.

Schmidt, R. (1992). Psychological mechanisms underlying second language fluency. *Studies in Second Language Acquisition, 14,* 357–385.

Sorace, A. (1985). Metalinguistic knowledge and language use in acquisition-poor environments. *Applied Linguistics, 6,* 239–254.

Swain, M., & Lapkin, S. (1995). Problems in output and the cognitive processes they generate: A step towards second language learning. *Applied Linguistics, 16*(3), 371–391. doi: 10.1093/applin/16.3.371

Tarone, E., & Parrish, B. (1988). Task-related variation in interlanguage: The case of articles. *Language Learning, 38*(1), 21–44.

Trenkic, D. (2000). *The acquisition of English articles by Serbian speakers* (Unpublished PhD thesis). Cambridge University.

Ullman, M. T. (2005). A cognitive neuroscience perspective on second language acquisition: The declarative procedural model. In C. Sanz (Ed.), *Mind and context in adult second language acquisition* (pp. 141–178). USA: Georgetown University Press.

VanPatten, B. (1994). Evaluating the role of consciousness in second language acquisition: Terms, linguistic features & research methodology. *Consciousness in second language learning,* 27–36.

Wallach, D., & Lebiere, C. (2003). Implicit and explicit learning in a unified architecture of cognition. In L. Jiménez (Ed.), *Attention and implicit learning* (pp. 215–250). Amsterdam: John Benjamins Publishing Company.

Willingham, D. B. (1998). A neuropsychological theory of motor skill learning. *Psychological Review, 105*(3), 558–584. http://dx.doi.org/10.1037/0033–295X.105.3.558

Zhang, R. (2015). Measuring university-level L2 learners' implicit and explicit linguistic knowledge. *Studies in Second Language Acquisition, 37*(3), 457–486. doi:10.1017/S0272263114000370

ZOE GAZELEY-EKE

DIGITISING THE EAP CLASSROOM: MAKING THE VLE MORE ACTIVE

INTRODUCTION

The development of learners' digital literacies is increasingly given high priority in many higher education institutions; with the Higher Education Academy stating that the use of technology-enhanced learning can improve the student experience (HEA, 2015). This paper will discuss the application of technology-enhanced learning and teaching in the EAP classroom. Using an action research approach, it examines how EAP tutors can assist international students in the development of 21st-century skills such as critical thinking, innovation, collaboration, autonomy, and flexibility (Dudeney, Hockly & Pegrum, 2013) within a digital context (JISC, 2009). It is intended that the information gathered from the research project could provide some useful insights for EAP tutors looking for new ways to increase the engagement of learners in the classroom and utilise their Virtual Learning Environment (VLE) in a more communicative and transformative way,

as opposed to its simply being a repository for course documents (Kirkwood & Price, 2014).

THE CONTEXT

The research project focuses on a mandatory credit-bearing EAP module, Advanced Business English for International Students, which is taken as part of a final-year direct entry International Business (BA) top-up course. The entrance requirement is the completion of years 1 and 2 of an equivalent undergraduate course and IELTS level 6.5, with some students gaining direct entry and others taking Pre-sessional English courses. Two-thirds of the learners are from China, with the remainder coming from Africa, the Middle East and Europe.

RATIONALE FOR THE RESEARCH

The action research project aims at exploring ways of encouraging learner engagement and developing formative assessment techniques through the use of technology. This use of technology also helps to achieve one of Coventry University's corporate objectives of ensuring that students are given the opportunity to learn through a diversity of relevant media, which would prepare them for the rapid changes in the increasingly digital workplace (Coventry University, 2011). This research also reflects the belief held by Dudeney et al. (2013) that teachers are preparing their learners for futures in which they do not know what types of jobs will exist.

Dudeney et al. (2013, p. 2) define digital literacies as 'the individual and social skills needed to effectively interpret, manage, share and create meaning in the growing range of digital communication channels'. Our EAP learners studying at UK universities are required to develop skills such as critical thinking, innovation, collaboration, autonomy and flexibility. Engaging with digital literacies requires an effective command of technologies in order to locate resources, communicate ideas and build collaborations. This focus on social constructivism in learning has been argued as 'ideally preparing students for a post-industrial context' (Pegrum, 2009, p. 27) and has turned learning via a computer from a passive activity to a shared culture of active contributors (Dudeney et al., 2013, p. 3).

RESEARCH AIMS AND OBJECTIVES

The aim of this action research project is to explore the impact of incorporating digital literacy skills into an EAP classroom. The researcher wanted to: investigate the learners' use of technology within and outside the classroom, experiment with different e-learning tools in lesson time to promote production of the target language, and collect feedback (via an online questionnaire) on the use of these new e-tools.

REDESIGNING THE VLE

The first change was to use the VLE in a more active way in the classroom. This required eliminating the 'scroll of death', which is often associated with the Moodle VLE, when long webpages require extensive scrolling to access all the information. This scrolling also reduces the learner's ability to see the 'big picture' (Moore, 2012). The move to the grid format and the inclusion of relevant Rich Site Summary (RSS) feeds, which show regularly changing web content relevant to their discipline, and Twitter feed, not only made the site more visually appealing, but also engaged learners in authentic reading. The addition of the EAP tasks and tools resulted in the VLE being at the centre of each EAP session.

EAP TASKS AND TOOLS

THE PLANNING PROCESS

The three EAP areas that were focused on were engaging learners in the planning process, the writing process and giving feedback. For planning, instead of using flipchart paper and pens, learners used two different open-source websites. In one activity, learners first discussed in pairs or small groups their views around academic writing style and the common errors found in their work. They then used Padlet (2016), a virtual wall, to share their group's ideas with the whole class. It was observed that the learners not only discussed what they believed academic style to be, but also went online to search for and post a link to another university's academic style guide. This encouraged a discussion on the use of online sources and acknowledging where ideas have been borrowed and, therefore, should be credited to others.

Another session which incorporated planning required learners in groups to use an e-tool to produce a mind map of their ideas at the beginning of the writing process in preparation for writing a report. This time, the Text 2 Mind Map (2016) was used. After producing the mind map, the learners could then save it to a PDF file and upload to a forum on the VLE, which allowed them to share and comment on each other's mind maps. Both of these tools gave learners the advantage of being able to save their plans, which are often lost when completed on paper, allowing the learners to refer back to them as the writing process continued.

THE WRITING PROCESS

The next part of the research was to explore how technology could be utilised in the writing process during an EAP lesson. It has been claimed that most instructors use Moodle's news forums to make announcements, post files for learners, collect learner submissions and not much more (Moore, 2012). The aim was to make the VLE more active for the learners by increasing the writing output in class time, whilst raising awareness of differing writing styles. In addition, it was hoped that encouraging collaborative writing would also lead to increased peer feedback.

The Moodle forum was used for groups to post their collaborative writing and, when finished, others could give feedback on the completed work. Following the peer feedback posted below, a discussion ensued regarding how the tool affected the

register of the writing and whether it was appropriate to give one-word responses with characters such as question marks.

Group 1. *According to Chief Executive the bank was forced to set aside cash to deal with the scandal as well as other fines and disputes. We recommend that they pay all pending fines and in the future avoid tax evasion scandals. Due to battered image by the scandal they should restructure its executive for better image.*

Group 2. *This is not a recommendation. Also these are problems that were faced by the bank. Need academic style.*

Group 3. *Solutions?*

Another e-tool used was Google Docs. The activity required the learners to work together in groups to produce different sections of a business report. The use of the anonymous function allowed writers to contribute to, edit and give comments freely on the document without their identity being displayed. The benefits to the learners were that they were working together to improve their writing, and the e-tools enabled quicker responses from their peers. Moreover, the tutor comments were posted to give formative feedback in real time, as opposed to marking the work after class.

FEEDBACK

In post-course evaluations, learners often state that they would like more feedback on their work during class. In this research project, different e-tools were trialled as methods of giving feedback. One function found on Moodle is the Instant Messenger (IM) chat session. Learners entered the chat session and contributed answers to questions set or gave their opinion. This was then projected for the whole class. It was hoped that, in addition to learners gaining more writing practice by using this method, the teacher could see who was engaging with the activity, and the learners might feel more comfortable than speaking out in front of the whole class.

Other functions used on Moodle were the quiz creation functions and the real-time quiz option. The quiz was used to turn paper-based manipulative/card-sort activities into electronic versions that gave immediate feedback, and the real-time quiz was adapted to check understanding of particular concepts. Finally, the Journal e-tool, which enables learners to upload a written reflection only the teacher can read, was used for learners to comment on their experience of submitting their first piece of assessed writing. This facilitated the tutor in gaining an insight into the learners' writing process and any issues they encountered.

FINDINGS

One objective of this research project was to gather information on the learners' use of technology. As could be presumed, all of the 30 respondents stated that they had some form of mobile device that they brought into university classes to use. When asked about their digital skills outside the classroom, a third of the learners revealed they had never participated in online forums, over half had never uploaded a video to the internet and two thirds had never used Twitter.

A further objective was to collect learners' feedback regarding the new e-tools used in the classroom. A Likert scale was used, in which respondents had to state

their level of agreement with a number of statements. Twenty-seven out of the thirty learners who completed the questionnaire agreed that the real-time quizzes helped to revise the content covered in the lessons. Eighty per cent believed that the IM chat function allowed them to contribute more to a class discussion, and over 80% agreed that the use of Google Docs was useful and that the journal-writing activity helped them to reflect on how they could improve their coursework time management.

A final objective was to obtain more qualitative feedback.

Samples of learner feedback:
What did you like about the module and why?

- *The module being informative and engaging and making my Business English learning and writing skills much better.*
- *Our teacher using the digital teaching is more realistic than normal class.*
- *I like the drop and drag exercise because it helped me a lot with my previous essay structure.*
- *I like the digital work we do in class and the discussion group work.*
- *Lots of resources in Moodle which I can access easily.*

The feedback appears to indicate that the learners perceived a positive influence on their academic writing skills with the use of the e-tools. In addition, the e-tools empowered them to participate in collaborative writing activities and group discussions. The responses also showed that learners appreciated the additional feedback given in the form of the self-testing element of the VLE, with many respondents asking for 'more quizzes'.

Along with the positive aspects, the learners were asked:

'What do you need/want to use to improve your digital literacy skills?'

- *To have digital literacy skill workshops so that students will be more better with it.*
- *Keep on practicing forums and online activities.*
- *More practice on digital literacy skills.*
- *Technical skill.*

As part of a Continuous Professional Development (CPD) observation by a teacher trainer from another institution, feedback was also obtained in which the following comments were made:

You have created an atmosphere ripe with autonomy and student collaboration is encouraged as far as possible. Your use of learning technology is exemplary and your students clearly gain great benefit from it.

Learners also accessed tasks via Moodle throughout the session. This is good practice as it gets students comfortable with using the VLE – an essential skill in H.E.

The research revealed that, whilst the learners all had mobile devices which they brought into the classroom, they seemed more receptive than productive when using digital technology outside of the classroom. The students did have some difficulties in using all of the different e-learning tasks. However, by the teacher encouraging group collaboration and providing more guidance, they became more confident in using the different e-tools as the course progressed. The individual e-learning tasks were ideal for the teacher to observe exactly how individual students were progressing.

Often, when using tools such as the mini-whiteboard (an A4 sized whiteboard), learners look at the person who has responded first to find out the answers. With the use of the Instant Messaging function, it was extremely difficult for them to see the other PCs or mobile devices. In addition, the real-time quizzes were a good way of assessing if learning had taken place, and had the added benefit of providing instant feedback.

Overall, this action research project has provided some useful information regarding the digital expertise that these learners have, and raised tutor awareness of what these students might need in terms of more support to develop their digital literacy skills. For example, online discussion forums are often used by teachers to generate discussion outside the classroom, but they are seldom fully utilised. It might be that learners from different academic backgrounds need more guidance or training in using these tools. During the project, it was found that learners contributed more to discussion forums during class time when in groups, than whilst alone outside the classroom.

LIMITATIONS AND CHALLENGES

This project involved a small sample of data collected from two class groups, so to this extent, it is limited in the outcomes that can be claimed. The challenges revolve around the ability to ensure that all learners have access to a mobile device or that the lessons can take place in a PC lab. Developing materials to be utilised by e-tools is very time-consuming, but it is hoped that, after the initial time requirements, they can be reproduced in a more time-efficient manner. Also, the ever-changing nature of learning technology can often mean that open-source access can change or be removed.

RECOMMENDATIONS

This action research project has resulted in a number of recommendations that could be made to further develop the use of digital literacy skills in the EAP classroom.

1. INCLUSION IN DIAGNOSTIC TESTING

During the diagnostic testing stage, there should be a survey given to learners to determine their proficiency in using various forms of independent learning technology. Digital literacy skills can only be developed if teachers are aware of their learners' starting points. Klapper claims that diagnostic tests allow tutors to shape the syllabus and learners to take remedial action when necessary (2006, p. 262).

2. TEACHERS NEED TO DEVELOP THEIR CATALOGUE OF E-LEARNING TASKS

This project included various e-learning tasks, but more research is required by teachers to ensure they are constantly developing their arsenal in this ever-changing field of teaching. Books such as *How to teach English with technology* can provide new ideas (Dudeney & Hockly, 2007). Taking ideas from educationalists such as Petty (2009a, 2009b) and applying e-tools will help to develop digital literacy skills. In addition, there are many online resources such as *learning technologies in EAP* (2016) (learningtechnologiesineap.org) with current blogs and tips on using learning technology within the field of EAP.

3. ENCOURAGE LEARNERS TO USE THESE TOOLS OUTSIDE OF THE CLASSROOM

Learners were keen to use the technology when encouraged in the classroom, but more should be done to encourage use outside the classroom. Specific tasks should be set initially to encourage autonomous learning. In addition, new tools should be exploited to help with their formative assignments.

CONCLUSION

This action research project set out to improve the level of engagement in the EAP classroom and to develop the digital literacy skills of the EAP learner. Positive feedback from both the learners and teacher trainers during CPD observations suggest that this is an area that should continue to be incorporated into the EAP classroom. There was evidence of increased writing output in class time, through the use of Instant Messenger and the Journal e-tool. Awareness of writing styles for different audiences emerged from the discussion surrounding the group responses to the forum. Learners have also engaged in more collaborative writing and been encouraged to give more peer feedback through e-tools such as Google Docs. It has led to increased engagement in the VLE by the learners, which is hoped to have resulted in not only the development of learners' digital literacy skills, but also improvements in their academic English.

REFERENCES

Coventry University. (2011). *Coventry University teaching, learning and assessment strategy, 2011–2015*. Coventry: Coventry University. Retrieved from http://www.coventry. ac.uk/Global/PDF%20Documents/9236-11%20Teaching%20Learning%20and%20 Assessment%20Strategy%202011-15%20v4%20hi%20res.pdf

Dudeney, G., & Hockly, N. (2007). *How to teach English with technology*. Harlow: Pearson Education Limited.

Dudeney, G., Hockly, N., & Pegrum, M. (2013). *Research and resources in language teaching: Digital literacies*. Harlow: Pearson Education Limited.

Google Docs. (2016). *Google docs*. Retrieved January 20, 2016, from http://www.google.com/ docs/about/

Higher Education Academy. (2015). Online learning. Retrieved September 1, 2015, from http://www.heacademy.ac.uk/workstreams-research/themes/online-learning

JISC. (2009). *Effective practice in a digital age: A guide to technology-enhanced learning and teaching*. Bristol: JISC.

Kirkwood, A., & Price, L. (2014). Technology-enhanced learning and teaching in higher education: What is 'enhanced' and how do we know? A critical literature review. *Learning, Media and Technology, 39*(1), 6–36.

Klapper, J. (2006). *Understanding and developing good practice: Language teaching in higher education*. London: CILT, the National Centre for Languages.

Moodle. (2016). Moodle [Learning platform]. Retrieved January 20, 2016, from https:// moodle.org/

Moore, M. (2012). Best practices in moodle course design. In M. Glynn (Ed.), *Ireland & UK: Moodlemoot Conference Publication* (pp. 4–16). Held April 2–4, 2012. Dublin: Dublin City University.

Padlet. (2016). *Padlet*. Retrieved January 20, 2016, from https://padlet.com/

Pegrum, M. (2009). *From blogs to bombs: The future of digital technologies in education*. Western Australia: UWA Publishing.

Petty, G. (2009a). *Evidence-based teaching: A practical approach*. Cheltenham, UK: Nelson Thorne Ltd.

Petty, G. (2009b). *Teaching today: A practical guide*. Cheltenham, UK: Nelson Thorne Ltd.

Text 2 Mind Map. (2016). *Text2mindmap*. Retrieved January 20, 2016, from https://www. text2mindmap.com/

MEHTAP KOCATEPE

EXTRINSICALLY MOTIVATED HOMEWORK BEHAVIOUR: STUDENT VOICES FROM THE ARABIAN GULF

INTRODUCTION

Homework is important. It can help to prepare learners for a following lesson, reinforce skills introduced in class, facilitate participation in class and develop lifelong skills (Epstein & Van Voorhis, 2001). Most educators agree that effective pedagogic practices comprise complementing classroom learning with some form of study beyond the classroom context (Benson, 2011). In the United Arab Emirates, homework is endorsed by the Ministry of Education (United Arab Emirates Ministry of Education, 2010) and by tertiary-level institutions as integral to education and student learning (Zayed University Office of Student Affairs, 2013).

Setting homework can be contentious. In the context in which this research was carried out, many teachers complain about students not doing homework and many students complain about teachers assigning

too much. In the literature on homework-related research, there are disagreements too. While some researchers have found that homework positively influences academic achievement (Cooper, Robinson & Patall, 2006; Trost and Salehi-Isfahani, 2012), others have questioned such a causal relationship (Geide-Stevenson, 2009; Kohn, 2006; Trautwein, Schnyder, Niggli, Neumann & Lüdtke, 2009).

Research on homework motivation has focused either on how students can be intrinsically motivated to enjoy doing homework, such as by providing choices (Patall, Cooper & Wynn, 2010), or on the role that external incentives play in motivating students to do homework. Grades (Radhakrishnan, Lam & Ho, 2009), peers and significant adults in learners' lives (Xu, 2010) and cultural contexts (Rapanta, 2014) have been identified as factors that influence a student's decision to do or not do homework. The complex relationship between such external factors and students' decision-making capacities, however, has not been explored.

The present research employed a qualitative research design to investigate how different types of extrinsic motivation influenced students' decisions to engage with homework. The focus of the research was solely on identifying extrinsic motivators. As Ryan and Deci (2000a) observe, most of the tasks that educators assign to students are not inherently interesting or enjoyable. This is especially true of homework. In fact, the majority of activities undertaken by adults are extrinsically motivated, as after childhood, the freedom to be intrinsically motivated is limited by social pressures and responsibilities (Ryan & Deci, 2000b). It is, therefore, important to investigate how external incentives shape adult language learners' decisions and behaviours to do homework (Vallerand & Ratelle, 2002).

SELF-DETERMINATION THEORY

Self-determination theory provides a useful framework for exploring what moves students to do homework. It helps to understand the underlying attitudes and goals that give rise to students' actions regarding homework. According to self-determination theory (Deci, Vallerand, Pelletier & Ryan, 1991; Ryan & Deci, 2000a, 2002), the orientation of an individual's motivation can be broadly categorised as being intrinsic or extrinsic. Intrinsic motivation refers to an individual's engagement in an activity for the pleasure and satisfaction derived from the activity itself. Extrinsic motivation underpins activities that are done to achieve a separable outcome. The two types of motivation are not binary opposites, but

rather, different points on a continuum of different kinds of motivation.

Figure 1 describes a taxonomy of motivation, ranging from being highly self-determined and autonomous (intrinsic motivation) to having no impetus to act (amotivation). Between these two ends of the continuum are four types of extrinsic motivation that vary in the degree of self-determination exercised by the individual.

External regulation underpins actions that are done to obtain an external reward, to satisfy an external demand or to avoid punishment. A student doing homework to attain a grade is displaying externally-regulated homework behaviour. This is the least autonomous form of extrinsic motivation. A second type of extrinsic motivation is *introjected regulation,* where an action is done to avoid shame, or to enhance one's ego and feelings of worth. For example, when a student does homework to avoid feeling guilty, the resulting emotional experience is negative.

A more self-determined type of extrinsic motivation is *identified regulation,* which involves a conscious valuing of a goal or regulation and an acceptance of the behaviour as personally or socially important. For example, a student who does grammar homework because she believes that producing accurate grammar is important has endorsed this activity as being personally relevant. Her decision to engage in the homework is to some extent self-determined. *Integrated regulation* is the most self-determined form of extrinsic motivation and results from when a person internalises the reasons for an action and assimilates them with her personally-endorsed values, goals, needs and identities. An example of integrated regulation would be a student doing homework because she believes it will

Amotivation	Controlled extrinsic motivation		Autonomous extrinsic motivation		Intrinsic motivation
	External regulation	Introjected regulation	Identified regulation	Integrated regulation	

←   →
No/Low self-determination   High self-determination

Figure 1 The self-determination continuum (Based on Ryan & Deci, 2002). [Source: Adaptation used with permission of Rochester Press]

make her a better university student. Actions that are regulated internally are the result of volition and lead to emotionally positive experiences.

Many of the studies that identify extrinsically-motivated behaviours as underpinning homework motivation dichotomise extrinsic motivation against intrinsic motivation. Extrinsic behaviours are described as undesirable, as they are believed to fail to develop lifelong habits and attitudes in learners or create a sense of enjoyment from doing homework (Coutts, 2004; Patall et al., 2010). These studies adopt a homogenous view of extrinsic motivation and fail to capture the variability in it.

There is a strong need for more research on homework motivation in second/foreign language learning contexts in tertiary education. Much of the existing research on homework has neglected the investigation of the more self-determined forms of extrinsic motivation. Secondly, much of the research on homework has focused on young school children in educational contexts in which their home languages are used (Cooper & Valentine, 2001; Trautwein & Lüdtke, 2009). A third gap in the literature is that there is limited research on homework practices in the Gulf Arab context. Rapanta (2014) has shown how doing homework in this region is not necessarily seen as

one's own decision, but as emanating from religious beliefs. However, this finding currently lacks empirical support.

The present research sought to identify the ways different types of extrinsic motivation potentially influence a group of female Emirati university students' decisions to do homework. My primary interest was in exploring the role that external incentives play in promoting self-determined forms of motivation, as such motivating factors result in active, volitional engagement and can lead to high-quality learning (Ryan & Deci, 2000a).

RESEARCH DESIGN

A qualitative inquiry was conducted to investigate how different types of extrinsic factors motivate students to do homework. I conducted the research in an English-medium university in the United Arab Emirates in a first-year English Composition class. The university is gender-segregated and the class consisted of 21 female Emirati students aged 18 to 22. All the students spoke Arabic as a first language. I assigned homework in almost every class, but did not grade it.

Data were collected using semi-structured interviews and homework logs. I conducted individual interviews with students mid-semester, as well as at the end of semester.

Sixteen students participated in the first set of interviews, which lasted approximately 20 minutes each. The interview question prompts are shown in the Appendix. The second set of interviews, which had an open structure and in which 15 students took part, lasted for 30–45 minutes. The homework log was in the form of an online Word document which students completed and submitted in class every week. Students used the log to make notes of whether or not they had done the homework assigned to them in the Composition course or in other courses, and the reasons why they did or did not do that week's homework. A total of 18 logs were submitted at the end of the semester.

DATA ANALYSIS

A deductive approach to data analysis was employed, where data were initially categorised into the four categories of extrinsic motivation. The data were then further categorised depending on commonly used themes. Data suggested that students may adopt any one of these forms of external regulation at any time, moving back and forth along the continuum of extrinsic motivation.

Only one comment suggested the adoption of integrated regulation in doing homework; 21 comments suggested homework was done for ego enhancement or internal coercion and, hence, were categorised as introjected regulation. In contrast, 92 comments suggested that homework was done for an external reward (external regulation) and, in 101 comments, students identified with the role and value of homework (identified regulation). In the analysis, I focus on the two most commonly identified types of extrinsic motivation underpinning students'

homework behaviour: identified regulation and external regulation.

IDENTIFIED REGULATION

This type of extrinsic motivation involves a conscious valuing of an activity or a goal and accepting it as personally or socially important. Students appeared to engage in homework that they perceived as contributing to academic studies. For example, one student said, 'Homework has benefits for me. It help me learn, to understand the lesson'. Homework that was perceived as contributing to learning in other courses or as having long-term career benefits also encouraged engagement.

Students also valued homework that was intellectually challenging. Activities that encouraged students to think critically about their responses, rather than copy and paste answers, were seen as valuable. Homework that encouraged student creativity and/or that asked for students' opinions on topics was also rated highly by students, especially if it incorporated the use of video, audio, image and other media. For example, a number of students referred to homework in which they had to create an infographic as 'important' and 'useful'.

The provision of guidance in how to complete homework through models, grids and templates also motivated students to recognise and identify with the value of doing homework. One student explained, 'I used the model summary a lot. It was clear and also reading-and-taking-notes homeworks were good. It help me read and understand.' Homework tasks which students saw as scaffolded increased their feelings of confidence and competence in doing homework. Such attitudes were influential in encouraging students to recognise and accept the potential value of doing homework.

The factors motivating these students to do homework remained extrinsic, as homework was done to achieve an outcome separate to the activity itself. Nevertheless, students' identification with the value of homework led to their exercise of a relatively high degree of autonomy in deciding to do a particular homework task. These students expressed willingness to do homework and the emotional outcome of this engagement was positive.

EXTERNAL REGULATION

The second largest category of responses was related to homework behaviour that was regulated by compliance to external demands. A frequently repeated phrase in the data was 'I have to do homework'. When prompted as to why they felt obliged to do homework, a common response was related to the teacher, as is the case in the following interview excerpt:

Student: *If the teacher told us to read, we have to.*

Interviewer: *Do you feel you have to? Why do you feel that way?*

Student: *Because the teacher said do it. I don't know. The teacher knows what is better for me. I'll do it because you or my maths teacher said do it.*

Interviewer: *What if you don't like the homework?*

Student: *I don't like homework anyway. But I do it.*

Other than teachers, some students appeared to do homework to 'make [their] parents proud'.

Another type of external incentive mentioned in the data was that of obtaining grades. One student explained: 'I do all the homework because if I fail in the tests, maybe homework grades will save me'. Other students also referred to doing homework to obtain homework grades. What is interesting is that grades were not awarded for homework in this particular composition class. However, students expected to be given a reward for their work. Potential long-term rewards were also an incentive for students to do homework. Many referred to the possibility of homework contributing to higher grades in exams or even higher salaries in employment.

While comments in this category did show that homework was completed, these students did not appear to gain any pleasure or satisfaction from doing so. In fact, 'dislike', 'hate', 'annoyed', 'didn't like' were used to describe their emotions when doing homework. Their decision to do homework was controlled by an external force, suggesting low autonomous behaviour.

DISCUSSION

The focus of the study was on identifying the external incentives that motivated a group of female university students in the United Arab Emirates to do homework. I focused specifically on identifying extrinsic factors, with the assumption that much of adult life is centred on completing tasks that are not inherently interesting. An identification of external motivators that move students to do homework willingly can help teachers in creating homework assignments that facilitate effective learning.

A striking theme in the data was that many students completed homework when they identified with the values and purposes related to a homework task.

When students perceived a homework task as personally or academically useful or as mentally challenging, they completed it with satisfaction and pleasure. When they recognised that they were provided with guidance and support in completing assigned homework, they engaged with the task more favourably and felt competent.

A second theme that emerged from the data was that students' homework behaviour was externally regulated. Homework was done to attain a material reward or to gain the approval of 'significant others'. This supports claims in the literature that family and society are at the crux of Emirati students' lives (Engin & McKeown, 2012). Fulfilling expectations of teachers and family members, in particular, were forces that moved students to do homework. While this type of motivation did lead to homework engagement, students' intentions were controlled by external factors, leading to a lack of autonomy in decision-making. Students who were moved by such factors reported resentment when doing homework.

It appears that students' decisions to engage with homework were influenced by students' perceptions of how a particular homework task fit in with broader social and academic contexts, or by factors related to the task itself. Decisions that derived from one's sense of self were minimal in the data. This explains why decisions to do homework based on desires of ego-enhancement (introjected regulation) or those that involved an assimilation of the activity with one's identity (integrated regulation) were less frequently referred to in the interviews and homework logs.

The data presented here point to the need for educators to design and assign homework that challenges students and arouses creativity, while providing academic support. Such homework can create opportunities for students to feel competent and in charge of their own learning. While awarding grades for homework completion might increase homework submission rates, it might not create meaningful and pleasant out-of-class learning experiences. As the data here suggest, homework that arouses feelings of self-efficacy and provides opportunities for the exercise of self-determined behaviour has the potential to create higher levels of engagement with learning.

RECOMMENDATIONS

One recommendation of this study is that, when teachers design homework, students need to be made aware of the personal, academic and/or social outcomes of the homework. Simply listing learning outcomes will not suffice. There need to be discussions of students' understandings of learning outcomes and of how the homework is relevant and significant in reaching these. A recognition of how a homework task fits in with their broader educational goals can encourage students to value homework.

A second important aspect of homework design is that students should be given guidance and support. Teachers should not assume that students already know how to shape their own learning experiences (Pearson, 2003). Providing step-by-step guidelines, sample answers, model texts, note-taking grids and other forms of academic support in completing homework can provide opportunities for scaffolding and increase students' sense of self-efficacy.

Homework that contributes to the development of competence and a sense of autonomy is important in moving student motivation towards the more self-determined end of the motivation continuum. Students who are less influenced by external rewards or punishments, those who recognise a purpose in doing homework are also those who have greater enjoyment, of and interest in, learning (Ryan & Deci, 2000a).

This study has also shown that homework will not be perceived and carried out in the same way by all learners. Indeed, it is not a one-size-fits-all task. It will inevitably have different impacts on student motivation, due to a range of academic and personal reasons. Providing students with choices in homework is one way of encouraging self-determined behaviours. Students could also be given the responsibility of devising homework tasks that they believe help to achieve particular learning goals.

A limitation of this study is that it took place in one classroom with a relatively small number of students and is not generalisable. Another limitation is that my dual role as teacher and researcher might have impacted on students' participation in the research and the data that I obtained. Some students might have felt pressured to participate as I was their teacher, while others might have sought to impress me by giving answers they believed I wanted to hear as an interviewer/teacher (Dörnyei, 2007).

This particular study has achieved the purpose of contributing to existing literature on homework, by providing a glimpse into the homework practices of a group of Gulf Arab language learners. Unlike Rapanta's (2014) claim, religion was not found to be a guiding force in the homework-related decisions of this

particular group of students. Rather, students exercised varying levels of self-determination in their decisions to do homework, while being motivated by external factors. As homework is an integral part of educational contexts, it warrants attention in both pedagogy and research.

CONCLUSION

This research reported on the extrinsic factors that motivate students to do homework and suggested ways of designing homework where students employ autonomous forms of extrinsic motivation. Homework tasks that explicate the ways in which the task can be personally and academically relevant to students, and that provide students with guidance and support in learning, have the potential to create effective out-of-class learning experiences. Future research is needed to identify whether these recommendations can indeed facilitate homework and learning out of class. Another area of future research can be investigating the time and effort students spend on doing homework and how this correlates with different motivation types that underpin homework behaviour.

REFERENCES

Benson, P. (2011). *Teaching and researching: Autonomy in language learning (applied linguistics)* (2nd ed.). Harlow: Pearson Education.

Cooper, H., Robinson, J. C., & Patall, E. A. (2006). Does homework improve academic achievement? A synthesis of research 1987–2003. *Review of Educational Research, 76*(1), 1–62.

Cooper, H., & Valentine, J. C. (2001). Using research to answer practical questions about homework. *Educational Psychologist, 36*(3), 143–153.

Coutts, P. M. (2004). Meanings of homework and implications for practice. *Theory into Practice, 43*(3), 182–188.

Deci, E. L., Vallerand, R. J., Pelletier, L. G., & Ryan, R. M. (1991). Motivation and education: The self-determination perspective. *Educational Psychologist, 26*(3/4), 325–346.

Dörnyei, Z. (2007). *Research methods in applied linguistics*. Oxford: Oxford University Press.

Engin, M., & McKeown, K. (2012). Cultural influences on motivational issues in students and their goals for studying at university. *Learning and Teaching in Higher Education: Gulf Perspectives, 9*(1), 1–15.

Epstein, J. L., & Van Voorhis, F. L. (2001). More than minutes: Teachers' role in designing homework. *Educational Psychologist, 36*(3), 181–193.

Geide-Stevenson, D. (2009). Does collecting and grading homework assignments impact student achievement in an introductory economics course? *Journal of Economics and Economic Education Research, 10*(3), 3–14.

Kohn, A. (2006). Abusing research: The study of homework and other examples. *Phi Delta Kappan, 88*(1), 9–22.

Patall, E. A., Cooper, H., & Wynn, S. R. (2010). The effectiveness and relative importance of choice in the classroom. *Journal of Educational Psychology, 102*(4), 896–915.

Pearson, N. (2003). *The idiosyncracies of out-of-class language learning: A study of mainland Chinese students studying English at tertiary level in New Zealand*. Paper presented at the Independent Learning Conference, Melbourne, Australia.

Radhakrishnan, P., Lam, D., & Ho, G. (2009). Giving university students incentives to do homework improves their performance. *Journal of Instructional Psychology, 36*(3), 219–225.

Rapanta, C. (2014). "Insh'Allah I'll do my homework": Adapting to Arab undergraduates at an English-medium university in Dubai. *Learning and Teaching in Higher Education: Gulf Perspectives, 11*(2), 1–8.

Ryan, R. M., & Deci, E. L. (2000a). Intrinsic and extrinsic motivations: Classic definitions and new directions. *Contemporary Educational Psychology, 25*, 54–67.

Ryan, R. M., & Deci, E. L. (2000b). Self-determination theory and the facilitation of intrinsic motivation, social development, and well-being. *American Psychologist, 55*(1), 68–78.

Ryan, R. M., & Deci, E. L. (2002). Overview of self-determination theory: An organismic dialectical perspective. In E. L. Deci, & R. M. Ryan (Eds.), *Handbook of self-determination research* (pp. 3–33). New York: The University of Rochester Press.

Trautwein, U., & Lüdtke, O. (2009). Predicting homework motivation and homework effort in six school subjects: The role of person and family characteristics, classroom factors, and school track. *Language and Instruction, 19*(3), 243–258.

Trautwein, U., Schnyder, I., Niggli, A., Neumann, M., & Lüdtke, O. (2009). Chameleon effects in homework research: The homework-achievement association depends on the measures used and the level of analysis chosen. *Contemporary Educational Psychology, 34*(1), 77–88.

Trost, S., & Salehi-Isfahani, D. (2012). The effect of homework on exam performance: Experimental results from principles of economics. *Southern Economic Journal, 79*(1), 224–242.

United Arab Emirates Ministry of Education. (2010). The Ministry of Education Strategy 2010–2020. Retrieved January 11, 2015, from https://www.moe.gov.ae/English/ SiteDocuments/MOE _Strategy.pdf

Vallerand, R. J., & Ratelle, C. F. (2002). Intrinsic and extrinsic motivation: A hierarchical model. In E. L. Deci, & R. M. Ryan (Eds.), *Handbook of self-determination research* (pp. 37–64). Rochester, NY: The University of Rochester Press.

Xu, J. (2010). Homework purposes reported by secondary school students: A multilevel analysis. *The Journal of Educational Research, 103*, 171–182.

Zayed University Office of Student Affairs. (2013). Student handbook 2013–2014. Retrieved January 11, 2015, from http://www.zu.ac.ae/main/files/images/enroll/Student_Handbook_ Eng_2013–2014.pdf

APPENDIX

SEMI-STRUCTURED INTERVIEW QUESTIONS

- How much homework do you get in the courses you are currently taking? How do you feel about the homework load of the English composition course?
- What type of homework have you enjoyed doing in Composition II? Can you give an example?
- What kind of homework have you disliked doing? Can you give an example?
- Why do you do homework? What do you expect to/want to get out of doing homework?
- You said you do homework to/for .... Why is this important? Can you explain?
- Let's look at your homework log. Which homework did you do? Why did you do this particular homework?
- Let's look at your homework log. Which homework did you not do? Why didn't you do this particular homework?

SECTION III
Approaches to genre and discourse

STEVE KIRK

WAVES OF REFLECTION: SEEING KNOWLEDGES IN ACADEMIC WRITING

INTRODUCTION

Reflective writing is emerging as an increasingly common assessment type in higher education. Assignments of this kind may prove challenging for students, particularly in later stages of an academic degree where, for example, essay writing may have been the norm up to that point. Scaffolding students from mere recognition of what might be required (e.g., via marking criteria and task rubrics) towards the realisation of disciplinary expectations in their writing is one of the key functions of EAP practitioners. This paper discusses an ongoing endeavour to facilitate such a shift for reflective writing with fourth-year integrated Masters students of anthropology. The principal contribution to EAP practice of the teaching intervention reported is a pedagogical toolkit that enables students to visualise the selection and arrangement of knowledge through

a piece of academic writing. This tool enacts for classroom practice the concepts of *semantic gravity* and *semantic gravity waves* (Maton, 2013; 2014), extending components of an increasingly influential framework in the sociology of education: Legitimation Code Theory.

REFLECTIVE WRITING — LOOKING FOR A TOOLKIT

Reflective writing assignments across departments at Durham University tend to be assessment tasks for modules linked to real or imagined work placements. Assignments are therefore based primarily on personal experience, may take a diary-type form (at least initially) and may require the student writer to reflect on past, present and/or future events, often as the basis for real or imagined future action. Nesi and Gardner characterise this kind of writing broadly as a *narrative recount*

(2012, p. 219*ff*), grouping these assessments with similar forms of writing, such as biographies and urban ethnography. They note that reflective assignments occur across all undergraduate years and at Master's level, but are most prevalent at final-year undergraduate level. This perhaps reflects the focus on employability-oriented skills development, and is the intention of such modules at Durham.

Writing of this kind can differ quite markedly from essayist-type writing (Lillis, 2001). Reflective assignments tend to require an explicitly personal and emotional voice, contrasting sharply with the explicitness of argument development and logic in the service of 'academic truth' characteristic of essay writing (Lillis, 2001, p. 81). Students at Durham University must compose informal reflections on lived experience, also often needing to weave in reference to academic reading. Perhaps unsurprisingly, therefore, the linguistic characteristics of this form of writing tend to be unlike most other genres of academic writing (Nesi & Gardner 2012, pp. 236–237). In looking to move from research insights to pedagogical practice, however, the corpus descriptions and patterns do little more than reinforce an intuitive sense of what reflective writing might look like in an academic context. Beyond short exemplars of reflective-type writing, they do not provide EAP practitioners with tools for practice.

In the broader literature on developing reflective practice and writing in higher education, a number of frameworks draw on Schön's work on the 'reflective practitioner' (1983) or on Gibbs' (1988) reflective cycle. One example is the 5R framework proposed by Bain, Ballantyne, Mills and Lester (2002), where each 'R' represents a different level of reflection, depending on the nature of the problem, task or desired outcome. In an educational context, students might be scaffolded through successive stages of *Reporting, Responding, Relating, Reasoning* and *Reconstructing*, on the way to higher levels of cognitive challenge and engagement. Given reported student difficulty with distinguishing 'reporting' from 'responding', Ryan and Ryan (2013) conflate these first two levels to offer a 4R model. This was the model I drew on for the intervention reported below.

Frameworks such as these focus on the ways that reflective practice can have a transformative impact (e.g., Kalantzis & Cope, 2008; Mezirow, 2006). It is the purposeful reflection in the service of personal change that distinguishes academic from 'everyday' reflection (Moon, 2006). However, in looking for tools that can make the valued practices more explicit and achievable, this work does not provide students with concrete ways of enacting this knowledge transformation in their writing. Existing approaches in EAP can help students see linguistic and textual patterns, but they do not offer a means for seeing distinctions in content or knowledge. New tools are needed.

LEGITIMATION CODE THEORY AND 'SEMANTIC GRAVITY'

Legitimation Code Theory (LCT) is a multidimensional toolkit that builds on, *inter alia*, the work of Basil Bernstein and Pierre Bourdieu. Legitimation Code Theory takes the social-realist position that knowledge is both socially produced and *real*, in the sense that forms of knowledge have effects that can be seen and explored. This has enabled the study of knowledge itself and how it is structured and developed across fields of practice and over time. The LCT concept drawn on here is that of *semantic gravity*: the extent to which knowledge practices are related to their social or symbolic context of acquisition or use (Maton, 2014, p. 110). This concept forms one component of Semantics, a dimension of LCT developed to conceptualise and empirically explore the ways in which knowledge is built by actors in social contexts, and how it may be developed and transformed over time (e.g., Maton, 2011; 2014).

Semantic gravity (SG) can be traced as continua of relative strengths, from weaker (SG–) to stronger (SG+) 'with infinite capacity for gradation' (Maton, 2014, p. 131). The stronger the gravity, the more meaning is dependent on its context; the weaker the gravity, the less dependent meaning is on its context. For example, mention in a student essay of 'cutting down trees in the Amazon' exhibits stronger semantic gravity than a reference elsewhere to 'deforestation'. Viewed *across* the text, a movement from the more concrete ('cutting down trees') to the more abstract ('deforestation') is an instance of weakening semantic gravity (SG↓); introducing the more abstract term first and then defining or illustrating it is an instance of strengthening semantic gravity (SG↑). The concept thus also enables *profiling* of meaning-making over time – in texts or, for example, in classroom practice or the historical development of a discipline. Semantic gravity has been used as an analytical tool in a wide range of contexts, from secondary school teacher training (MacNaught, Maton, Martin & Matruglio, 2013) and problem-solving in engineering (Wolff & Luckett, 2013) to freemasonry (Poulet, 2016) and political discourse in the South African parliament (Siebörger & Adendorff,

2015). There are also a growing number of teacher-practitioners recontextualising LCT Semantics to enhance their work with students (e.g., Blackie, 2014; Szenes, Tilakaratna & Maton, 2015), academic staff (e.g., Clarence, 2015) and teachers of EAP (Kirk, 2015).

Figure 1 represents three notional *semantic gravity profiles*: a *high gravity flatline* (A1), a *low gravity flatline* (A2) and a *semantic gravity wave* (B). Empirical research into, for instance, student writing is suggesting that higher-achieving work across subject areas is structured into such waves of recurrent *semantic shifts* between more concrete and more abstract meanings (e.g., Maton, 2013; Maton, 2014). In contrast, writing that 'flatlines', e.g., by remaining confined to anecdotal examples (profile A2) or to abstractions (profile A1), has been shown not to be rewarded in the same way. Looking to the *semantic range* between highest and lowest strengths may also be important in understanding educational achievement, since particular disciplines or tutors may require that certain *semantic thresholds* be reached (Maton 2013, p. 19).

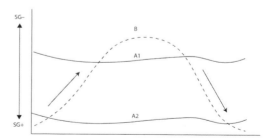

Figure 1 Three illustrative semantic gravity profiles (adapted from Maton, 2014, p. 143) [Source: Reproduced by permission of K. Maton]

The empirical form taken by semantic gravity depends on how the concept is enacted for practice. In my teaching intervention, this was realised as relative strengths of context-dependent meanings in anthropology student writing. A recount of personal experience, for instance, was seen as exhibiting stronger gravity; drawing on theoretical concepts from course reading was seen as exhibiting weaker gravity. Extending work that has also used semantics for student disciplinary learning (Szenes et al., 2015), I divided the SG+/SG– continuum into three 'sections', introducing a heuristic mid-level. This level represents meanings which *generalise* over specific episodes or illustrations, but which are not entirely abstracted from a contextual base. Represented in Figure 2, this small, but important, innovation developed from working to enact semantic gravity for the classroom in a way that would retain conceptual integrity, while also being practically useful for students. Drawn in class as a four-line 'stave diagram', the sectioning serves two pedagogical purposes. Firstly, it enables heuristic identifying and 'categorising' of different forms of knowledge with students, without losing sight of there being a continuum. Secondly, it captures the semantic range within which

generalisations over experience occur, e.g., 'leadership', 'teamwork' or 'confidence'. It is these such insights that students must identify and reflect upon through their writing.

Crucially, however, identifying only skills or insights from personal experience may be insufficient for obtaining higher grades. Semantic gravity provides a means of articulating why this is the case, since such generalised meanings remain anchored to a real-world context: gravity remains relatively strong. It is pushing interpretations of personal experience higher, further weakening semantic gravity, e.g., via engagement with academic theory, that may be needed in many disciplines to access higher grades. This is not simply a tick-box requirement: it may be that this higher threshold must be reached for personal change to occur. By engaging with *uncommonsense* knowledge (Bernstein, 2000), using academic concepts or theory as lenses through which to re-view and reassess experience, students can genuinely transform their understanding of a critical incident or pattern of experience, enabling new understandings and the potential for new or revised future action.

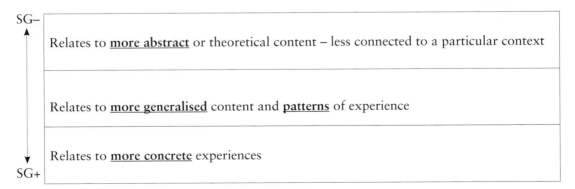

SG–

Relates to **more abstract** or theoretical content – less connected to a particular context

Relates to **more generalised** content and **patterns** of experience

Relates to **more concrete** experiences

SG+

Figure 2 Heuristic sectioning of the semantic gravity continuum

PEDAGOGICAL INTERVENTION

The integrated Masters module *Anthropology and Professional Practice* was first run at Durham University in 2013/14. Average cohort size is around 10–12 students, with a mix of home and international students. Summative requirements include evidence of job searches, a CV and a cover letter for a workplace or research post. Forty per cent of the grade is allocated to a 2,000-word reflective statement that must summarise key knowledge and skills gained from students' undergraduate study, and suggest how these might prepare them for a future workplace context. Students draw experience for this statement from a personal reflective log, which they keep throughout the module. Evidence suggests this kind of task may well be a common feature across disciplines and across institutions (Nesi & Gardner, 2012, p. 221).

Given concerns about students' reaction to and handling of an unfamiliar form of assessed writing in their final year, the module lecturer approached the University English Language Centre and a two-hour introductory session was agreed to supplement existing module provision. Early planning drew on course documents and insights from the module leader, who sat in on the session and provided insights for discipline-specific student questions. In the class, participants were introduced to a version of Ryan and Ryan's 4R model (2013) as a basic structural template for section writing, but most attention was focused on how different *forms* of knowledge can be woven together in a piece of academic reflective writing. Drawing tacitly on semantic gravity throughout (see below), we then explored how students

could act on this awareness during their reflective log keeping and assignment drafting.

In the first iteration of the session (2013/14) there were no exemplars of anthropology student writing to work with, so participants worked with a short sample model of reflective writing drawn from the British Academic Written English (BAWE) Corpus (Nesi & Gardner, 2012, p. 224). In the second iteration (2014/15) we were able to work with student writing from the previous cohort. One example of higher-scoring work that I explored with students appears below.

> Sanctions were imposed in February 2014 by Applegate Jobcentre on a seasonal ex-employee of mine who is currently unemployed. [...] I acted as a mediator and negotiator between my colleague and the Department for Work and Pensions. Before studying anthropology, I would have felt and believed that the advisor who imposed sanctions was prejudiced towards the unemployed. Now, I look through a theoretical lens to understand everyday events and practices. I abstracted the concept of structural violence (Das et al., 2000; Galtung, 1999; Farmer, 2004) enforced by government policy and its institutions to explore how political, economic and cultural structures result in the occurrence of avoidable violence often seen within human rights and the deprivation of basic human needs. The jobcentre advisor is simply an agent authorised by the state to impose sanctions and reduce Britain's annual benefit spending through the coalition government's welfare reform policy.

> I offered to help my past colleague by writing letters of appeal and speaking on his behalf. Having learned through study to write descriptively and critically, and to understand

government policies, a successful outcome was applied and his jobseekers allowance was reinstated after four weeks. [...] Using my new skills and drawing on my fieldwork experiences [...] has enhanced my understanding of theory, concepts and subject-specific knowledge. I now feel confident and experienced for a career in the international job market rather than in Moorsby.

(Author data. Place names changed to preserve anonymity.)

Built up on the whiteboard as a series of gravity waves, represented in Figure 3, students saw how the writer's selection and sequencing of reflections and insights could be visualised as movements between relatively context-dependent meanings ('sanctions … in February 2014') through more generalised and abstracted meanings less dependent on a particular context (e.g., 'structural violence'), to recontextualised understandings that 'wave down' again towards more context-dependent meanings ('I offered to help …'). The extract ends by then 'waving back up', to comment on the increased confidence gained through the chosen critical incident. Tracing the peaks and troughs of the waves was achieved together by agreeing, for instance,

'how abstract' (SG–) or 'how close to a personal experience' (SG+) different stretches of text were.

Enacting LCT concepts for the EAP classroom in this way, I chose not to use the terms 'semantic(s)' or 'gravity', to avoid unnecessary unpacking of technical terms and potential student confusion. Instead, my *language of enactment* (Maton, 2014, p. 209) recast SG+ as 'closer to experience' or 'more concrete', and SG– as 'more abstract/theoretical'. I labelled the sections on the vertical semantic continuum as 'experience', 'patterns/generalisations' and 'concepts/theory'. To enable students to begin appropriating and applying the tools for themselves, I then elicited examples of anthropology programme experience (e.g., 'lectures'; 'presentations'; 'fieldwork'). Students decided on skills gained through this experience (SG↓ – e.g., 'public speaking'), identified possible theories that might be used to reinterpret this experience (further SG↓ – e.g., 'essence of communication'), and then discussed the possible relevance of these insights for future practice (SG↑). Figure 4 on page 115 reproduces the whiteboard sketch we ended up with.

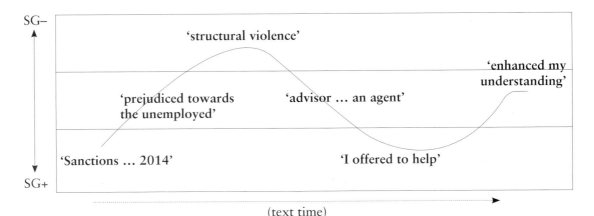

Figure 3 Anthropology student writing extract as a gravity wave profile

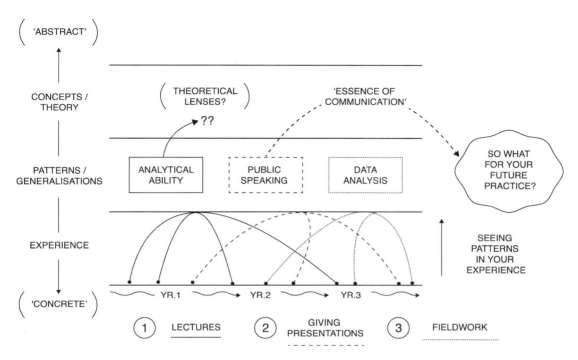

Figure 4 Whiteboard sketch (reproduced): Semantic gravity waving with students

Having established a shared metalanguage with participants, the 'meaning profiles' of higher- and lower-achieving work were then compared, drawing some inspiration from the research methodology proposed by Tribble and Wingate (2013) for learning from student writing. Students identified for themselves the 'low flatlining' that resulted from writing too anecdotally. Similarly, they became aware of how familiarity with more theoretical essay writing might lead them inadvertently to 'high flatlining'. Through profiling, class discussion and, later, examining of the marking criteria, students recognised that the valued practice is not writing at one level or another, but, rather, demonstrating the knowledge-transforming movements up *and* down between these levels. Maton conjectures that it is these waves of increasing and decreasing semantic gravity that enable cumulative knowledge building and knowledge transfer (2013; 2014). This may be why reflective practice and writing can be a potentially powerful form of learning *through* assessment in higher education.

IMPACTS AND IMPLICATIONS

The impact of the interventions has been highly positive. The lecturer reported students immediately reworking drafts after attending the session, armed with a practical means of reanalysing their own writing. An additional, unforeseen benefit was the effect on subsequent tutorials, where assignment drafts were discussed. The module leader found that the new, shared metalanguage enabled focused conversations about what needed to change in students' writing:

I'm just giving formative feedback on the reflective overviews and the 'wave' analogy has been utterly invaluable. Thank you. I have seen several pennies drop over the past few days when I've pointed out an experience flatline or a theory flatline and they go 'ohhh yeeess!!'.

It has been an incredibly useful conceptual model.

Students also fed back very positively. One participant from the second iteration of the session commented:

I liked that there was something visual as I find this much easier to process and understand. I think it has provided a clear way in which I can structure my paragraphs/themes.

Insightfully, another wrote:

It was very helpful having the three levels described visually, it made it much easier to understand. I particularly liked that the waves can depict these levels on a continuous scale, so you can easily visual [sic] that something is a low level of theoretical analysis, for example, rather than simply 1, 2, 3.

Students understanding that there can be differing *degrees* of theoretical analysis is an illustration of the practical, yet conceptually rich, insights made possible through the approach outlined above. Students also commented on reading more in preparation for the assignment than they had done previously. Asked what had been most beneficial, one participant wrote:

Knowing the extent to which anthropological theory needs to be addressed and intertwined with personal experience.

Semantic gravity profiling enables students literally to *see* what is valued and required in an unfamiliar writing form. This recontextualising of LCT concepts into teaching is transforming how reflective writing is introduced and scaffolded more widely at Durham University. The approach has been replicated to develop similar sessions for students in applied linguistics, biology, criminology, psychology and sport. It also has much broader relevance for EAP writing pedagogy, given that the analysis and approach can be enacted for *any* genre or text-type. We are beginning to explore the possibilities in our summer pre-sessional materials.

While the context discussed here is perhaps not representative of a 'typical' EAP class, the mixing of home and international students is becoming increasingly common – at Durham University and elsewhere – as recognition grows that academic discourse is nobody's first language (Bourdieu & Passeron, 1994, p. 8). The potential of the approach is arguably all the more significant by having relevance for *all* students across the university, something being called for more widely in the literature (e.g., Wingate, 2015). Applications and enactments of LCT for EAP are in their infancy, but several research projects are under way[1]. By offering ways to conceptualise and make visible educational knowledge practices for researchers, teachers and learners, LCT is likely soon to figure more prominently in EAP-oriented research and pedagogical practice.

---

[1] My own doctorate is one example. I use LCT to explore relations between the potential and the enacted curriculum in EAP teaching practice.

REFERENCES

Bain, J. D., Ballantyne, R., Mills, C., & Lester, N. C. (2002). *Reflecting on practice: Student teachers' perspectives*. Flaxton, ND: Post Pressed.

Bernstein, B. (2000). *Pedagogy, symbolic control and identity: Theory, research, critique*. Revised edition. Oxford: Rowman & Littlefield.

Blackie, M. (2014). Creating semantic waves: Using legitimation code theory as a tool to aid the teaching of chemistry. *Chemistry Education Research and Practice, 15*, 462–469.

Bourdieu, P., & Passeron, J. C. (1994 [1965]). Introduction: Language and the relationship to language in the teaching situation. In P. Bourdieu, J.-C. Passeron & M. de Saint Martin (Eds.), *Academic discourse* (pp. 1–34). Cambridge: Polity Press.

Clarence, S. (2015). Exploring the nature of disciplinary teaching and learning using legitimation code theory semantics. *Teaching in Higher Education, 21*, 123–137. http://dx.doi.org/10.1080/13562517.2015.1115972

Gibbs, G. (1988). *Learning by doing: A guide to teaching and learning methods*. Further Education Unit. Oxford: Oxford Polytechnic.

Kalantzis, M., & Cope, B. (2008). *New learning: Elements of a science of education*. Cambridge: Cambridge University Press.

Kirk, S. (2015). *Waving across fields of practice: Three tales of semantics*. Paper presented at Legitimation Code Theory Colloquium 1 (LCTC-1), Cape Town, South Africa, 17–19 June, 2015.

Lillis, T. M. (2001). *Student writing: Access, regulation, desire*. London: Routledge.

Macnaught, L., Maton, K., Martin, J. R., & Matruglio, E. (2013). Jointly constructing semantic waves: Implications for teacher training. *Linguistics and Education, 24(1)*, 50–63.

Maton, K. (2011). Theories and things: The semantics of disciplinarity. In F. Christie & K. Maton (Eds.), *Disciplinarity: Functional linguistic and sociological perspectives* (pp. 62–84). London: Continuum.

Maton, K. (2013). Making semantic waves: A key to cumulative knowledge-building. *Linguistics and Education, 24*(1), 8–22.

Maton, K. (2014). *Knowledge and knowers: Towards a realist sociology of education*. London: Routledge.

Mezirow, J. (2006). An overview of transformative learning. In P. Sutherland, & J. Crowther (Eds.), *Lifelong learning: Concepts and contexts* (pp. 24–38). London: Routledge.

Moon, J. (2006). *Learning journals: A handbook for reflective practice and professional development*. London: Routledge.

Nesi, H., & Gardner, S. (2012). *Genres across the disciplines: Student writing in higher education*. Cambridge: Cambridge University Press.

Poulet, C. (2016). Knowledge and knowers in tacit pedagogic contexts: The case of freemasonry in France. In K. Maton, S. Hood & S. Shay (Eds.), *Knowledge-building: Educational studies in Legitimation Code Theory* (pp. 214–230). London: Routledge.

Ryan, M., & Ryan, M. (2013). Theorising a model for teaching and assessing reflective learning in higher education. *Higher Education Research & Development, 32*(2), 244–257.

Schön, D. (1983). *The reflective practitioner*. San Francisco, CA: Jossey-Bass.

Siebörger, I., & Adendorff, R. D. (2015). Resemiotizing concerns from constituencies in the South African parliament. *Southern African Linguistics and Applied Language Studies*, *33*(2), 171–197.

Szenes, E., Tilakaratna, N., & Maton, K. (2015). The knowledge practices of critical thinking. In M. Davies & R. Barnett (Eds.), *The palgrave handbook of critical thinking in higher education* (pp. 573–591). London: Palgrave Macmillan.

Tribble, C., & Wingate, U. (2013). Learning from student texts: A genre-based approach to 'mainstreaming' academic writing instruction. BALEAP Pre-Conference Workshop, Nottingham University, UK, 9 April, 2013.

Wingate, U. (2015). *Academic literacy and student diversity: The case for inclusive practice*. Clevedon, UK: Multilingual Matters.

Wolff, K. & Luckett, K. (2013). Integrating multidiscipinary engineering knowledge. *Teaching in Higher Education, 18*(1), 78–92.

Sheena Gardner

Applying linguistics in TEAP: The case of student reports

Introduction

The BALEAP accreditation scheme has been designed to support the continuing professional development of those involved in Teaching English for Academic Purposes (TEAP) (BALEAP, 2014). As the Competency Framework in Figure 1 suggests, understanding academic practices is a fundamental component of being an informed EAP practitioner, but it is only the beginning ('A'). Such understandings need to be applied, to be used in analysing student needs (B), and in designing programmes (D). These inform course delivery (C), which is central, as indicated in Figure 1. Evaluation of programmes and course delivery will then prompt further research on academic practices in general and in local contexts in particular. And so the cycle continues in theory, although, in practice, the relationships are seldom as streamlined.

Research on academic practices is popular, prolific and well published. Early developments include a focus on register

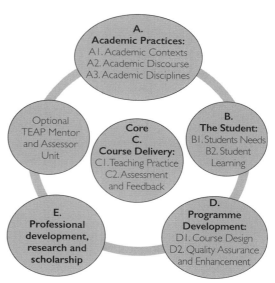

Figure 1 TEAP Competency Framework (BALEAP, 2014, p. 9)

[Source: Used with permission from BALEAP]

analysis *inter alia* (Benesch, 2001, pp. 5–23), with a 'huge growth in research into the genres and practices of different academic contexts' (Hyland, 2006, p. 4). This continues to expand in scope, detail and number of publications (Paltridge, 2014) in fields such as academic literacy practices, ethnographies, systemic functional linguistic genre analyses, and multidimensional studies of registers. These accounts of academic language mushroom, and yet they still seem to have only scratched the surface of its fascinations and complexities.

This raises questions about how TEAP can benefit from the abundance of riches in published research on the nature of academic language. From the perspective of published research, accounts may end with sentences such as 'this should be of benefit to teachers of EAP', but it is not always exactly clear if they will be, or how. Equally, from an EAP perspective:

> [m]any EAP courses still lack a theoretical or research rationale and textbooks too often continue to depend on the writer's experience and intuition rather than on systematic research.
>
> (Hyland, 2006, p. 5)

In other words, the progression from A to B, C, D and E in Figure 1 is neither self-evident, nor universal practice.

With a focus on written student reports, this paper considers how linguistic descriptions of texts can be applied in TEAP. It outlines a series of related studies, and suggests ways in which each could inform TEAP practice. The studies fall under two funded projects[1] that relate to the BAWE corpus[2] of successful student writing (Nesi & Gardner, 2012), and are presented here in the order in which

they were conducted, including work on macrostructures, genre families, registers and teaching materials. The actual uptake from such studies is often unpredictable, and the aim is not to dictate a prescribed methodology, but rather to reconsider in the context of specific studies how linguistics can be applied in teaching EAP.

MACROSTRUCTURES

An initial skim reading of texts often focuses on the organisation as indicated in section headings. These provide the assignment macrostructure, and can be easily extracted from the BAWE corpus. An initial assessment of the three assignment macrostructures in Table 1 suggests that the Applied Linguistics assignment is an empirical study report, the Biology assignment is an essay and the Business assignment is a SWOT analysis.

A linguistic analysis of the macrostructures, and the forms and functions of section headings in the BAWE corpus led to the development of a classification of macrostructures (Gardner & Holmes, 2010), and the differentiation of headings that are frequent and widespread (such as *Introduction, Results*) from those that are more genre specific (e.g., *Opportunities, Threats*) and from those that are more discipline specific (e.g., *contested language use, Endosymbiotic Theory*).

---

[1] The two related funded projects are
  a) An investigation of genres of assessed writing in British Higher Education (ESRC RES-000-23-0800), which included the development of the BAWE corpus and classification of genre families, and
  b) *Writing for a Purpose*: materials to improve the quality of discipline-specific student work, (ESRC ES/J010995/1), which involved the development of materials that are available on the British Council LearnEnglish website under the tab '*Writing for a Purpose*'.
[2] The British Academic Written English (BAWE) corpus of successful student writing contains assignments from across 34 disciplines, four levels of study, and 13 genre families. See www.coventry.ac.uk/BAWE for information about the corpus and how to access it in class or for research purposes.

Table I Three BAWE assignment macrostructures

Applied Linguistics	Biology
Task 2. An interview concerning an area of contested language use.	*Endosymbiotic Theory*
	Abstract
Introduction	Introduction
Experiment	History of Endosymbiotic Theory
Method	Factors in favour of mitochondrial and chloroplast
Results	endosymbiosis
Comments	Summary
Conclusion	Reference
Business	
Executive Summary	
Main Report	
Customer Margin	
Payback and Net Present Value (NPV) of the Project	
Factors That May Change Over The Life Of The Project	
Strengths, Weaknesses, Opportunities and Threats (SWOT)	
a) Strengths	
b) Weaknesses	
c) Opportunities	
d) Threats	
Reaction of Competitors	
Conclusion	
Appendix	

We discovered that the use of section headings increases from first-year undergraduate to final year and postgraduate, as assignments get longer and more reports are written. We also discovered that assignments in the sciences, including essays such as the Biology essay in Table 1, were more likely to use section headings than those in humanities or social sciences. Further details and examples are given in Gardner and Holmes (2009).

An understanding of the variation in macrostructures achieved by skimming student texts from the target context can provide a practical framework for use in needs analyses, programme design and course delivery. When specific macrostructures have been identified, the next step is to examine the purpose and staging of the assignments.

GENRE FAMILIES AND GENRES

It is tempting to assume that assignments with 'similar' section headings belong to the same genre, and that differences are essentially disciplinary. Conversely, we might assume that assignments from the same discipline with a 'similar' macrostructure belong to the same genre family. More detailed reading is required, however, before such claims can be made.

Following *Introduction* and *Conclusion*, the most frequent words in section headings were, in order of frequency, *Results, Analysis/es, Method/ologies* and *Discussion/s*. Although Essay is the most populated genre family in the BAWE corpus, students in areas such as Engineering and Accounting, where there are large numbers of international students, write more reports (e.g., Nesi & Gardner, 2012, p. 52). Table 2 shows typical headings in these 'IMRD' (Introduction-Methodology-Results-Discussion) reports from three disciplines.

Table 2 IMRD macrostructures in three disciplines (adapted from Gardner & Holmes, 2009, p. 260)
[Source: Used by permission of Bloomsbury Publishing Plc]

Biology	Engineering	Psychology
Abstract	Abstract	Abstract
Introduction	Introduction	Introduction
	Theory	
Materials	Apparatus	Method
and Method	and Methods	
Results	Observations	Results
	and Results	
	Analysis of	
	Results	
Discussion	Discussion	Discussion
(Conclusion)	Conclusion	
(Future Work)		
References	References	References

Further examination of the texts, and discussion with students and lecturers in the departments, reveals that such macrostructures correspond to two different genres. The first is a short report on an experimental study, such as a laboratory report in Biology or a questionnaire study in Psychology, written typically in first or second-year university, where the topic is often given to all students and the focus in the text is on the Methodology and Results. In such genres, a Discussion section might consist of only one or two sentences. The second is a longer, final-year report, typically written in the upper years, where students have to develop their own topic and draw specifically on published literature, and where the Introduction and Discussion sections assume much more significance and might constitute half the paper.

The purpose of these two genres is different. In the first, students are learning the conventions of their discipline – what to do and how to write it up. In the second, they are demonstrating how they can make an original contribution. The second may well include the more explanatory language of the first, in its middle sections, but the framing Introduction and Discussion sections are where they have to evaluate, persuade and situate the findings in context. Therefore, as writing tasks, they are quite different. Details and examples are given in Gardner (2012) and Nesi and Gardner (2012, Chapter 5).

A similar difference is found within Essays and within Case Studies, where lower-level assignments have a more pedagogical focus, while longer, final-year assignments are written for a wider academic or professional audience. Such findings warn about the dangers for teachers of using published research as models for student writing, and reinforce the message in Flowerdew (2000) of the benefits of teaching using high-quality assignments from the target context.

Having identified macrostructures and genres, the next step is to examine the lexico-grammatical features of the different registers that realise these genres.

REGISTERS

It is evident from the above that the registers of student writing differ not only according to genre and level of study, but also according to discipline. Here are extracts from two second-year undergraduate student assignments from different disciplines[1]:

To determine how adjectives are used … I decided to first build a wordlist using Concap for the broadsheet and online news services samples as I felt this would allow me an overview to evaluate my results which would in turn give me the opportunity to investigate any interesting features.

(BAWE Applied Linguistics)

In order to investigate whether self-esteem levels were lower and deviant eating behaviours were higher in first year university girls than a control group of non-university girls, between subjects multivariate analysis of variance (MANOVA) and Pearson's correlation co-efficient were used to analyse data.

(BAWE Psychology)

The Applied Linguistics extract uses the first person to recount decisions (*I first decided to …*) and to provide a rationale (*as I felt this would allow me to …*). These wordings create a more personal impression than the extract from Psychology, where

the language is more formulaic (*in order to investigate whether …*), and the research procedures used (*between subjects multivariate …*) are stated and generally not justified.

Many studies have been conducted on the lexico-grammar of the BAWE corpus (as listed on the www.coventry.ac.uk/BAWE website), but there is still more to do. Throughout Nesi and Gardner (2012), details can be found of the lexico-grammar of the texts in the BAWE corpus, but this is not exhaustive, and EAP teachers and students can also explore the corpus themselves to seek answers to specific questions. Using SketchEngine, a search for *I decided* and for *I felt* shows that, although not frequent in general, they are relatively frequent in Linguistics, but do not occur at all in Psychology assignments in BAWE.

Disciplinary contrasts such as these raise questions that can be asked either of lecturers in the target context or in class for students to become aware of and discuss. Both assignments received 'very good' marks as coursework, but it is possible that, if the Psychology assignment had used first person and mental process verbs such as *felt*, the marks might have been lower. As also evidenced in these extracts, there is less need to justify methods in Experimental Psychology, where there is a dominant research tradition, in contrast with Corpus Linguistics, where paradigms are in greater competition (Becher & Trowler, 2001) and methods can be more 'trial-and-error' (Swales, 2004, p. 97). (See Nesi & Gardner, 2012, Chapter 5 for related discussion of clipped and elaborated text in methods sections of reports.)

[1] The extracts from student assignments are reproduced with the permission of students concerned.

Having begun to identify register features, the next question might be, are there ready-made materials for teaching these genres?

MATERIALS: WHAT THE TEXTBOOKS OFFER

On consulting several widely-used EAP textbooks, I found that some ignore IMRD type reports entirely. Others bullet-point headings, but with no examples, the intended genre is not evident (e.g., IMRDC – Introduction, Methods, Results, Discussion, Conclusion – in Bailey, 2011, p. 258). Where the genre is evident and illustrated, only one is given: for example, a Chemistry Lab Report (with Purpose, Equipment and Materials, Procedure, Results, Conclusions) is described in Chaplen (1981, pp. 68–69); while Hewings (2012, pp. 116–117) provides section headings for a research report (Abstract, Acknowledgements, Title, Introduction, Literature Review, Methodology, Results, Discussion, Conclusion, References, Appendices) with examples of some sections from Business and from Applied Linguistics. The physical limitations of textbooks mean that general textbooks cannot be expected to include examples of the generic and disciplinary diversity of good student writing. In contrast, online materials on student report writing can provide many more examples.

ONLINE MATERIALS

The WRiSE (Writing a Report in Science and Engineering) project at Sydney University (http://www.usyd.edu.au/learningcentre/wrise/), informed by Sydney School genre analysis, has detailed guidance on student reports from several disciplines in science and engineering, as does the Monash University Language and Learning Online website (http://www.monash.edu.au/lls/llonline/writing/index.xml), with a wider range of disciplines. Each highlights linguistic features of reports deemed useful, clearly linked to the stages of the genre.

Materials based on a greater range of genres and disciplines are found in the *Writing for a Purpose* online materials (Nesi & Gardner, 2014; British Council, n.d.), which were developed with the British Council LearnEnglish team and Andy Gillett, author of the UEfAP website, from the findings of the BAWE corpus project. The resulting materials include not only information about the purposes and genres of student writing from all 13 genre families, but also guidance on structures and useful vocabulary for each. One of Nesi's contributions was to identify frequent phrases from the different genre families and enable users to connect with many instances of these from across the disciplines. An example from reports in the Methodology Recount family is shown in Appendix 1. Figure 2 shows useful phrases and Figure 3 shows concordance lines from across disciplines for *the aim of the/ this experiment/report is/was*. These are potentially very useful for classes with students from different subject areas.

APPLICATIONS IN TEAP PRACTICE

The aim of this paper was to explore, with specific reference to student reports, (a) how linguistic accounts of academic practices (A in Figure 1) evidenced in research related to the BAWE corpus of successful student writing can inform the other TEAP competencies implied in Figure 1, and (b) how linguistic analyses can be applied in teaching EAP.

It has been suggested that an investigation of student assignment macrostructures provides an accessible starting point, and that the use of headings such as *Introduction, Methods, Results* and *Discussion* are a general indication of student empirical reports. In order to identify specific genres, it is necessary to read beyond such section headings to determine the purposes of the assignments and the relative importance of each section. For many disciplines, two distinct 'IMRD' type assignments can be identified. These belong to two distinct genre families: Methodology Recounts (which focus on the methodology and results) and Research Reports (which require students to develop a research focus within the literature, conduct the study, and discuss its contribution to the discipline in some detail). The third main type of analysis proposed involves an examination of the registers of the assignments.

An understanding of academic practices (A in Figure 1), exemplified here in the identification of the macrostructures, genres and discipline-based registers students on EAP courses will need to control, is important in conducting needs analyses (B in Figure 1). These IMRD report genres are frequent in many science and engineering disciplines that are popular with international students. They are also a crucial starting point for programme development (D in Figure 1) and course delivery (C in Figure 1). The applications can be direct – for instance, in a programme design that groups students by year of study and disciplinary group to teach those disciplinary genres required. Flowerdew (2000) provides a noteworthy example of how 'model' student Engineering reports can be exploited as a teaching resource in the EAP classroom. The applications can be semi-direct, for example, by grouping students into cross-disciplinary groups that share the need for specific genres, and encouraging them to explore disciplinary variations within genres (as suggested in a genre-instantiation approach, Gardner, 2016). Or they can be more indirect – for instance, by raising awareness of genre variation and enabling students to explore their own target disciplinary contexts.

With this wide range of potential applications, all EAP courses should be able to benefit from the wealth of published research on academic practices, as illustrated here in terms of assignment macrostructures, report genres and registers. A reliance on popular textbooks would be misguided in as much as the student report genre families appear to be seriously under-represented, particularly in contrast to the online materials websites that draw explicitly on discipline- and genre-based research on academic practices.

REFERENCES

Bailey, S. (2011). *Academic writing: A handbook for international students* (3rd ed.). London: Routledge.

BALEAP (2014). *TEAP accreditation scheme handbook*. Retrieved April 20, 2015, from https://www.baleap.org/wp-content/uploads/2016/04/TEAP-Scheme-Handbook-2014.pdf

Becher, T., & Trowler, P. (2001). *Academic tribes and territories: Intellectual enquiry and the cultures of disciplines* (2nd ed.). Buckingham: Open University Press/SRHE.

Benesch, S. (2001). *Critical English for academic purposes: Theory, politics and practice.* Mahwah, NJ: Lawrence Erlbaum.

British Council (n.d.). *Writing for a Purpose on the LearnEnglish website.* Retrieved December 26, 2015, from http://learnenglish.britishcouncil.org/en/writing-purpose/writing-purpose

Chaplen, F. (1981). *A course in intermediate scientific English.* London: Longman.

Flowerdew, L. (2000). Using a genre-based framework to teach organizational structure in academic writing. *ELTJ, 54*(4), 369–378.

Gardner, S. (2012). Genres and registers of student report writing: An SFL perspective on texts and practices. *Journal of English for Academic Purposes, 11*(1), 52–63.

Gardner, S. (2016). A genre-instantiation approach to teaching English for specific academic purposes: Student writing in business, economics and engineering. *Writing and Pedagogy, 8*(1), 117–144.

Gardner, S., & Holmes, J. (2009). Can I use headings in my essay? Section headings, macrostructures and genre families in the BAWE corpus of student writing. In M. Charles, S. Hunston, & D. Pecorari (Eds.), *Academic writing: At the interface of corpus and discourse* (pp. 251–271). London: Continuum.

Gardner, S., & Holmes, J. (2010). From section headings to assignment macrostructures in undergraduate student writing. In E. Swain (Ed.), *Thresholds and potentialities of systemic functional linguistics: Applications to other disciplines, specialised discourses and languages other than English* (pp. 268–290). Trieste: Edizioni Universitarie Trieste (EUT).

Hewings, M. (2012). *Cambridge academic English.* Cambridge: Cambridge University Press.

Hyland, K. (2006). *English for academic purposes: An advanced resource book.* London and New York: Routledge.

Nesi, H., & Gardner, S. (2012). *Genres across the disciplines: Student writing in higher education.* Cambridge: Cambridge University Press.

Nesi, H., & Gardner, S. (2014). Balancing old and new activity types on an academic writing website. In M. Kavanagh & L. Robinson (Eds.), *The janus moment in EAP: Revisiting the past and building the future. Proceedings of the 2013 BALEAP conference* (pp. 187–198). Reading: Garnet Publishing Ltd.

Paltridge, B. (2014). Research timeline: Genre and second-language academic writing. *Language Teaching, 47*(3), 303–318.

Swales, J. M. (2004). *Research genres: Explorations and applications.* Cambridge: Cambridge University Press.

APPENDIX I

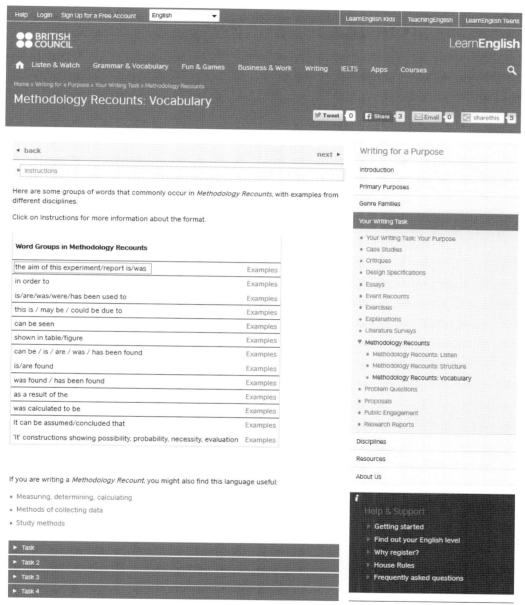

Figure 2 Vocabulary links for the Methodology Recount genre family (British Council, n.d.)
[Source: Used with permission of the British Council]

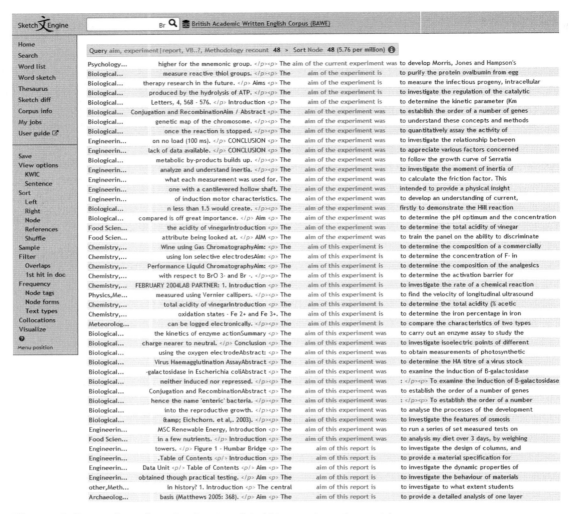

Figure 3 Concordance lines for *the aim of the/this experiment/report is/was*
There is a link from the first vocabulary item in Figure 2 to the concordance lines above (British Council, n.d.) that connects the learner to the BAWE corpus in SketchEngine.

[Source: Reproduced with permission from SketchEngine, www.sketchengine.co.uk]

Katrien L. B. Deroey

How representative are EAP listening books of real lectures?

Introduction

It has often been noted that EAP listening textbooks do not provide a realistic model of lectures (e.g., Alexander, Argent, & Spencer, 2008; Field, 2011; Flowerdew & Miller, 1997; Nesi, 2001; Salehzadeh, 2013; Thompson, 2003). Issues include the use of short and scripted texts, artificially slow and clear speech, and unusually frequent and explicit structuring. While we need to balance authenticity with pedagogical appropriateness, it stands to reason that 'exposing students only to simplified lecture texts certainly does students a disservice' (Salehzadeh, 2013, p. xix).

This paper explores the correspondence between the language in published EAP lecture-listening courses and authentic lecture discourse. Specifically, it compares signposts of important lecture points attested in a large lecture corpus with those in listening courses. Although

importance marking is but one feature of lecture discourse, identifying key points is a vital listening skill and issues with the representation of discourse structuring in lectures have already been noted: EAP lectures are said to be comparatively coherent and explicit (Flowerdew & Miller, 1997) as well as more heavily and carefully signalled (Flowerdew & Miller, 1997; Thompson, 2003) with more transparent phrases (Field, 2011).

Importance markers are here defined as 'lexicogrammatical devices that overtly mark the importance, relevance, or significance of points that are presented verbally or visually' (Deroey, 2015, p. 52). Crucially, they organize discourse while also evaluating it (cf. Crawford Camiciottoli, 2007). Hence, signposts without evaluative force such as enumerators (e.g., 'firstly', 'the next point is') were not included, nor were instances where entities in the real world were evaluated (e.g., 'an important philosopher') instead of the lecturer's discourse (e.g., 'an important point').

Readers will be aware that authenticity is a multi-faceted concept, of which text authenticity is but one aspect (cf. Widdowson, 1998). Here, I have simply defined authentic lectures as those delivered on degree courses and not adapted for language-learning purposes (cf. Basturkmen, 2010). I should point out, however, that even these lectures cannot provide our students with a totally authentic listening experience, as they are removed from the original context and may not be fully representative of lectures in their disciplines and institutions (MacDonald, Badger & White, 2000).

In what follows, I provide an overview of the corpus and listening courses used for this study and compare importance markers in the two. The paper concludes with pedagogical implications.

MATERIALS AND METHODS

LECTURE CORPUS

The importance markers are from the British Academic Spoken English (BASE) Corpus of 160 lectures. The lectures are mostly delivered by native speakers and are from four broad disciplines: arts and humanities, social studies, physical sciences, and life and medical sciences. To capture as wide a range of markers as possible, an extensive manual search of 40 lectures was followed by an automated analysis of all lectures (see Deroey & Taverniers, 2012 for details). The latter search was done with the concordancing tool Sketch Engine (https://the.sketchengine.co.uk).

LISTENING COURSES

Six EAP listening courses were manually examined for phrases presented as signalling key points; lists of both phrases

and examples in exercises were included. The courses were selected from recent materials available at my institution and intentionally included integrated skills courses and books aimed at various levels. In this study, I distinguish between courses that are not corpus based and those that are. The former do not include authentic lectures (as judged by the information from the books' introductions, the transcripts and audiovisual materials), and do not mention using a lecture corpus for their development or language presentation. The latter state they are based on language use in authentic lectures and also include such lectures. Table 1 on page 131 summarizes the main features of the six listening courses. Note that research-based means the courses clearly incorporate findings from their own study of a lecture corpus or findings from existing studies on lecture listening and/or lectures.

RESULTS

IMPORTANCE MARKERS IN THE LECTURE CORPUS

The 160 lectures yielded 782 importance markers. Depending on their main constituent, I distinguished noun, verb, adjective and adverb markers. Reflecting the different lexicogrammatical patterns formed with these main constituents, subtypes were distinguished for each class, apart from adverb markers. For example, verb markers formed patterns such as V n/clause (imperative verb followed by a noun/pronoun or clause), 1st pers pron V n/clause (first person singular pronoun followed by a verb and noun/pronoun or clause) and TO-INF n/clause (a to-infinitive with a noun/pronoun or clause). A complete overview of attested marker types and lexemes can be found in Deroey and Taverniers (2012).

Table I Listening courses used in the study

Book	Level	Authentic lectures?	Corpus based?	Research based?	Other details
Study listening (Lynch, 2004)	≥ IELTS 5.0	✗	✗	✓	Lecturers have different native-speaker accents
Lecture Ready (Sarosy & Sherak, 2013)	1: CEF B1.1 2: CEF B1.2 – B2.1 3: CEF B2.2	✗	✗	✗	Lectures are said to be 'realistic'
Academic listening strategies (Salehzadeh, 2013)	n/a	✓	✓	✓	Includes lectures from MICASE[1]
Cambridge academic English C1 (Hewings & Thaine, 2012)	CEF C1	✓	✓	✓	Native and non-native speaker lecturers; lectures from the CAEC[2]
EASE: Listening to lectures (Kelly, Nesi, & Revell, 2000)	n/a	✓	✓	✓	Lectures from BASE
English for academic study: Listening (Campbell & Smith, 2012)	IELTS 5.0–7.5	✗	✓	✓	Some BASE lectures, but adapted

[1]Michigan Corpus of Academic Spoken English; [2]Cambridge Academic English Corpus

For the sake of simplicity, I have here given examples only of common realizations. The five main types, constituting roughly 77% of all markers, are listed in Table 2 with their most frequent lexemes.

As Table 2 on page 132 shows, subjectless imperatives (1) are by far the most popular importance markers, followed by formulaic phrases of the type 'the point is' (2).

(1) *this is a very innovative building and* **remember** *that Arup Associates were the architects who then moved on to design Broadgate so this was a pioneering building that influenced what was going to happen in Broadgate in London*

Table 2 Predominant importance markers (N=782)

Type	N	%
Remember/notice/note	264	33.7
The point/question is	162	20.7
I want to emphasise/stress; (as) I (have) pointed out	70	8.9
The important/key point/thing is	64	8.2
You have to remember	41	5.2

(2) *you take protein from mice and inject it into a rabbit that rabbit will generate an immune response to that protein from mice* **the point is** *we have to be able to respond to anything that challenges us*

Markers where the main verb denotes the lecturer's intention to stress a point (3) or which contain an adjective denoting importance (4) are far less commonly used.

(3) **i emphasized** *the the the impact on developing countries partly 'cause that's what we're interested in*

(4) *this top line is for sorry for re relatively low emissions and high emissions of C-O-two and you know we may be somewhere in between but it this quantifies the effects and* **the important thing is** *that in terms of winter rainfall it seems that most of the effects are going to be concentrated in the in the south and south east of of of the country*

Instances where the listener is directly addressed with 'you' are even less common:

(5) *when you look at neonates and old people because obviously their surface area if you're very small are very sma sm small old frail lady or small baby becomes important so* **you need**

to remember *it's per surface area and you will lose marks if i ask for a G-F-R and you give me mls per minute and not mls per minute per surface area*

The most common verb, metalinguistic noun and importance adjective are *remember, point* and *important*.

'IMPORTANCE MARKERS' IN THE LISTENING COURSES

Courses that are not corpus based
Study listening (Lynch, 2004)

Lynch distinguishes three ways in which lecturers 'can underline or emphasise points in their argument' (p. 39):

- by speaking about the subject matter itself: 'the central problem is that'; 'a basic point is that'; 'one essential fact is that'; 'another key issue/crucial difference is the';
- by speaking to the audience: 'it's important to bear in mind that'; 'it's worth(while) …ing that'; 'remember that'; 'don't forget that'; 'you shouldn't lose sight of the fact that'; and
- by speaking about themselves: 'I want to stress/emphasise/underline'; 'my point is; what I'm getting at is'.

Lynch has a varied overview of importance markers and his classification in terms of their interactive orientation corresponds to that proposed by Deroey (2015), which is derived from the markers attested in BASE. He includes 'remember that', the most common importance marker in BASE, and 'my point is', a variant of the second most common marker 'the point is' (see Table 2). Other markers listed are fairly explicit and are relatively infrequent in the lecture corpus.

Lecture ready (Sarosy & Sherak, 2013)

Lecture ready 1 contains the following signals of important information (pp. 109, 111, 112):

'this is important'; 'this is very important'; 'the idea … is very important'; 'here is a key question'; 'this idea is key to'; 'step one is the most common and important'; 'it's important to note that'; 'I want to point out'; 'I'd like to focus on'; 'you should write this down'; 'it is important to write these in your notes now'; 'I'll say that again'; 'let me repeat that'; 'let me repeat that idea'.

Lecture ready 2 provides these signposts (pp. 83, 85, 86):

'this is important'; 'one important point is'; 'another important finding was'; 'the bottom line is'; 'here's the bottom line'; 'the point I want to stress the most is'; 'it's important to note that'; 'pay attention to this'; 'I want you to notice that'; 'listen to this'; 'I want to point out that'; 'I want to stress that'; 'you should write this down'; 'now write this down'; 'let me repeat that'; 'I'll say that again'; 'this will be on the test'.

Lecture Ready 3 offers a list of 'expressions that signal repetition for clarification or emphasis' (p. 43):

'in other words'; 'what I mean is'; 'so what I'm saying is'; 'that is'; 'as I said'; 'let me say that another way'; 'in other words'; 'which is to say'.

Markers in *Lecture Ready* also include phrases signalling repetition. While repetition may indeed suggest importance, no instances of such phrases were found in the 40 lectures I examined manually. The other markers are mostly very explicit and either did not appear in BASE (e.g., 'you should write this down') or were comparatively rare in the lectures (e.g., 'this is important', 'pay attention to this', 'I want to stress that').

Corpus-based courses
Academic listening strategies (Salehzadeh, 2013)

Salezadeh gives examples of organizational phrases that help students 'see the forest [the main points] for the trees' (p. 49):

'today I'm going to talk about X because'; 'first I want to talk about'; 'so, let's get on with today's topic'; 'I'm gonna illustrate three reasons for; so why is this important?'; 'OK, next I wanna talk about'; 'let's move on to the other aspect'.

She further presents 'emphasis/evaluative comment[s]' that can signal a new topic is coming (p. 106):

'the important thing here is'; 'what you don't want to forget'; 'be careful about'; 'here's the tricky part now'; 'this causes some very serious problems'; 'some people think that we have too many specialists'; 'what I'm interested in and hoping for is that China will play a major leadership role'.

Salezadeh's examples are mainly of discourse organizational phrases signalling the different lecture points, rather than evaluating their importance. Naturally, structural signals such as 'first I want to talk about' can also make a point more prominent, but only two examples are given where importance is clearly signaled ('the important thing here is'; 'what you don't want to forget'), and these are not representative of common markers in BASE.

Cambridge academic English C1 (Hewings & Thaine, 2012)

Only two examples of 'signposting language' are given which resemble importance markers. They 'indicate a focus' on an idea and part of a quote: 'what we are interested in'; 'and here comes probably the most important sentence' (p. 152).

EASE: Listening to lectures (Kelly, Nesi & Revell, 2000)

The importance markers are from the British Academic Spoken English corpus:

'the key point is'; 'the main point is'; 'one of the most important points is'; 'an important point is'; 'a point worth noting is'; 'that's the main point here'; 'the big question is'; 'what's crucial is'.

Although this course is based on BASE lectures, again only explicit markers with adjectival evaluation are listed, hence misrepresenting how importance marking more usually – and less explicitly – happens in lectures.

English for academic study: Listening (Campbell & Smith, 2012)

From an 'informal analysis' of the corpus, the authors conclude a 'substantial use of informal and idiomatic language by lecturers' and 'less use of (and consistency in the use of) discourse markers to organize information than we might have expected'. Consequently, they have de-emphasized

'listening for discourse markers as a means of identifying key idea to note down' (Teacher's book, p. 7).

The key to exercises on identifying 'signposting language used to highlight key points' (Student's Book, pp. 26, 31) yields the signposts below; however, the lecture in question appears not to be authentic:

'just as important'; 'the important point here'; 'remember'; 'firstly'; 'finally'; 'this brings me to my last point'; 'in addition'; 'so'; 'another thing is'; 'one further issue'; 'one advantage is'; 'for example'; 'you also need'.

This overview is rather a mixed bag, with phrases introducing new points and examples, as well as signalling importance. However, apart from Lynch, this is the only course which includes the most frequent marker in BASE, 'remember'. There are only two other examples of importance markers and they are of the infrequent type containing adjectives.

DISCUSSION

A key finding of this study is the lack of correspondence between the predominant importance markers in the lecture corpus and those in the listening courses. Only one of the more common markers from the lectures, *viz.* adjective + metalinguistic noun (e.g., 'the key point is') occurs in almost all courses. Interestingly, this prototypical and relatively explicit marker probably comes to mind intuitively when considering how lecturers might signpost key information. Nevertheless, in the lecture corpus, this is a relatively minor importance marker (c. 8%) compared to multifunctional markers of the type 'remember' (c. 34%) and 'the point is' (c. 21%). These can have different meanings depending on their context and prosody (e.g., 'remember this' vs. 'do you remember'; 'this is important' vs. 'the purpose is'). Yet, they rarely feature in the materials and mostly occur with lexemes that (almost) never occurred in the lecture-derived markers (e.g., 'pay attention to this'; 'listen to this'; 'now write this down') or in forms that are more easily identifiable as marking importance (e.g., 'my point is'; 'a point worth noting is') than their unmodified counterpart (e.g., 'the thing is'). In addition, more explicit markers with importance adjectives are overrepresented in the courses, considering that only about one fifth of all importance markers from the lectures contain an adjective. By contrast, markers based on verbs (e.g., 'remember, I want to point out that'; 'you shouldn't lose sight of the fact that') are underrepresented in the courses.

Comparing different courses, the ones for more proficient listeners (*Lecture ready 3* and *Cambridge academic English C1*) did not really treat importance marking, and corpus-based courses did not excel in including markers that reflect the variety and prevalence of those used in real lectures. Perhaps the latter finding is not so surprising. On the one hand, materials writers may have neither the time nor the skills for systematic linguistic study, and are thus likely to pick up on the more prototypical signposts in their corpus. On the other hand, research into lecture language is in its infancy, so we cannot expect much of it to have been incorporated into textbooks.

CONCLUSION AND RECOMMENDATIONS

This study explored to what extent listening courses contain language that is representative of authentic lectures. Naturally, the investigation would need to be extended to more courses and discourse features to reach firmer conclusions. However, the analysis of importance markers suggests a mismatch. While listening courses mainly contained explicit, intuitively obvious, and prototypical importance markers (e.g., 'the important point is'; 'pay attention to this'), the lecture corpus yielded a wide variety of markers of which the predominant ones were 'muted' (Swales & Burke 2003, p. 17), multifunctional signals (e.g., 'the thing is'; 'remember').

English for Academic Purposes practitioners have an important role in raising awareness of such issues and adapting materials where appropriate and possible. First, we should establish how confident we are that our listening course reflects real lecture discourse, by examining the introduction, scripts and audiovisuals. Unfortunately, if the current sample is representative of listening courses at large, authors don't usually state where they got their examples of language use from. Second, students need to be made aware of the potential discrepancy between the EAP lectures and those on their degree courses. For example, when teaching discourse-structuring signals, we could note that their lecturers may use different ones, some of which may not be as explicit. Third, keeping abreast of research into lecture listening and discourse can help us point out and prepare students for such discrepancies. In the case of importance marking, for instance, it seems worthwhile to train them to recognize the different meanings of phrases such as 'the thing is' and 'remember'. Fourth, and importantly, we can use freely available lectures and lecture transcripts (e.g., BASE, MICASE, Coursera) to design (supplementary) activities that are adapted to our aims, context and students. Flowerdew & Miller (1997, p. 44) recommend the inclusion of longer, authentic extracts in addition to the shorter, 'cleaned-up' ones that typify many textbooks, so that students can 'develop strategies to deal with the "messiness" of real lectures'. To make working with authentic texts manageable, Alexander et al. (2008) propose ways of controlling authenticity in terms of texts, goals, interactions, processes, and tasks (see also Moore, 2015). Suggestions include live lectures by invited speakers, modifying the pace of delivery, delivering lecture scripts yourself, dictation of small parts with key vocabulary and content before listening, and providing advance notes with the main points and structure.

This paper has aimed to increase EAP practitioners' and materials developers' insight into how representative published lecture listening materials are of authentic lectures. The findings suggest that their representativeness is limited and highlight the need to include authentic lectures and research on lecture discourse in preparing students for the demands of their lectures.

ACKNOWLEDGEMENTS

The recordings and transcriptions used in this study come from the British Academic Spoken English (BASE) corpus. The corpus was developed at the Universities of Warwick and Reading under the directorship of Hilary Nesi and Paul Thompson. Corpus development was assisted by funding from BALEAP, EURALEX, the British Academy and the Arts and Humanities Research Council. The corpus is accessible at https://the.sketchengine.co.uk/open/.

LISTENING COURSES USED IN THIS STUDY

Campbell, C., & Smith, J. (2012). *English for academic study: Listening. Course book.* Reading: Garnet Publishing Ltd.

Campbell, C., & Smith, J. (2012). *English for academic study: Listening. Teacher's book.* Reading: Garnet Publishing Ltd.

Firth, M. (2012). *Cambridge academic English: An integrated skills course for EAP. Lecture skills video worksheet.* Cambridge: Cambridge University.

Firth, M., Sowton, C., Hewings, M., & Thaine, C. (2012). *Cambridge academic English: An integrated skills course for EAP. C1 advanced. Teacher's book.* Cambridge: Cambridge University Press.

Hewings, M., & Thaine, C. (2012). *Cambridge academic English: An integrated skills course for EAP. C1 advanced. Student's book.* Cambridge: Cambridge University Press.

Kelly, T., Nesi, H., & Revell, R. (2000). *EASE volume one: Listening to lectures.* Coventry: University of Warwick.

Lynch, T. (2004). *Study listening: A course in listening to lectures and note-taking.* Cambridge: Cambridge University Press.

Salehzadeh, J. (2013). *Academic listening strategies: A guide to understanding lectures.* Ann Arbor: University of Michigan Press.

Sarosy, P., & Sherak, K. (2013). *Lecture ready 1: Strategies for academic listening and speaking* (2nd ed.). Oxford: Oxford University Press.

Sarosy, P., & Sherak, K. (2013). *Lecture ready 2: Strategies for academic listening and speaking* (2nd ed.): Oxford: Oxford University Press.

Sarosy, P., & Sherak, K. (2013). *Lecture ready 3: Strategies for academic listening and speaking* (2nd ed.). Oxford: Oxford University Press.

REFERENCES

Alexander, O., Argent, S., & Spencer, J. (2008). *EAP essentials: A teacher's guide to principles and practice.* Reading: Garnet Publishing Ltd.

Basturkmen, H. (2010). *Developing courses in English for specific purposes.* London: Palgrave Macmillan.

British Academic Spoken English Corpus (BASE). Retrieved from https://the.sketchengine. co.uk/open/#

Coursera. Retrieved from https://www.coursera.org

Crawford Camiciottoli, B. (2007). *The language of business studies lectures. A corpus-assisted analysis.* Amsterdam: John Benjamins Publishing Company.

Deroey, K. L. B. (2015). Marking importance in lectures: Interactive and textual orientation. *Applied Linguistics, 36*(1), 51–72.

Deroey, K. L. B., & Taverniers, M. (2012). Just remember this: Lexicogrammatical relevance markers in lectures. *English for specific purposes, 31*(4), 221–233.

Field, J. (2011). Into the mind of the academic listener. *Journal of English for Academic Purposes, 10*(2), 102–112. doi:10.1016/j.jeap.2011.04.002

Flowerdew, J., & Miller, L. (1997). The teaching of academic listening comprehension and the question of authenticity. *English for Specific Purposes, 16*(1), 27–46.

MacDonald, M., Badger, R., & White, G. (2000). The real thing?: Authenticity and academic listening. *English for specific purposes, 19*(3), 253–267.

Moore, J. (2015). *Making authentic academic texts manageable* [Blog post]. Retrieved 2 April, 2016, from http://lexicoblog.blogspot.co.uk/2015/11/making-authentic-academic-texts.html

Nesi, H. (2001). EASE: A multimedia materials development project. In K. Cameron (Ed.), *CALL – The challenge of change* (pp. 287–292). Exeter: Elm Bank Publications.

The Sketch Engine. Retrieved September, 1, 2015, from https://the.sketchengine.co.uk

Swales, J. M., & Burke, A. (2003). 'It's really fascinating work': Differences in evaluative adjectives across academic registers. In P. Leistyna & C. F. Meyer (Eds.), *Corpus analysis: Language structure and language use* (pp. 1–18). Amsterdam: Rodopi.

Thompson, S. E. (2003). Text-structuring metadiscourse, intonation and the signalling of organization in academic lectures. *Journal of English for Academic Purposes, 2*(1), 5–20.

Widdowson, H. G. (1998). Context, community, and authentic language. *TESOL Quarterly, 32*(4), 705–716.

OLGA BURAKOV

TEACHING FIGURATIVE LANGUAGE IN AN ENGLISH FOR ACADEMIC PURPOSES CLASSROOM

INTRODUCTION

Sylvia Plath's poem, 'Metaphors' (Plath, 1960), is a favourite among editors of poetry anthologies, English literature teachers and students. It is not surprising that the poem resonates with many readers of different ages and literary tastes as, in the space of only nine lines, it delivers a complex study of the emotionally-charged topic of impending motherhood. The poet accomplishes this feat by means of the dazzling juxtaposition of metaphors to do with money, animals and food, the precise meaning of which is not easy to grasp. How should the reader interpret, for example, the speaker's view of herself as a 'fat purse' and her equation of her unborn child with a freshly-minted coin? Is the speaker trying to tell her reader that she herself is merely a container, or that her child is her most precious possession? What about the speaker comparing herself to an elephant or cow? Some might revere these creatures as sacred or majestic beings, while others might merely see them as an exploitable commodity. Likewise, when the speaker refers to herself as a piece of fruit or a loaf of bread, it is unclear if these metaphors are meant as light-hearted references to the physical changes in her body or her uneasy sense of a self in a state of flux or dissolution. Finally, what is the reader to make of the concluding line, in which the speaker sees herself as a passenger on a train from which she cannot disembark? Is it indicative of her devil-may-care attitude towards her future as a mother, a final statement of acceptance of the inevitable, or a desperate cry for help? In every line of the poem, Plath provokes such questions in the reader through her choice of metaphor.

This type of engagement with a text is usually reserved for the English literature classroom and not for the English for Academic Purposes (EAP) classroom, in which metaphors are still often frowned upon as a staple of a 'colourful' idiomatic language (Littlemore & Low, 2006, p. 4) best avoided by academic writers. Would spending class time on metaphors then be of any value to an EAP practitioner, whose job it is to prepare undergraduate and postgraduate students for their careers in a variety of technical and scientific fields as engineers, pharmacists, public administrators, computer scientists and business managers? What purpose does figurative language serve for the majority of international students, who are required to read academic research articles and reference textbooks, rather than analyze poems? This paper will try to provide some answers to these questions. More specifically, building on the growing research on metaphors and language learning (Hoang, 2014; Low, Littlemore & Koester, 2008; Littlemore & Low, 2006; Holme, 2004; Boers, 2004), it will suggest that an analysis of an academic writer's use of figurative language might facilitate not just a learner's vocabulary learning (Boers, 2004; Littlemore & Low, 2006; Kalyuga & Kalyuga, 2008; Gao & Meng, 2010). It can also facilitate the learners' identification of the writer's stance or position, a task which EAP learners often find daunting. Finally, this paper will also suggest that raising learners' awareness of figurative language and metaphors in academic texts might also help international undergraduate and postgraduate EAP learners to develop their own critical position *vis-à-vis* these texts.

FIGURATIVE LANGUAGE AND NON-LITERARY TEXTS

Unlike lecturers in the Schools of English whose job it is to hone their students' understanding of the place and the function of figurative language in general, and of metaphors in particular, in a variety of literary texts, the majority of EAP instructors are responsible for the development of academic skills of international learners reading and writing scientific or technical texts. Such texts tend to prioritize 'linearity over circularity; explicitness … over evocation; closing down of possible meanings rather than open-endedness; certainty over uncertainty' (Lillis, 2001, p. 115).

Why, then, should EAP practitioners integrate the study of figurative language or of metaphors into their lessons? It is possible to argue, of course, that the job of EAP practitioners is to introduce their students to a variety of genres, including the non-technical or the non-scientific ones. To put it differently, as educators, teachers of EAP have the responsibility to introduce their students to academic narrative genres which require a more creative approach, and also allow the students to demonstrate their developing expertise as critical thinkers and their growing understanding of non-literal uses of language. As Nesi and Gardner (2012) have effectively demonstrated, creative assignments are valued within UK academia, where more and more programmes aim to prepare students for life outside of the university walls. Nesi and Gardner interviewed academic staff across a variety of disciplines about the types of reading and writing projects they required their students to complete. They report that:

> … (t)he value placed on innovation in higher education was evident in the interview comments of academic staff who considered essays to be too traditional (Sociology) and limiting (English) … The academic staff we interviewed were proud to tell us about

their exciting new ideas for a crime fiction assignment in a Sociology module, and for a Law assignment in the form of a play script of a legal case.

(Nesi & Gardner, 2012, p. 215)

At the same time, as Nesi and Gardner acknowledge in their study, creative approaches to learning are still somewhat of a rarity in today's academia, and even the proponents of creative projects themselves are not entirely comfortable with their literary assignments. For instance, a Computer Science lecturer described the literary tasks she set her students as 'wacky', while the Theatre Studies lecturers interviewed by Nesi and Gardner referred to their writing assignments as 'writing dangerously' (2012, p. 215). The language used by both lecturers clearly betrays the academics' discomfort in relation to the literary, a discomfort which might be, to some extent, shared by a number of EAP practitioners (Littlemore & Low, 2006). In fact, as Littlemore and Low note in their study of metaphors and second language learning, 'metaphors are still felt by some [language instructors] to be largely literary and thus recondite, obscure, and difficult. According to this view, metaphor reflects an advanced use by a minority of speakers and there is little justification for exposing most learners to it' (ibid. p. 4).

However, a growing body of studies from across a variety of disciplines has shown that figurative language in general, and metaphors in particular, are widely used not only in academic lectures (Low, Littlemore & Koester, 2008), but also in academic textbooks, where they serve a variety of purposes. Carew and Mitchell (2006) identify four distinct metaphors repeatedly used by engineers to understand

and to explain the concept of sustainability. These metaphors refer to sustainability as 'weaving', 'trading', 'guarding', and as 'observing limits' (Carew & Mitchell, 2006, pp. 223–226). Similarly, in an earlier paper, Keen (1996) has shown that metaphors are frequently used in computer sciences and software engineering textbooks. Metaphors identified by Keen include prototyping as 'a journey', a software project as 'a game', software engineer experts as 'wizards', system design as 'building a house', data as 'having fluid properties of a liquid flow' and, finally, 'the anthropomorphic metaphor of a computer thinking in an analogous manner to the human brain' (Keen, 1996, p. 331).

Aside from engineering, other disciplines, such as business and architecture, use conceptual metaphors to describe how different types of companies and/or spaces are designed, organized and managed (Hey, Linsey, Agogino & Wood, 2008). In addition, a wide range of metaphors is also commonly used in science and medicine, not only to describe what scientists and doctors do, but also to conceptualize illness and the process of diagnosis. According to Sontag's by now canonical studies of illness and of HIV/AIDS, some of the more common metaphors used in medicine are military metaphors that equate medical treatment with war, an illness with an external threat, an invasive army, an enemy, or simply a killer (Sontag, 1979; 1989). Other common metaphors used in medical textbooks constitute doctors as detectives and medical diagnosis as a police investigation (Hodgkin, 1985). Hodgkin quotes one example from a medical textbook that does just that: 'This sinister disease requires a rigorous history to be taken plus a searching examination together with a high index of suspicion in order to spot the tell-tale clues and make the correct diagnosis' (p. 1820). Finally, metaphors are widely used in education, with students being routinely referred to as customers, disciplines as fields, research as output, and the teaching process as a journey, a search or even a quest.

Given the ubiquity of metaphoric language in a variety of disciplines, it seems beneficial for EAP lecturers to raise their students' awareness of the dominant non-literal expressions within the texts they are assigned to read. Such awareness-raising may simultaneously aid the learners' vocabulary acquisition and improve their reading skills (Hoang, 2014; Gao & Meng, 2010; Kalyuga & Kalyuga, 2008; Boers, 2004). However, as was suggested in the introduction to this paper, paying attention to metaphors can also help learners when they are asked to critically evaluate a text and its writer's stance. Before moving on to explain this last point in more detail, however, it is important to first address the reason why writers use metaphors or what purpose metaphors serve in academic texts.

THE FUNCTION OF METAPHORS IN ACADEMIC TEXTS

Early studies of metaphors by Lakoff and Johnson (1980) have emphasized that metaphors are used to conceptualize abstract ideas such as time, for example. This view was more recently supported by Holme (2004), who argues that metaphors can be thought of as a 'method of finding and naming concepts that are crucial to how we structure reality, such as reason or time' (p. 13). Indeed, the use of metaphors to explain sustainability by Engineering students described by Carew and Mitchell (2006) performs just this function. However, metaphors do much more than offer an

explanation of difficult concepts. They also, as Holme succinctly notes, 'control those structures in order to foster or protect a given social order' (2004, p. 13). Put another way, metaphors in academic texts do not just describe difficult concepts in a compressed way. In addition, they shape and define what their writers think to be true, and thus reveal how writers perceive these difficult concepts. In other words, metaphors expose the ideological and/or disciplinary assumptions and attitudes embedded in a text. Describing a virus as a killer and claiming that a doctor is waging a war against an invasive tumour (Hodgkin, 1985, p. 1820), for example, reveal a set of attitudes which privileges aggressive action and emphasizes the physician as the one in control, while the patient remains largely invisible and agentless. Similarly, describing sustainability as 'weaving' (Carew & Mitchell, 2006, pp. 223–224) locates it within a system of values that privileges connectivity, whereas a description of sustainability as 'trading' foregrounds the process of exchange, which may or may not entail financial compensation. In a similar way, referring to students as customers and to research as output reveals a particular way of thinking about what researchers do and who students are, a way of thinking that transforms the university into a business or a corporation.

To conclude this discussion of the ideological work performed by metaphors in academic texts, a brief mention of the use of metaphors in scientific articles on genetically modified (GM) food is perhaps warranted, as it is a topic which is commonly researched, read, and written about by learners in a variety of pre-sessional EAP classes. Many academic journal articles debating the controversial topic of GM products deploy metaphors of war and of impurity. One such article, which I use with my EAP learners, is by Pandey, A., Kamle, Yadava, Muthukumar, Kumar, Gupta, Ashfaque & Pandey, B. K. (2010). In this article, the authors purport to analyze what GM food does, making their support for GM food clear already in their abstract, where they use a military metaphor that turns GM crops into an effective weapon governments and scientists can deploy against multiple dangers: 'world's hunger, malnutrition problems, environmental pollution and phytoremediation in agriculture are the challenges for scientists as well as governments. Those can be combatted by application of genetic engineering in crops' (Pandey et al., 2010, p. 444). As some of my EAP learners like to point out, with its military metaphoric connotations, the verb 'combat' in the quote above is a clear example of how proponents of GM crops seek to condition consumers' response to such products.

On the other hand, opponents of GM food often utilize metaphors of pollution when addressing the topic of GM food. One such metaphor is that of GM food as 'Frankenfood', which was adopted by the popular Western media, and led to the 2004 publication of *The Frankenfood Myth: How Protest and Politics Threaten the Biotech Revolution* by Miller and Conko. In addition to this culture-specific metaphor, there are many, arguably more universal, references to non-GM food as 'clean,' or to the mixing of non-GM seeds with GM seeds as 'contamination', which critics of GM crops frequently use to bolster their arguments (Levidow, 2000, pp. 325–351). Students are quick to perceive that such metaphoric expressions seek to 'delegitimize... agricultural biotechnology,

while catalysing public debate about choices for the future of nature and society' (Levidow, 2000, p. 325).

METAPHORS AND EAP CLASSROOM APPLICATIONS

Raising EAP learners' awareness of the ideological work performed by metaphors in a text can thus help them in two ways. For students who have difficulty identifying the writer's stance and position in an academic text where the writer does not explicitly declare that he or she will argue for or against something, repeated or dominant metaphors offer a way to pinpoint the writer's position. This, in turn, allows learners to begin thinking about and unpacking the often implicit ideological assumptions or ideological purposes at work in the text. Secondly, and, perhaps even more importantly for those students who are expected to demonstrate not just their understanding of what they have read, but also to apply critical thinking to their reading, the study of metaphors can empower them to develop their critical stance towards the text and its writer's argument. For example, EAP learners can be asked to consider how the metaphors of clean food or of a killer virus enforce certain lines of thinking about their topics while discouraging other points of view, what alternative phrases or words could have been used by the writers, and what language the students themselves would use if they were asked to write on the topic. Such activities encourage students to develop their own critical thinking skills by empowering them to reflect on the fact that what they are reading is not always an accurate reflection of reality or the only possible way of thinking about, say, GM food or viruses.

Rather, it is a position that the writer of a particular academic text wants them to subscribe to.

When EAP instructors ask their learners to identify the stance of a writer in an academic text or to critically evaluate the argument of an academic text, they can first draw their students' attention to one or two examples of figurative language in the text. The instructor's next step should be to elicit from the learners similar or additional instances of this way of talking about the subject from the text to see if this is a common linguistic feature (Goatly, 2000; Holme, 2004). Next, the students might be asked to interpret the meaning of these metaphors – are they universal or culture specific, positive or negative – and to think about what this type of language tells them about the writer's system of values or the ideological purpose of the text (Holme, 2004; Littlemore & Low, 2006). Finally, students should always be encouraged to consider alternative possibilities as a way of establishing their own critical position in relation to the text.

CONCLUSION

In conclusion, this paper has shown that figurative language plays an important role in a variety of technical and scientific texts on a variety of topics in a variety of disciplines. Moreover, an analysis of a given writer's use of figurative language might help the reader to identify the writer's stance or position, and, perhaps more importantly, might also help students for whom English is not their first language to develop their own critical position in relation to the text. After all, if figurative language in general, and metaphors in particular, can teach us anything, it is that they can be used both to promote the established norms and to challenge the ideology behind them.

REFERENCES

Boers, F. (2004). Expanding learners' vocabulary through metaphor awareness: What expansion, what learners, what vocabulary? In M. Achard & S. Niemeier (Eds.), *Cognitive linguistics, second language acquisition and foreign language teaching* (pp. 211–232). Berlin, New York: De Gruyter.

Carew A., & Mitchell, C. (2006). Metaphors used by some engineering academics in Australia for understanding and explaining sustainability. *Environmental Education Research, 12*(2), 217–231.

Gao, L., & Meng, G. (2010). A study on the effect of metaphor awareness raising on Chinese EFL learners' vocabulary acquisition and retention. *Canadian Social Science, 6*(2), 110–124.

Goatly, A. (2000). *Critical reading and writing*. London: Routledge.

Hey, J., Linsey J., Agogino A. M., & Wood, K. L. (2008). Analogies and metaphors in creative design. *International Journal of Engineering Education, 24*(2), 283–294.

Hoang, H. (2014). Metaphor and second language learning: The state of the field. *TESL-EJ, 18*(2), 1–13.

Hodgkin, P. (1985). Medicine is war. *British Medical Journal, 291*, 1820–1821.

Holme, R. (2004). *Mind, metaphor and language teaching.* New York: Palgrave Macmillan.

Kalyuga, M., & Kalyuga S. (2008). Metaphor awareness in teaching vocabulary. *Language Learning Journal, 36*(2), 249–257.

Keen, C. (1996). Treatment of metaphors in software engineering education. *Conference Proceedings, Institute of Electrical and Electronics* Engineers, 329–335. Hobart: University of Tasmania.

Lakoff, G., & Johnson, M. (1980). *Metaphors we live by.* Chicago: University of Chicago Press.

Levidow, L. (2000). Pollution metaphors in the UK biotechnology controversy. *Science as Culture, 9*(3), 325–351.

Lillis, T. (2001). *Student writing: Access, regulation, desire.* London: Routledge.

Littlemore, J., & Low, G. (2006). Metaphoric competence, second language learning and communicative language ability. *Applied Linguistics, 27*(2), 268–294.

Low, G., Littlemore, J., & Koester, A. (2008). Metaphor use in three UK university lectures. *Applied linguistics, 29*(3), 428–455.

Miller, H., & Conko, G. (2004). *The Frankenfood myth: How protest and politics threaten the biotech revolution.* Westport, Connecticut: Praeger Publishers.

Nesi, H., & Gardner, S. (2012). *Genres across the disciplines: Student writing in higher education.* Cambridge: Cambridge University Press.

Pandey, A., Kamle, M., Yadava, L. P., Muthukumar, M., Kumar, P., Gupta, V., Ashfaque, M., & Pandey, B. K. (2010). Genetically modified food: Its uses, future prospects and safety assessments. *Biotechnology, 9*(4), 444–458.

Plath, S. (1960) 'Metaphors'. In X. J. Kennedy & D. Gioia (Eds.) (1994), *An introduction to poetry* (p. 101). New York: Harper Collins College Publishers.

Sontag, S. (1979). *Illness as metaphor.* New York: Farrar, Straus & Giroux.

Sontag, S. (1989). *AIDS and its metaphors.* New York: Farrar, Straus & Giroux.

Jill Northcott, Pauline Gillies and David Caulton

Feedback on feedback: The role of ESAP tutor feedback in improving postgraduate student academic writing ability

Introduction

Feedback is considered central to student learning and academic achievement. With the continuing increase in the numbers of both distance and face-to-face international Masters students, providing effective online formative feedback to develop second language (L2) English academic writing skills has become a crucial concern. Identifying the characteristics of effective feedback is an important first step in spreading good practice more widely. Whilst there is a general consensus that effective feedback is personalised, specific and timely (Busse, 2013; Hyland, 2013b), there is little agreement about whether written correction has any transferable effects from the immediate assignment to long-term improvement of writing. Studies into student and teacher perceptions of feedback effectiveness have sometimes produced conflicting results, because the experimental design removes feedback 'from the contexts in which it has meaning for students' (Hyland, 2013b, p. 182). The need for experimental controls may, for example, restrict the choice of texts and tasks, requiring selected groups of students to produce several versions of the same text for no obvious purpose. The teaching and learning environment, however, provides a very meaningful context for research in this area, addressing some of these concerns.

The very practical teaching and learning concerns of EAP and other writing teachers have resulted in something of a revival in feedback-related research recently. The original debate was begun by Truscott (1996, 2007, 2010), who maintained that written corrective feedback (WCF) was ineffective in improving writing. Ferris (2006, 2007) wrote directly in response to Truscott, taking the opposite view. The debate has since been joined by Bruton (2009), Lee (2008), McMartin-Miller (2014), Hyland & Hyland (2006) and Hyland (2013a and b), among others. There is now a general consensus that WCF can, in fact, contribute to improving some areas, such as grammatical accuracy. However, the contribution of different written feedback strategies to overall writing improvement is still unclear (Lee, 2014).

This paper reports on the initial phase of a grounded theory-inspired study. Our primary aim was to explore the perceptions of effectiveness of online formative feedback on postgraduate academic writing provided by English Language Education (ELE) tutors, in order to identify effective feedback techniques. Developing understanding and skills in providing feedback might, in turn, contribute to the improvement of postgraduate students' academic writing ability. A better understanding of how to effectively tailor our approach to different disciplinary areas and programme needs should also ensue.

We focused on two academic writing courses run by ELTC in collaboration with the College of Medicine and Veterinary Medicine (CMVM) and the School of Social and Political Science (SPS). The courses run as early as possible in the academic year in order to provide students with structured support in writing an essay before formally assessed assignments are due. Participation is voluntary as the courses are non-credit bearing. Assignments with prescribed reading are provided by the academic department. ELTC tutors provide online feedback on four weekly tasks and assignments which build an academic essay, section by section. Subject tutors give feedback on the final 1,500-word essay. The SPS course includes three joint ELTC/subject specialism face-to-face sessions providing further opportunities for feedback and an open forum for questions about academic writing conventions, style and content expectations.

METHODOLOGY

DATA COLLECTION

The data consist of the four short written texts submitted by each student from two separate online academic writing courses. These are Scientific Academic Writing for Masters by Research in Medicine, Dentistry and Veterinary Medicine (SAW) and Academic Writing for Social and Political Sciences (AWSPS). The texts include the comments, changes and corrections from the ELTC tutor. SAW uses an online system (Grademark), whereas AWSPS assignments are sent to tutors as emailed Word attachments and returned with comments and changes tracked. Each tutor manages a group of ten students. A total of 145 students enrolled on AWSPS; 94 completed the first assignment and tutors provided feedback on a total of 224 texts. Of the 137 enrolled on SAW, 81 completed the first assignment. Tutors provided feedback on 234 texts. All the students are in the first month of their one-year postgraduate programmes.

In addition to the writing samples, short Feedback on Feedback questionnaires (Appendix 1) were sent to students on three separate occasions during the course to elicit comments on the feedback they were receiving. Numbers are presented here for transparency purposes only. Our interest was in information-rich cases (Patton, 2002) in the real-world setting. There were 26 completed questionnaires for AWSPS and 21 for SAW. A final course evaluation questionnaire was sent to all students participating in the course. Ten were returned from AWSPS, four from SAW. We also looked at comments students made in emails, and took into consideration comments made during face-to-face exchanges.

Data analysis procedures
Adopting a modified Grounded Theory approach (see Northcott, 2001), we conducted an initial trawl of the data, beginning from the returned Feedback on Feedback questionnaires, to identify any emerging themes and generate categories through open coding. These initial categories were then refined and developed and applied to sets of data, checking for both positive and negative instances. We divided the data for coding between us, and all three researchers looked independently at some sample data to ensure that we were interpreting the data and applying the codes in similar ways. Research memos were written throughout the process, and the three researchers met regularly to discuss the findings and hypotheses/theories generated, creating the 'genuine interweaving of data collection and theorizing of the kind advocated by Glaser and Strauss' (Bryman & Burgess, 1994, p. 6).

Feedback on Feedback questionnaires and final course evaluation questionnaires (where available) were then matched to students and tutor groups to examine written work and tutors' feedback. We narrowed our focus to those students who had expressed a strong sense that their written work had improved as a result of the course, and took the further step of examining texts for uptake of feedback. Two examples are provided in the next section. Whilst there is general agreement that effectiveness of feedback is very hard to pin down, we hoped to discover whether there was any evidence that the students' expressed perceptions of improvement reflected their actual written performance. Students did not produce second versions of the individual assignments, but were encouraged to incorporate suggestions for changes and corrections into the developing essay, which allowed us to distinguish between those who acted on the feedback and those who did not.

Examination of written feedback began with the students' texts and tutor comments to identify patterns. These were matched afterwards with student comments on the effectiveness of the feedback and the course. As the work progressed, we read the relevant literature, particularly in relation to the written corrective feedback debate, and compared our emergent findings. As much of the WCF research is conducted in secondary school and early undergraduate years' settings and focuses on grammatical and lexical correction, we interpreted WCF more widely for the postgraduate context to indicate correction of the use of academic conventions, sentence structure and argumentation, as well as grammar and lexis. Initial categories developed were refined and grouped to produce the scheme in Table 1.

The following excerpts from SAW coding exemplify CONFID. Comments from students (S) are taken from the Feedback on Feedback questionnaire returns and matched with the tutor comments (T) on the unit assignment:

> **S1.** *have been out of higher education for a while and was concerned that my academic writing would be below par. The feedback I had from the first assignment was reassuring and I will approach essays and other writing tasks with more confidence now. I would say that my writing will improve because it won't be such a fraught experience for me.*
>
> **T.** *This is well written and well organised in logically sequenced paragraphs … Well done for what you have produced so far.*
>
> **S2.** *I included some information about studies conducted and references for my work in assignment 2! It gave me confidence!*
>
> **T.** *… you refer to a number of studies suggesting a link between oral inflammation and CV disease and then go on to state your reservations about the link. It might help to create greater balance in the essay if you also introduced research findings which suggest that there is no evidence for a link. The main point I'd like to make is that you will have to include reference details for the studies you mention …*

RESULTS AND DISCUSSION

Focusing on those students who had explicitly expressed satisfaction with the feedback provided by ELTC tutors, we observed that particular combinations of the codes identified from our examination of the data were prevalent. In the cases we examined, WCF was appreciated, whether this was provided by drawing attention to errors through highlighting, direct correction or indirect correction. Initially, we focused on looking for differences in responses to indirect versus direct feedback, expecting students to respond more favourably to the first. Ferris (2006, p. 98) maintains that

Table 1 Categories and codes

Categories	Codes
Positive comments from tutor leading to increased motivation and improvement	POS
Corrective feedback leads to perceived improvement and elimination of mistakes	CF
Refreshed knowledge of academic conventions and style	REFRESH
Developed awareness of academic expectations	EXPECT
Critical awareness developed	CRITAWARE
Confidence developed	CONFID
Improved but lack of detail	NONSPECIFIC
Extended academic vocabulary	VOCABEXTEND
Positive use of names	NAMED
Suggestions for improvement	IMPSUGG
Any comments related to feedback on this	CONTENT
Tutor comments/instruction/correction to improve academic style	ACADEMIC

there is 'a strong case for the superiority of indirect feedback over direct feedback', as it allows learners to engage with the rules and apply them to their own correction of errors, resulting in deeper learning (Ferris, 2001). We expected student satisfaction with improvements to their writing to focus on this area. However, our data suggested that any kind of correction, including proofreading for errors, appeared to result in perceived improvement and student satisfaction with feedback. Further investigation revealed that other factors also needed to be present. These appeared to focus more on the interpersonal aspects of the online relationship established between the individual tutors and students. Students reacted favourably to a personalised approach. This is exemplified by the tutor engaging positively with the student text, as evidenced by using the student's first name and giving positive comments, as well as providing both direct and indirect feedback. A typical example of well-received feedback follows:

> *An interesting and comprehensive introduction, well done, Masako. You have included all five elements indicated in the task rubric. Your writing is mostly clear; check my highlighted points. Make sure you proof-read; I've made some changes and suggestions (mostly on verb agreement/prepositions). Let me know if you have any questions.*

Establishing a relationship, developing confidence and individualising feedback to take account of the student's L1 and cultural background, as well as their professional background, appeared to play a role. Informal discussions revealed how tutors used their experience of working in different cultures and with different professional

groups to guide their responses to individual students. We developed the theory that it is a combination of POS/NAMED/CF with ACADEMIC + CONFID, which leads to both student satisfaction and improvement. However, applying the theory to our data and checking for both positive and negative instances led to a further modification, as these two contrasting cases from the SAW data illustrate. In both cases, students profess satisfaction with improved academic writing, and both tutors demonstrate a high level of engagement with the student and their writing by providing positive comments and correcting errors in language and use of referencing.

CASE ONE

The feedback leads to professed increased confidence and improved writing in the case of the first student:

> **T1.** *Hi (student's first name). Well done. Overall, this is well written. (tutor's first name)*
> **S1.** *... motivational, encouragement and compliments make me believe that I can do it!*
> **S1.** *(in response to the question: How did you use the feedback?) I implemented recommended changes & corrections/techniques explained will be most useful/ ... rewrote based on suggestions and recommendations about what to think about, sentence structure, vocabulary, paragraph structure, etc.*

Appropriate indirect and direct feedback is provided:

> **T1.** *Your English is impressively accurate. Your citation skills, however, need some polishing. There are examples of incorrect citation throughout your writing. You need to revise the Harvard referencing system. A useful website is: www.epax.co.uk ... you need to reorder as well as restructure this part of the sentence.*

My suggestion is: These rights are basic, fundamental …

CASE TWO

Tutor 2 remains positive and encouraging, in spite of the fact that the student has not taken any steps to implement the feedback:

T2. *Thank you for submitting your 4th task. To make a few general comments I think you could maybe go back and look at previous corrections on tasks – particularly task 2. I think much of the advice I gave you for that doesn't seem to have been applied – I especially recognise a few sections in paragraph 1 of task 4 which I have already commented on. I know it is time consuming but you will find the suggestions helpful. Have a look again at task 2 at my suggestions and the same for 1 and 3 and see if you can make changes to incorporate in your task 4 so that over the course the improvement builds up from task to task.*

Appropriately worded indirect and direct WCF is provided:

T2. *I think you would benefit from having another look at the material for task 4 – especially the hedging as you do need to be a bit more cautious in your writing … for example, in paragraph 2, genetically modified organisms which seem to experience pain would be more appropriate than the sweeping statement you have made.*

However, there is no evidence of uptake of feedback in the case of Student 2:

S2. *(in response to the question: How did you use the feedback?) I checked my mistakes and I noticed my deficiencies in order to improve my writing for the next time.*

(in response to the question: Is the feedback helping you to improve your academic writing?) Because next time I will write an essay I will have in mind not to do the same mistakes.

We compared the final essay submitted to the SPS subject specialists for assessment with the initial task submitted to the ELTC tutor. This involved writing a short response to the essay question. The two versions were very similar.

As expected, feedback uptake had proved complex. We had found examples where, although all of the elements of feedback we had discovered to be important were present, it was clear that the student had not acted on the feedback to make changes and corrections to their writing. We found, however, little evidence of what Truscott (1996, p. 355) refers to as 'the inherent unpleasantness of correction'. On the whole, our postgraduate students appreciated the correction provided, even when there was little evidence that they had acted upon it.

Lee (2008), researching Hong Kong secondary classrooms, concluded that the teacher's personality and pedagogy can indirectly influence student reactions to teacher feedback (p. 156). We concur with Lee (p. 146) that 'feedback is a social act' and most effective when a cooperative dialogue between tutor and student is established. This is as true of the online as the face-to-face classroom context. Establishing a persona online to project a friendly and involved, yet critical, friend appeared to be as central as principled WCF to good feedback practice in our postgraduate context.

CONCLUSION

Our research has indicated that it is both possible and desirable for EAP practitioners to investigate their own specific contexts with the aim of improving practice. We conclude that it is the combination of a personalised, confidence-building approach to providing consistent and principled corrective feedback with a focus on developing awareness of academic conventions and style which can result in effective feedback. However, we would add the proviso that there needs to be evidence of student uptake for effectiveness to be demonstrated. In line with previous research (Lee, 2014), we were unable to identify the exact contribution of different feedback strategies to overall writing improvement. Nor can we say with certainty that the improvement in writing we observed will carry over to later written assignments. We do, however, feel that we have a stronger awareness of what works for this specific context. We are keen to stress that, in identifying the characteristics of tutor feedback contributing to student satisfaction with improved academic writing ability, we are essentially investigating our own practice, and our examples of good practice come from our colleagues. Involvement as practitioners in researching our own teaching contexts is a key component in improving our online feedback practice. We make no case for the generalisability of our claims within the WCF debate, but we hope our approach will be of relevance for practitioners in similar contexts to ours.

We have produced and are trialling initial feedback guidelines based on this research and practice (Appendix 2), and these were disseminated and discussed before the 2015 course. Our collaborative academic writing courses are continuing to provide some rich opportunities for subject and EAP specialist cooperation. Future planned developments include a session with SPS academic staff in response to SPS tutor requests for more guidance on feedback. We are also intending to investigate further some of the other categories in our data, and apply our findings to new sets of data. In addition, we plan to track the progress of some of the students to explore the contribution of the courses to performance in credit-bearing assignments later in the year.

ACKNOWLEDGEMENTS

This research was partially funded by the University of Edinburgh's Principal's Teaching Award Scheme (PTAS).

REFERENCES

Bruton, A. (2009). Improving accuracy is not the only reason for writing, and even if it were … *System, 37,* 600–613.

Bryman, A., & Burgess, R. (Eds.) (1994). *Analyzing qualitative data.* London & New York: Routledge.

Busse, V. (2013). How do students of German perceive feedback practices at university? A motivational exploration. *Journal of Second Language Writing, 22,* 406–424.

Ferris, D. (2001). Teaching writing for academic purposes. In J. Flowerdew & M. Peacock (Eds.), *Research perspectives on English for Academic Purposes* (pp. 298–314). Cambridge: Cambridge University Press.

Ferris, D, (2006). Does error feedback help student writers? New evidence on the short- and long-term effects of written error correction. In K. Hyland & F. Hyland (Eds.), *Feedback in second language writing: Contexts and issues* (pp. 81–104). Cambridge: Cambridge University Press.

Ferris, D. (2007). Preparing teachers to respond to student writing. *Journal of Second Language Writing, 16,* 165–193.

Hyland, K. & Hyland, F. (2006). Contexts and issues in feedback on L2 writing. In Hyland, K., & Hyland, F. (Eds.) *Feedback in second language writing: Contexts and issues* (pp. 12–20). Cambridge: Cambridge University Press,

Hyland, K. (2013a). Faculty feedback: Perceptions and practices in L2 disciplinary writing. *Journal of Second Language Writing, 22,* 240–253.

Hyland, K. (2013b). Student perceptions of hidden messages in teacher written feedback. *Studies in Educational Evaluation, 39,* 180–187.

Lee, I. (2008). Understanding teachers' written feedback practices in Hong Kong secondary classrooms. *Journal of Second Language Writing, 17,* 69–85.

Lee, I. (2014) Editorial. Feedback in writing: Issues and challenges. *Assessing writing, 19,* 1–5.

McMartin-Miller, C. (2014). How much feedback is enough? Instructor practices and student attitudes towards error treatment in second language writing. *Assessing Writing, 19,* 24–35.

Northcott, J. (2001). Towards an ethnography of the MBA classroom: A consideration of the role of interactive lecturing styles within the context of one MBA programme. *English for Specific Purposes, 20,* 15–37.

Patton, M. (2002). *Qualitative research and evaluation methods.* Thousand Oaks: Sage.

Truscott, J. (1996). The case against grammar correction in L2 writing classes. *Language Learning, 46,* 327–369.

Truscott, J. (2007). The effect of error correction on learners' ability to write accurately. *Journal of Second Language Writing, 16,* 255–272.

Truscott, J. (2010). Further thoughts on Anthony Bruton's critique of the correction debate. *System, 38,* 626–633.

APPENDIX I

FEEDBACK ON FEEDBACK QUESTIONNAIRE

Evaluation of Tutor Feedback

Unit _

Please tick (✓) the relevant box and provide further information where asked.

1. Is the feedback you have received useful?

Very Useful	Useful	Not very useful	Not at all useful

2. Is the feedback clear?

Very clear	Clear	Not very clear	Not at all clear

3. Have you been able to act on the feedback?

Yes	No
How did you use the feedback?	If not, please briefly tell us why:

4. Is the feedback helping you improve your academic writing?

Yes	No
Please tell us why:	Please tell us why not:

5. Is there any way you think the feedback can be improved?

APPENDIX 2

DRAFT FEEDBACK GUIDELINES

The initial 'guidelines' below are based on our Improving Feedback Research Project which looked at tutor feedback on both SPS and SAW. Please note that they are *only* guidelines and they are based on the examples of good practice we found and learned from.

1. Read the piece through and give a general comment before attempting any detailed corrective feedback (CF). Remember that the students are writing in their own disciplinary areas and the focus is on developing their academic *writing* skills.
2. Begin your feedback with a friendly greeting and sign off to establish an online relationship.
3. Use first names.
4. Make it clear to the student what you intend to comment on/have commented on.
5. Instil confidence by commenting first on what you think the student has done well.
6. Comment on academic expectations.

   e.g.,

   - Have they understood and answered the question? (In the UK, the question *is* the essay title – this is not necessarily the case in other academic cultures.)
   - Is there a balance of arguments (if that is what the question requires)?
   - Are they expressing an argument/making a knowledge claim and using sources to support/critique it (rather than simply explaining the source material/reviewing the literature)?
   - Have they followed through their arguments or made unsubstantiated knowledge claims without fully developing their arguments?
   - Comment on effective/ineffective paraphrasing and summarising.
   - Comment on writing style and use of non-academic, informal or spoken language.
   - Comment on organisation and paragraphing.
   - Corrective feedback.

As well as a general comment, you will usually give in-text feedback (Track Changes for AWSPS; Grademark for SAW).

1. If you use a coding system/abbreviations, make sure the student is familiar with the codes you use.
2. Tell the student whether you are correcting errors comprehensively or selectively.
3. The literature on CF makes a distinction between **direct** and **indirect** feedback. Direct feedback is necessary for **untreatable** errors (ones the student cannot correct themselves because there are no 'rules'). **Reformulation/Recasting** can also be considered under this category.
4. **Indirect** feedback may be better for **treatable** errors. You can link to a web source (dictionary/grammar site/concordance/other ELTC or IAD resource) as part of your indirect feedback.
5. You can give both direct and indirect feedback on the same point, e.g., citation errors.

Content

The separation of language from content creates a false dichotomy and it is clearly important not to lead students to view the two as separate, as this may lead to rhetorical inappropriateness. However, we are all aware of not wanting to go beyond our competence levels. You can comment in several ways:

1. Summarise the student's argument: 'If I understand you correctly, you are saying/arguing ...'.
2. Ensure students are answering the question set and have not misunderstood some basic concepts (e.g. 'welfare state' in one of the SPS questions).
3. Ensure that students have not ignored the counter arguments.

NB. Some students are very satisfied with ELTC tutor feedback and then quite shocked to get a stricter evaluation from the SPS tutor who marks the essay. Feed forward – tell them what to do to improve wherever you can. Students, we observed, are suspicious of praise without advice about what they can do better.

Highly proficient and native-speaking students

You often need a more hedged style for feedback with these students. They are very identified with their writing and can be sensitive to criticism! Phrases that confuse L2 speakers work well: 'You might like to consider ...'

Simon G. J. Smith and Christopher J. M. Smith

The literature review as an integrated EAP/ disciplines assessment

Introduction

This study identifies and addresses certain challenges faced by international students on Year 3 direct-entry Engineering & Computing courses. As students' English proficiency varies widely, those with more advanced communicative ability may question the need for a credit-bearing EAP module, unless there are explicit links to the subject modules. Other students may have only a limited awareness of English academic writing conventions, and/or little experience of independent study. These challenges may be exacerbated when modules are assessed separately, as has typically been the case in our institutional setting (and, indeed, in earlier deliveries of the course that is the subject of this paper).

The collaborative approach taken in this study, with an EAP and a discipline tutor working together 'to prepare students for particular tasks or courses' (Dudley-Evans & St. John, 1988, p. 44), reflects Hyland's (2002) approach to specificity in EAP, whereby delivery is tailored to teaching in the disciplines. However, collaboration on content may not be enough: authentic assessments have a positive impact on learning outcomes (Gulikers, Bastiaens & Kirschner, 2004), and we believe that clear links between EAP assessments and content modules do enhance authenticity. In the absence of such links, there is a risk that students will see EAP as a standalone module, or – even worse – consider English learning and assessment an irksome and purposeless exigency of UK-based study.

A keyword in our study is 'integration'. By this, we mean an assessment which is used jointly across modules, rather than being confined to a standalone module (typically an EAP module). It is also integrated in the sense that what is a summative assessment for one module, may in effect serve as a formative assessment on another module. Over the few years preceding the study, the EAP module had, in fact, been operated as a general EAP course, often drawing on Business texts and resources, with little concession to the specific academic English needs of Engineering & Computing Faculty students.

Initially, the challenge for the authors, as EAP and subject tutors on the courses, was to identify a subject module that particularly lent itself to both collaborative content delivery and to integrated forms of assessment with the EAP module. Operationally, this choice is not just about synergy in content, but also about timing: how much time is required for any collaboration to be meaningful to students, whether the sequences of module teaching delivery lend themselves to collaboration. The timing of assessments, although not necessarily the detail of what is to be assessed, is of course determined months or years in advance by central university processes, so it is necessary to ensure compatibility here.

The module which best met these requirements, both operationally and in terms of content, was the dissertation module. This study, therefore, presents a collaboration between the dissertation module and the EAP module taken by students on Engineering & Computing Faculty Y3 direct-entry courses.

There are specific considerations for an undergraduate dissertation module with a majority of international students: the dissertation is a 'substantial piece of independent work' (Heinze & Heinze, 2009, p. 2), and a paradigm with which international students may not be familiar, requiring high-quality and culturally-sensitive feedback (Sloan, Porter, Robins & McCourt, 2014). Sloan et al.'s postgraduate students expressed a desire for better explanations of assessment criteria, more opportunities for feedback, as well as more help identifying research objectives. Additionally, Sloan et al. observed that students had difficulty making links between their research objectives and literature review (LR), and in relating their own results to the work reported in the LR.

In the present study, dissertation feedback (in the form of weekly scheduled supervisions) was given throughout the year-long dissertation module. In addition, summative and relatively formal formative feedback was given by the module team at various stages along the way. One key waystage was the end of the first semester, when students were required to submit an Interim Report (IR) for the dissertation module, containing draft versions of the project aims, background, and literature review. The LR, therefore, was the section of the IR selected for collaborative feedback and assessment. The 'integrated assessment' of the present study refers to a coursework task, the LR, which is initially submitted to the EAP tutor. It is integrated in the sense that it is treated as a summative assessment on the EAP module, and formative feedback is also given, so that it can be redrafted and re-submitted as part of the Interim Report. After further feedback, the LR ultimately forms part of the final submitted dissertation.

Swales and Feak (2000, p. 116) note that the LR is often perceived as 'a boring but necessary chore', and is not the section of a dissertation that typically attracts praise. It is, however, the place where students motivate their research, and 'position [it] clearly on the academic map of knowledge creation' (Ridley, 2008, p. 1). The student needs to read widely yet selectively, determining what the key texts are, and 'weigh up the contribution that particular ideas, positions or approaches have made to their topic' (Hart, 2001, p. 9). Hsiao and Yu (2015) conducted a study of the discourse (move) structures of LRs compiled by their students in Taiwan, building on the work of Swales's CARS model (1990). They set out the typical difficulties encountered by non-native speakers in LR writing, which include paraphrasing, vocabulary, sentence structure and establishing an appropriate research niche. The present paper focuses on the collaborative aspects of our work (around assessment), and no discourse or move analysis is attempted here. This is noted as a limitation to be addressed in future work.

In what follows, we evaluate LR integrated assessment, paying particular attention to the following overarching research question:

1. Is the literature review an appropriate vehicle for an integrated EAP–disciplines assessment?

We also address two ancillary questions, which emerge from the two research instruments used:

2. From text analysis: What types of changes to the draft LR did students make in response to feedback?

3. From stakeholder feedback: What were the perceptions of students and dissertation supervisors regarding the integrated assessment?

THE STUDY

The study took the form of an action research project, conducted over two academic years (Y1: 2013–14; Y2: 2014–15). In Y1, there were 15 student participants; in Y2, there were 19.

Teaching and guidance on compiling the LR was provided in both the EAP class and the dissertation module – both modules offered a weekly two-hour workshop. Instruction in the dissertation module sessions focused on understanding the purpose of the LR, searching for sources, and finding a research gap in which to situate the project. In the EAP module, the focus was more on organizing and grouping sources, as well as the mechanics of citation and referencing, and the appropriate use of integral and non-integral citations. Workshops on defining project objectives and on structuring the LR were (in Y2 only) co-taught by the EAP and subject teacher, allowing for more individual attention, as well as demonstrating the concrete nature of the collaboration to students. Co-teaching took the form of invited sessions, once where the dissertation tutor visited the EAP class, and once vice-versa, giving a short presentation on an aspect of academic writing or dissertation structure, which was followed by a discussion open to all.

Figure 1 on page 162 shows the teaching, coursework submission and feedback chronology in the two years of the study. The reader's attention is drawn to the hatched area in the figure, showing the significant difference in January feedback arrangements in the two years of the project. In Y1, only written feedback was given by the EAP tutor on the LR. Written feedback was in the form of a brief paragraph of general suggestions for improvement, along with a copy of their submission annotated with more specific hints and suggestions (using the QuickMark Manager in Turnitin). In Y2, this was supplemented by verbal feedback in a supervision setting, where students had the opportunity to discuss their LR writing (in terms of language, structure

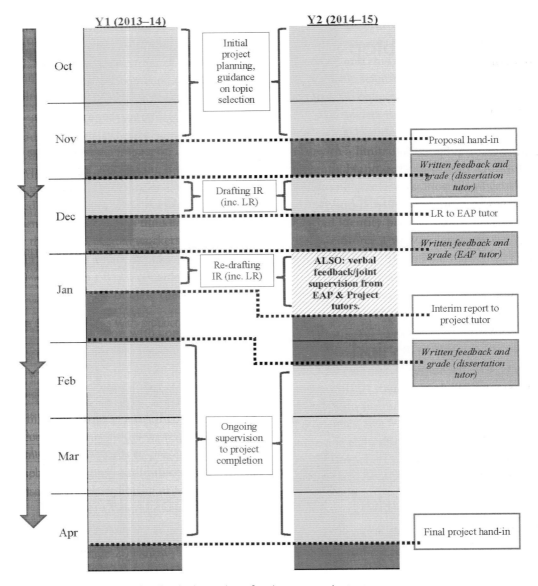

Figure 1 Submission and feedback chronology for the two project years

and content) with the EAP tutor and the project supervisor or dissertation module tutor in the scheduled teaching/supervision session (individually or in small groups). An extra week was allowed in Y2 for students to redraft the LR and submit it as part of the Interim Report.

A word limit of 2,000 words was set in the LR coursework brief. Word limits for the IR and final dissertation were higher, as they incorporated other chapters of the dissertation. As to criteria, the LR was assessed on task response (30%), cohesion and coherence (20%), language range and accuracy (30%) and sources and referencing (20%). The last-named criterion included the mechanics of referencing, as well as appropriate use of quotation and paraphrase, and good balance of integral and non-integral citations, while selection of sources and critique of relevant literature were assessed under Task Response. Again, criteria for the IR and final dissertation related to the whole submitted work, not just the LR chapter, and did not relate to post-feedback improvement.

Two types of qualitative analysis were performed. A textual analysis, using the MS Word Track Changes function, compared the version of the literature review submitted to the EAP module with the version submitted as part of the IR to the dissertation module later, to see which feedback suggestions from the EAP module tutor were actually implemented. The textual analysis was not motivated by a formal methodology; it simply assigned the modifications made by students to broad categories, which were in part inspired by the same criteria that were used to grade the writing (in the EAP module).

Complementarily, we sought the perceptions of two sets of stakeholders: dissertation supervisors (individually through interview) and students (through survey/focus group).

FINDINGS

In the text analysis, we classified the changes made between the submissions in December (LR, to EAP tutor) and January (IR, to dissertation module tutor). The results are summarized in Figure 2. 'Grammar', here, includes formatting, spelling, and other more mechanical linguistic amendments: in Y1, three-quarters of the submissions were amended to reflect this kind of feedback, with almost the same proportion in Y2. This outcome is expected, as such amendments intuitively depend more on seeing the written feedback. There is also little difference between the two year groups in terms of the proportion of both reorganization (where entire paragraphs were moved, potentially resulting in a major restructuring of the writing – clearly a more onerous and less popular type of revision effort!) and clarification amendments (where sentence-level structure was improved); this is a slightly surprising finding, as ideas for improving structure certainly came up in discussions with students, but we assume that this kind of feedback needs to be supplemented by more explicit written direction. Verbal feedback seems to be having an impact on the addition of new sections and incorporation of new and relevant references, for these were key weaknesses in many of the submitted LRs, and constituted key discussion points in the verbal tutor–student feedback dialogues, held only in Y2.

Students were provided with an annotated version of their document, which carried error codes such as AS (academic style), PUNC (punctuation) and WW (wrong word). In one Y1 example, a student responded correctly to a WW error, revising 'including' to 'namely' prior to an exhaustive list, such that the discourse marker should have a specifying rather than an exemplifying role. In another case of WW feedback, also in Y1, the reporting verb 'present' had been used to introduce a claim. In this case, the feedback did not assist the

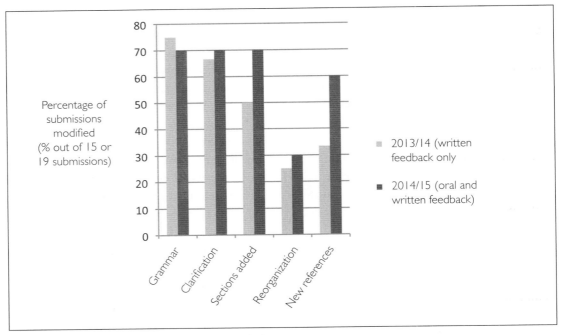

Figure 2 Summary of findings from text analysis

student, who changed the verb to 'illustrate', which was still incorrect. If there had been the opportunity to discuss the error with the student, an explanation of the discourse moves might have helped them to better understand the vocabulary issue here.

It is fair to say that written-only feedback does not always have the desired effect. We found that comments are often ignored when they are not understood, or, echoing a finding of Hyland and Hyland (2006), the offending text is simply deleted without an attempt to revise. Overall, students were much more likely to attend to mistakes of grammar and mechanics in response to written feedback than they were to structural or macro-level issues, and even in the former category, there were often opportunities to clear up misunderstandings that were not available with written comments.

In the stakeholder perception feedback, these findings were corroborated: in Y1, the students (seven respondents) indicated that they primarily focused on micro-structural revisions (in rank order: grammar, spelling, referencing and sentence structure). According to one supervisor, they were 'putting more effort into proof-reading to identify grammatical and spelling mistakes', but also 'including or removing paragraphs so the ideas are more focused and the message flows better'.

The timing of the informal written feedback, over the Christmas break, was identified by one supervisor as a possible reason for the lack of more substantial revisions. It was apparent from the interviews and focus groups that many students were satisfied with the integrated assessment, with one student, for example, commenting 'both feedback [on the two modules] they complement each other, looking at the same thing from two different perspectives'. Only one student complained that he had been unclear about the connection between components ('no happy with the integrated approach as link between both was not clear').

It seemed, however, that in Y1, the collaborative nature of the assessment approach was not adequately explained to the students (and possibly some of the supervisors), and that the students saw the assignments as discrete tasks: the suggestion was made that, for Y2, increased and more visible collaboration between the teams would benefit students and supervisors (one supervisor commented 'I do like the approach, but I do think from the students' point of view they should see us working together ... perhaps in induction [week]').

Despite these misgivings, all three supervisors in Y1 commented on benefits to the students: better use of academic style, an improved understanding of the notion of the research space and its relationship to their own primary research, as well as improvements in the overall standard of final reports.

The changes to delivery in Y2 (see Figure 1) reflected this feedback from Y1. They included collaborative teaching (EAP and discipline tutor each participated in the other's scheduled class), shared assignment briefing and joint feedback, where the EAP module tutor, dissertation supervisor and student discussed the LR together. A student respondent from Y2 commented that this kind of interactive feedback '[for] an international student was very useful', and promoted the development of better paragraph structure. Similarly, according to a responding supervisor, the students felt that they were being supported and that this made the dissertation less daunting.

DISCUSSION

The clearer and more visible collaboration between the teams in Y2 was needed to demonstrate to the students the integrated nature of the assessment and the benefit to them (not just in terms of grades, but also for their wider academic development). Moreover, when the timing and the nature of the feedback were adapted to the student group in Y2, supervisors and tutors found that (for this international group) the combined written and verbal feedback supported the students and overall programme outcomes more effectively – in line with Hyland and Hyland (2006) and Cho (2011).

The negative reaction of a minority of students in Y1 indicates that acceptance of a collaborative approach to teaching and assessment is not guaranteed. This may be because students do not perceive tutors' desired learning outcomes, such as research skills and independent thinking, along with proficiency in the linguistic constructs and vocabulary of the disciplines, as representative of their future professional needs. Thus, clearer links to employability may foster better student engagement, as noted also by Gulikers et al. (2004).

The study has responded to our research questions as follows:

RQ1: In general terms, the study has shown that the LR can be an appropriate focus for a collaborative EAP–disciplines assessment.

RQ2: A comparison of the texts before and after EAP tutor feedback indicates that feedback was used, but that the timing and method of feedback are critical in students understanding these changes fully. Suggestions given in written feedback only were sometimes ignored or, mirroring findings of Hyland and Hyland (2006), responded to by the deletion of the section or sentence containing the words requiring revision. As Cho (2011) found, oral feedback from the tutor is more likely to be acted on, as the tutor's intended message can be negotiated in discussion.

RQ3: Positive feedback was received from participating students and staff. Regarding the two modes of feedback offered, one student commented, 'The formal feedback was a sheet of paper. Informal feedback was better because it was more on an individual basis'. A supervisor commented 'Quality of English in final report is far better than I have seen in the past.'

CONCLUSIONS, LIMITATIONS AND FUTURE WORK

Operational considerations influence the effectiveness of any collaborative effort and the positive perceptions of the stakeholders. The sequencing of assessments must respond to institution-specified deadlines, and assessment loading needs to be balanced across modules in proportion to the amount of credit they bear. Timetable commitments of module tutors and supervisors need to

be taken into account in team teaching, especially where oral feedback sessions are concerned.

A limitation of this study was that the comparative text analysis was based on intuitive and somewhat arbitrary categories, and did not adopt a recognized applied linguistics methodology. Certain post-feedback error corrections, for example, could in a more careful analysis have been attributed to a clearer student understanding of the discourse moves expected in certain contexts. In future work, we will attend to the discourse structure of LRs, and the impact of feedback on revision, through an appropriate move-analysis framework, such as that of Hsiao and Yu (2015) or Kwan (2006). Such an analysis would enable us to determine and analyze more formally the most characteristic revision types, and the structure of LRs pre- and post-revision.

Additionally, we will evaluate the potential of dissertation chapters other than the LR (such as the research design chapter) as candidates for this collaborative approach addressing a wider question: what contribution can EAP–disciplines collaboration make to the various stages of a research project, and to the maturation of the international student as a clear writer, strong critical thinker and globally employable individual?

REFERENCES

Cho, N. H. (2011). *An exploration of the nature of teacher/peer feedback interactions on pre-sessional English for Academic Purposes (EAP) courses in UK higher education* (PhD Thesis). Oxford Brookes University.

Dudley-Evans, T., & St. John, M. (1998). *Developments in English for specific purposes: A multi-disciplinary approach*. Cambridge: Cambridge University Press.

Gulikers, J. T. M., Bastiaens, T. J., & Kirschner, P. A. (2004). A five-dimensional framework for authentic assessment. *Educational Technology Research and Development, 52*(3), 67–86. doi:10.1007/bf02504676

Hart, C. (2001). *Doing a literature search: A comprehensive guide for the social sciences.* Thousand Oaks, CA: Sage.

Heinze, A., & Heinze, B. (2009). Blended e-learning skeleton of conversation: Improving formative assessment in undergraduate dissertation supervision. *British Journal of Educational Technology, 40*(2), 294–305. doi:10.1111/j.1467-8535.2008.00923.x

Hsiao, C., & Yu, H. (2015). Move distribution and configuration of literature reviews at four levels. *Taiwan International ESP Journal, 7*(1), 51–77.

Hyland, K. (2002). Specificity revisited: How far should we go now? *English for Specific Purposes, 21*(4), 385–395. doi:10.1016/s0889-4906(01)00028-x

Hyland, K., & Hyland, F. (2006). Interpersonal aspects of response: Constructing and interpreting teacher written feedback. In K. Hyland (Ed.), *Feedback in second language writing: Contexts and issues* (pp. 206–224). New York: Cambridge University Press. doi:10.1017/cbo9781139524742.013

Kwan, B. S. C. (2006). The schematic structure of literature reviews in doctoral theses of applied linguistics. *English for Specific Purposes, 25*(1), 30–55.

Ridley, D. (2008). *The literature review: A step-by-step guide for students.* Thousand Oaks, CA: Sage.

Sloan, D., Porter, E., Robins, K., & McCourt, K. (2014). Using e-learning to support international students' dissertation preparation. *Education and Training, 56*(2/3), 122–140. doi:10.1108/et-10-2012-0103

Swales, J. M. (1990). *Genre analysis: English in academic and research settings.* New York: Cambridge University Press.

Swales, J. M., & Feak, C. B. (2000). *English in today's research world: A writing guide.* Ann Arbor, MI: University of Michigan Press.

SECTION IV
Achieving specificity

KEN HYLAND

INNOVATING INSTRUCTION: SPECIFICITY AND ENGLISH IN THE DISCIPLINES

In this paper, I want to discuss a new approach to EAP curriculum and a key idea in the reform of our undergraduate programme at Hong Kong University: the idea of specificity.

First, some background. In September 2012, universities in Hong Kong launched a four-year undergraduate curriculum to replace the existing three-year system. This reduced the secondary school experience by one year and refocused on a more student-oriented approach to undergraduate education. The change is a major shift in educational philosophy. It is an attempt to move away from a specialized British undergraduate curriculum and adopt a more holistic approach to the educational experience. Instead of selecting their major on arrival, students enrol in a broad disciplinary area and take a variety of first-year courses before they choose a major. This first year 'Common Core Curriculum' is a range of optional courses designed to facilitate the transition from school to university and to provide students with a humanistic education. This is a huge leap in the dark – very few countries have totally restructured their secondary and tertiary education systems in such a radical way all at once. Almost 30,000 new students entered university in 2012, admitted under two different systems, following two different curricula and spanning two different time frames. A considerable challenge.

English is the medium of instruction in Hong Kong universities, and central to students' study and academic success, although students often find study in English to be a struggle. A major part of the new curriculum, therefore, is the provision of English. At the University of Hong Kong (HKU), this was given double the amount of time and increased from six to twelve credits. The changes encouraged us to think about the kind of English that we should be teaching. What kind of English would most benefit our students? At the University of Hong Kong, our answer to this question was to help them in their academic studies by taking the idea of specificity seriously. Half the credits students take in English were going to be in the form of 'English in the Discipline'. This recognizes that, because academic communication conventions differ hugely across disciplinary communities, identifying the particular language features, discourse practices, and communicative skills of target cultures becomes central to teaching English in universities.

CURRICULUM CHANGES

Under the new curriculum, all 3,000 first-year students at HKU take a Core University English (CUE) course for six credits. This is a University-wide programme designed to bridge the gap between school-based English and the disciplinary studies they will encounter in their second year. At the Centre for Applied English Studies (CAES) we prepared for the changes with a committed, research-led engagement with the reform process.

Here, we want students to see that writing at university is very different from writing at school. We want them to take responsibility for clarity in their writing and give them the resources to do this. This means helping them to see that academic writing in English, compared with other contexts and languages tends to:

- be more explicit about its structure and purpose;
- use more citations to support arguments;
- focus on actions rather than actors;
- use fewer rhetorical questions than students tend to use in school essays;
- be intolerant of digressions;

- be cautious in making claims;
- package processes as things using nominalization;
- spell out steps in an argument and connections between sentences with metadiscourse.

So, in this course, we introduce students to concepts like nominalization, impersonalization, hedging, citation, and so on.

Thus, CUE is a 'bridging course' in English which brings students up to speed with general academic English. After the first-year core curriculum, students select and study for their majors and take one of the 30 new 'English in the discipline' (ED) courses which are offered in the second, third or fourth year, depending on the preference of the client faculty. These focus on the specificity of the language they need for their disciplines. These ED courses either:

- run parallel with a particular course or
- collect courses together from a particular discipline.

The idea behind this is to try and offer students a more discipline-sensitive approach to English through collaboration with faculties and research-informed course design.

EVIDENCE FOR SPECIFICITY

Having provided a sketch of the context, I will offer some evidence for the value of a specific approach, drawing on four very different sources: the variations in the features used by academics from different disciplines creating the same genre, how academics seek to project a disciplinary identity in their bios, the differences in tutors' writing expectations and feedback practices in different disciplines, and the disciplinary-specific writing assignments which confront undergraduate students. While only the last two of these feed directly into the design of our undergraduate programme, all reinforce the importance of specificity as a core principle which informs our understanding of teaching EAP and which underpins our approach to teaching and learning.

A. Genre features

First, rhetorical choices vary enormously across disciplines because they express very different epistemological and social practices. This means that students learn their disciplines as they learn its discourses. While the hard–soft distinction is a blunt instrument to elaborate these differences, it helps reveal some of the ways that authoring involves writers relating their rhetorical choices to wider social and academic understandings. Some examples of these differences are shown in Table 1, based on the analysis of features in a corpus of 120 research articles from the ten leading journals in eight disciplines, comprising 1.4 million words (Hyland, 2004; 2005).

Most predictably, we find that authors in the soft knowledge disciplines intrude into their texts through use of 'I' or 'we' almost three times more frequently than scientists.

This allows them to claim authority through personal conviction and to emphasize their contribution. It sends a clear signal of the writer's perspective and distinguishes that perspective from others. But, while self-mention can help construct an authoritative self in the humanities, authors in the hard sciences generally downplay their personal role to establish the objectivity of what they report, uncontaminated by human activity. They're concerned with generalizations rather than individuals, and this is done by distancing the writer from interpretations using the passive, dummy 'it' subjects, and attributing agency to inanimate things like tables, graphs or results. So, in subordinating their voice to that of nature, scientists rely on the persuasive force of lab procedures, rather than the force of their writing.

Similarly, citation practices also differ enormously, reflecting the extent to which writers can assume a shared context with readers. 'Normal science' produces public knowledge through cumulative growth; problems emerge from earlier problems and this enables writers to rely on readers recovering the significance of the research without extensive referencing. They are often working on the same problems and are familiar with the earlier work. In the humanities and social sciences, on the other hand, research is less linear, the literature

Table 1 Selected features across fields (per 1,000 words)

Fields	Self-mention	Citation	Self-citation	Hedges	Boosters	Directives
Arts/ Humanities	34.2	11.1	0.4	17.5	6.9	1.2
Science/ Engineering	12.1	5.8	0.6	10.25	4.5	2.5

more dispersed and the readership more heterogeneous, so writers can't presuppose a shared context to the same extent, but have to build one far more through citation. This also helps account for the much higher proportion of self-citation in the sciences (12.5% of all citations in the sciences compared with 4.3% in the humanities). The linearity of research means that scientists are constantly building on their previous work far more than writers in the soft knowledge fields.

Table 1 also shows that hedges and boosters index disciplinary practices, with both occurring more frequently in the arts and humanities papers. *Hedges* are devices which withhold complete commitment to a proposition; they imply that a claim is based on plausible reasoning rather than certain knowledge, while *boosters* stress certainty and commitment to statements. Because they represent the writer's direct involvement in a text, they are twice as common in the social sciences than in hard sciences. So, hedges indicate the degree of confidence the writer thinks it might be wise to give a claim, while opening a discursive space for readers to dispute interpretations. One reason they are more common in the soft fields is that there is less control of variables, more diversity of research outcomes, and fewer clear bases for accepting claims than in the sciences. Writers can't report research with the same confidence of shared assumptions, so papers rely far more on recognizing alternative voices. Arguments have to be expressed more cautiously by using more hedges. But because methods and results are also more open to question, writers also use more boosters in some circumstances to establish the significance of their work against alternative interpretations, using forms like 'definitely', 'prove' and 'certain' to restrict alternative voices.

In the hard sciences, positivist epistemologies mean that the authority of the individual is subordinated to the authority of the text and facts are meant to 'speak for themselves'. This means that writers often disguise their interpretative activities behind linguistic objectivity. Scientists put greater weight on the methods, procedures and equipment used, rather than the argument to suggest that results would be the same whoever conducted the research.

Less frequent use of hedges and boosters is one way of minimizing the researcher's role, and so is the preference for modals over cognitive verbs, as these can more easily combine with inanimate subjects to downplay the person making the evaluation. Modals, then, are one way of helping to reinforce a view of science as an impersonal, inductive enterprise, while allowing scientists to see themselves as discovering truth, rather than constructing it.

The final feature reflects the difference between hard- and soft-knowledge areas regarding the extent to which succinctness and precision are valued, or even possible: directives. These instruct the reader to perform an action or to see things in a way determined by the writer and are expressed through imperatives (like *consider, note* and *imagine*) and obligation modals (such as *must, should* and *ought*). They direct readers to three main kinds of activity:

- **textual acts** direct readers to another part of the text or to another text;
- **physical acts** direct readers how to carry out some action in the real world;
- **cognitive acts** instruct readers how to interpret an argument, explicitly positioning readers by encouraging them to *note, concede* or *consider* some argument in the text.

They are not only more frequent in science texts, but also function differently. So while directives represent a writer's intrusion into a text and so might be expected to be more frequent in the soft fields, they are also a potentially risky tactic, as they instruct readers to act or see things in a certain way.

If we exclude Philosophy, 60% of directives in the soft-knowledge texts direct readers to a reference or table, rather than telling them how they should interpret an argument. So examples like these are common:

(1) *See Steuer* 1983 for a discussion of other contingencies' effects. (Marketing)

Look at Table 2 again for examples of behavioristic variables. (Marketing)

For transcription conventions *please refer* to the Appendix. (App. Linguistics)[1]

Those in the sciences, on the other hand, largely guide readers explicitly through an argument, emphasizing what they should attend to and the way they should understand it:

(2) What has to be recognized is that these issues ... (Mech Eng)

Consider the case where a very versatile milling machine of type M5 ... (Elec Eng)

A distinction must be made between cytogenetic and molecular resolution. (Biology)

This is because the linear, problem-oriented nature of the natural sciences enables research to occur within an established framework, allowing authors to presuppose considerable background knowledge among their readers. Arguments can therefore be formulated in a highly standardized code. Moreover, directives facilitate directness, contributing to the succinctness which is valued by both editors and information-saturated scientists.

These variations suggest that, although a general academic English programme can go some way to sensitizing students to key rhetorical features of research writing, it can never hope to accommodate the very distinctive ways that disciplines have of seeing and talking about the world. Such differences point to the advantages of seeking to align our courses as closely as possible to these epistemological variations in academic practices.

B. DISCIPLINE AND IDENTITY

Another argument for the significance of disciplinary specificity is the different ways in which individuals present a scholarly identity. Clearly, this is not directly related to the development of our ED courses, but how members of different disciplines understand themselves in relation to their communities is a powerful indication of the value of treating the university as structured by specific fields of study. It not only points to the very clear dissimilarities in what disciplines value in their members and which individuals aspire to achieve, but also reflects what subject tutors might look for in the ways that students present themselves in their writing and behaviour.

The expression of identity can be most clearly seen in academic bios, a genre where, in 50 to 100 words, academics present a narrative of expertise for themselves. It is particularly interesting, as it sits in stark

---

[1] Text extracts are taken from two corpora: one of research articles and the other of article bios. These are described more fully in Hyland 2004 and Hyland & Tse 2012.

Table 2 Acts by Disciplines (Per 1,000 words)

	App. Ling.	Elec. Eng.	Philosophy	Total
Employment	16.5	8.3	14.9	**13.2**
Research	13.1	9.2	8.7	**10.3**
Publications	6.7	2.1	11.9	**6.9**
Education	5.1	8.2	4.0	**5.8**
Achievement	1.5	2.7	0.6	**1.6**
Community service	1.1	2.2	1.4	**1.5**
Personal profile	0.6	1.4	0.8	**0.9**
TOTAL	**44.6**	**34.1**	**42.3**	**40.2**

contrast to the article itself, which has been stripped of identifying information for blind review. In this section, I refer to a study of 600 bios, with 200 from leading journals in each of Applied Linguistics, Electrical Engineering and Philosophy (Hyland & Tse, 2012). The corpus was also stratified by status, using four categories from senior academics to technicians and students.

First, we looked at what aspects of themselves writers included, as these show kinds of identities likely to be approved by peers. Table 2 shows that virtually everyone mentioned employment and, together with research interests, this comprised over half of all moves in the corpus. While there was increasing mention of research, employment, publication and achievements with increasing status, discipline was the most significant influence on what authors included in their bios.

The biggest disciplinary difference was the weight engineers give to education. For them, this was typically linked with the area of study, thereby demonstrating a specific expertise and insider competence:

(3) She received the PhD degree (on thin-oxide technology and novel quasi-nonvolatile memory) from the University of California, Berkeley in 1999.
Irene Ntoutsi received her PhD in Informatics from the Department of Informatics, University of Piraeus, Greece.

This reflects a hard-science apprenticeship model, where the education of PhD students is also an opportunity to research and publish as part of a team, making education more central to their bios. We also find engineers giving more importance to personal information. Interestingly, almost all engineers mentioned their birthplace and often the year of birth. In contrast, applied linguists crafted identities around their research interests, with claims for credibility through insider expertise comprising about a third of all acts in their bios. Philosophers, on the other hand, tend to emphasize their publications. Generally, these are monographs and involve a greater investment of time than the multi-authored and frenetically-paced hard sciences articles, thus perhaps counting for more when constructing a self.

Identity is expressed not only in terms of *what* academics say about themselves, but also about how they say it, and one way of understanding identity in this way is to look at verbs, or process types. Systemic Functional Linguistics recognizes a distinction between *mental* and *material* processes:

- mental processes – are verbs relating to sensing (e.g., think, believe, feel);
- material processes – are concerned with doing (e.g., work, write, study);
- a third form are *relational* processes and these express *being*.

These choices matter in identity performance so, for example:

a) 'she is interested in …' (a mental process), constructs the author as an active, thinking being exercising conscious choice in a research interest, whereas

b) 'she works in the area of …' (a material process), suggests a highly visible and energetic researcher acting on the world, and

c) 'her research interests are …' (a relational process) is more impersonal, downplaying the author's role to highlight something that belongs to her.

Overall, writers used relational and material processes in 95% of all clauses, stressing what they *are* and what they *do*. This is because bios have something to say about *who the author is*, or rather, how he or she wants to be seen. Other process types are far less significant in this corpus (Table 3). Philosophy, the most individualistic of the three disciplines studied, contained a higher proportion of relational processes, while Engineering, the most collaborative, contained the least.

Relational clauses present identity claims as they construe 'being', where a writer claims to *be* something, such as an assistant professor, doctoral student, etc. These claims are strengthened by the use of *identifying* over *attributive* choices, particularly among professors, where they are over twice as frequent:

(4) Bonnie Urciuoli is Professor of Anthropology at Hamilton College. (AL)

She is the author or co-author of over 40 technical papers and is the holder of two patents. (EE)

These choices give a definiteness and uniqueness to what is being claimed. They *identify* the writer by signalling that this is an important part of who they see themselves as. The bios of students and

Table 3 Process types by discipline (per 1,000 words)

	AL	EE	Phil	TOTAL
Relational	30.8	23.7	32.6	27.9
Material	23.6	23.6	22.0	23.2
Mental	2.1	0.7	1.4	1.2
Verbal	1.1	1.4	0.7	1.1
Behavourial	0.1	0.0	0.1	0.0
Existential	0.0	0.0	0.0	0.0
TOTAL	57.7	49.4	56.8	53.4

support staff, in contrast, use attributive options to signal class membership, rather than a unique identity:

(5) Sampath is a member of the Institute of Industrial Engineers. (EE)

He is a Ph.D. student in Teaching English as a Second Language at UBC.

So status has some impact on identity representation but, once again, it is discipline which is the major influence on choice. Applied linguists often used mental types, representing themselves as thinking academics, rather than as intellectual workers grinding out a quota of papers and presentations:

(6) Her recent work considers the intersections of civic rhetoric and digital spaces. (AL)

His fascination with computers leads him to examine why some technologies are taken up while others are abandoned. (AL)

While this projects a distinctively intellectual identity to the writer, engineers used more verbal forms to present themselves as arguers and talkers:

(7) She is now lecturing at Sanjesh College of Computing and Statistics, Tehran, Iran. (EE)

He proposes the use of selectively grown epitaxial layers … (EE)

Verbal choices highlight agency, helping to construe the author as an active scholar. The biggest variations, however, were in relational processes. Interestingly, philosophers used identifying relational clauses twice as frequently as linguists and four times more than engineers. Explicitly naming themselves as something is obviously

key to identity and perhaps reflects the more individualistic ethos in philosophy. Here research represents the creative insights of the author and this is very different to the more humble scientific ideology, which sees results as the collective endeavours of a team using appropriate procedures.

So, while the bio seems a standardized genre with a limited range of options, these apparently bland descriptions are cross-cut by rank and gender but, most significantly, by discipline. These unconscious and largely neglected identity practices thus, once again, help to reinforce a view of language use which is based on disciplinary specificity and an individual's membership of a rhetorical community.

C. Tutor expectations

Another major disciplinary difference is tutors' attitudes to writing and feedback. In a recent study at HKU, I found broad differences looking at the attitudes and practices of 20 academics, five from each of four faculties comprising eight disciplines (Hyland, 2013). All teachers set written assignments – always as assessment and often as the only assessment. But soft-knowledge tutors were agreed that this is not just a measure of quality control, but of developing skills of disciplinary argument, as these respondents recognized:

> Writing is absolutely key, it embodies the discipline: the main discipline product. Teaching History is about teaching students to write. What I expect them to gain ultimately, as well as the ability to express themselves, is the ability to engage more effectively with discourses in the past. You can't do that unless you can articulate precisely what the discourse means. (History)[2]

---

[2] The research reported in this paper was conducted in accordance with the ethical standards for research set out by the University of Hong Kong and all quotes are cited with the permission of the interviewees.

I think writing is very important. It reflects the ways which students structure and express their thoughts. So, I am less concerned about correct spelling and grammar, what I am very concerned about is teaching them to write logical essays which take a research question and address it in a structured and thoughtful way with evidence and logical conclusions. (Business)

For teachers in the sciences, writing was less important, and the fact that students were writing in a second language was often treated as a minor issue:

If they have problems with language errors, that means they are not working hard enough. They are 21 year olds. I mean they should have a high level of ability already, not just what they have learnt since coming here. When I assess their writing I have to treat everybody equally so grade grammar less, a very small percentage, maybe 5%. (Engineering)

Looking at the feedback itself, it was typically less frequent and more cursory on the science assignments: just ticks or question marks and often just a grade. The texts seem hurriedly checked, rather than carefully read. Teachers in the social sciences, however, offered more explicit commentary on language and these comments were largely seen as aspects of disciplinary writing, rather than just aiming for correct grammar:

I suppose my feedback focuses on trying to help them clearly state a claim or idea and then how they can develop it in an appropriate style. So, it's about encouraging clarity of thought and clearly defining a question to discuss. (English)

In contrast, tutors in the hard sciences rarely required drafts and gave no feedback:

Actually I don't ask for a draft. Their report is an assignment and they are graded on this. If we give them a chance to write a draft, if we correct a draft, we are just giving a grade to our own work. We don't write their exams for them so why write their reports? (Engineering)

For some, especially in the sciences, setting assignments was a way of seeing if students had understood the course. Feedback had doubtful significance:

I don't think it makes a lot of difference to be honest. It all depends on the students. Some students will come and talk about it and will go away and change it. Some students seem not to care too much. I guess if the students thought it was helpful more of them would ask for feedback. (Bio)

In fact, tutors often delegated feedback to teaching assistants, and several did not see improving students' disciplinary literacy as their job at all:

How helpful is the written feedback for improving students work? I've no idea. I don't teach them how to write. They go to academic writing classes I think. I don't think my feedback would help them to write. (Eng)

While reflecting the ideas of individual faculty members, the views reported here nevertheless display clear patterns of attitudes and practices towards writing by tutors acting as community members. Again, there are differences which underpin the need to adopt a specific approach to English language teaching as a way of best meeting the needs of students.

D. Assignment types

Perhaps specificity is most obvious in the *kinds* of writing that students are asked to do. Most obviously, different fields value different kinds of argument and set different writing tasks, so the humanities and social sciences stress analyzing and synthesizing multiple sources, while the sciences value activity-based skills like describing procedures, defining objects, and planning solutions.

We also know that different fields make use of different genres, so that in their large-scale corpus study of 30 disciplines in UK universities, Nesi and Gardner (2012) found 13 different 'genre families', ranging from case studies through empathy writing to reports. These differ considerably in their social purpose, genre structure and the networks they form with other genres. Even in fairly cognate fields, students write quite different texts. In looking at the assignments given to medical students, for instance, Gimenez (2009) found that nursing and midwifery students were given very different writing assignments. Again, this underlines the different ways students are assessed and different expectations of how they should write.

Theory into practice

Turning from the research back to HKU, I have space for just one example of an English in the Discipline course to show what specificity means in practice.

English for Clinical Pharmacy is a new third-year ED course focusing on common spoken and written genres in drug information, and developed in collaboration with colleagues from the faculty of Medicine over two years. This represents a massive investment in time and energy and, as we experienced with other collaborations,

really depends for its success on imaginative individuals in the client faculty who are able to recognize the value of writing and communication skills to their students. We did, however, seek to avoid team teaching and tandem classes, due to the potential for faculty withdrawal and CAES being left to write a new course to replace it. Clearly, because CUE is related to broader academic presentation skills, it is less vulnerable to changes in personnel and the goodwill of faculty members. *English for Clinical Pharmacy*, however, represents a good example of what can be achieved through good relations and mutual respect.

Early in the course, we teach specific word knowledge and strategies for learning and applying new terms. This enables students to more easily select the vocabulary and arguments they need to write drug information genres and cite information from different sources to give drug recommendations. Learning is through a drug information project which was jointly devised with the Pharmacy Department. Drug evaluation is a basic part of a pharmacist's career, as many of the documents they write have to be based on some form of drug evaluation. So students, working in pairs, evaluate and recommend two drugs that can be used to treat the same medical condition. To make sure the exercise is meaningful, the drugs assigned to the students are selected by the Pharmacy Department. The Pharmacy department also advised us on the writing task – this is a hospital bulletin article – as this is a common genre for clinical pharmacists who are working in a hospital.

Thus the project provides an opportunity for learners to develop and practise useful and highly disciplinary specific research and academic writing skills. They have to search for and select relevant drug information from reliable sources, compare drugs, and write a comparative drug evaluation article for publication in an online pharmacy bulletin. To ensure the authenticity of all this, the project has not only been jointly designed by Pharmacy and English tutors in partnership, but is also co-assessed together.

Conclusions

The idea of disciplinary specificity has become important in EAP, as we have become more sensitive to the ways students write as members of social groups. Essentially, we can see disciplines as language-using communities, and the term helps us join writers, texts and readers together. Communities provide the context within which students learn to communicate and to interpret each other's talk, gradually acquiring the specialized discourses of the group. It has to be admitted that the notion of discipline is not altogether straightforward, but successful academic writing does not occur in a vacuum. Instead, it largely depends on the individual writer's projection of a shared context as they seek to embed their writing in a particular social world.

To work in a discipline, then, we need to be able to engage in these practices and, in particular, in its discourses. So disciplines structure academic work within wider frameworks of beliefs and practices. They also provide the conventions and expectations that make texts meaningful. This means that we need to understand the distinctive ways they have of asking questions, addressing a literature, criticizing ideas, and presenting arguments, so we can help students participate effectively in their learning.

I hope to have shown in this paper that the ways that we use language are situated in domains of knowledge and ways of talking about knowledge which differ across disciplines. I have also sought to locate this discussion in the current context of one language centre and its context. The bottom line here is that EAP has nothing to do with topping up generic language skills. It is about developing new kinds of literacy: equipping students with the communicative skills to participate in particular academic cultures.

References

Gimenez, J. (2009) Beyond the academic essay: Discipline-specific writing in nursing and midwifery. *Journal of English for Academic Purposes*, 7(3), 151–64.

Hyland, K. (2004) *Disciplinary discourses: Social interactions in academic writing*. Ann Arbor, MI: University of Michigan Press.

Hyland, K. (2005). *Metadiscourse*. London: Continuum.

Hyland, K. (2013). Faculty feedback: Perceptions and practices in L2 disciplinary writing. *Journal of Second Language Writing*, 22, 240–253.

Hyland, K., & Tse, P. (2012). 'She has received many honours': Identity construction in article bio statements. *Journal of English for Academic Purposes*, 11, 155–165.

Nesi, H., & Gardner, S. (2012). *Genres across the disciplines. Student writing in higher education*. Cambridge: Cambridge University Press.

DAVID DONNARUMMA AND EMMA BLYTH

AN EVALUATION OF AN ONLINE, IN-SESSIONAL ENGLISH FOR LEGAL STUDIES COURSE IN BANGLADESH

INTRODUCTION

As universities expand and deliver many of their degree programmes online internationally, there is an increasing need to support students who may not have the required language skills for their programme. There is a lack of research on online language learning (Sun, 2014), and the intensive nature of EAP courses means that instructors can have difficulty finding the time needed to integrate technology in their teaching and course design (Gilbert, 2013), with little time remaining for research in online EAP provision. This study is an evaluation of the design and development of an online in-sessional English for Specific Academic Purposes (ESAP) course for distance-learning Bachelor of Laws (LLB) students in Bangladesh. The evaluation of a course is the process of determining the relationship between different programme mechanisms,

the procedures and theory constructed by the individuals involved in a programme, and the outcomes used to demonstrate the value of the programme (Kiely & Rea-Dickens, 2005). This study draws upon quantitative and qualitative student feedback to offer insights and advice for future online EAP course developers.

The English for Legal Studies (ELS) course is designed around two terms (2 x 10 weeks) of material, with each week consisting of four hours of self-directed content, a live weekly webinar (1.5 hours) and approximately two hours of forum work. The development of the course started in February 2014, and it was delivered to 25 Bangladeshi students starting in September 2014. The LLB degree is fully online, but the University does have a partnership centre in Bangladesh that provides classroom and computer facilities where learners can come and study together.

LITERATURE REVIEW

The challenge of teaching in-sessional
EAP courses is often one of motivating
students to study, when they are already
fully engaged with their chosen degree
programme. Research has demonstrated
that the content on these courses should be
relevant to learners' goals and that this is
most likely to motivate them (Flowerdew &
Peacock, 2001). However, there is a balance
to be had between delivering subject-
specific content and language development,
and EAP tutors can struggle with limited
field-specific knowledge (Murray &
McPherson, 2004).

A genre-based approach focuses on
academic writing in a specific subject area.
This may involve identifying patterns of
structure and language within discipline-
specific texts and teaching students how to
identify and use these patterns. Texts vary
according to their purpose and context,
and good writing is not only to do with
grammar, but should be appropriate
to the purpose (Ivanič, 2004; Hyland,
2004). The Teaching and Learning Cycle
(originally developed by Rothery, 1994) is
such a genre-based approach (see Figure
1). Learners are first introduced to the
context, and the field (i.e., specific subject
knowledge) is continually built through
different activities. At the first stage,
deconstruction, students are introduced
to the genre, which is broken down in
detail. In the next stage, joint construction,
they are led through a series of scaffolded
activities to practise the new language
and genre. In the final stage, independent
construction, they practise writing the genre
independently with little or no scaffolding.
The purpose of the cycle is for students to
take control of the genre, to be able to write

the genre, as well as critically reflect on it
(Rose, 2008).

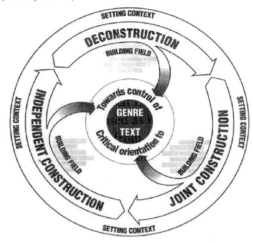

Figure 1 Teaching and Learning Cycle (Rothery, 1994, p. 107)
[Source: Reproduced by kind permission of the NSW Department of School Education, Sydney, Australia]

By using such an approach, students
should be more prepared for their target
discourse community (Hyland, 2007) and
more motivated to learn (Bruce, 2002), as
the content will be more relevant to their
target field.

Traditionally, the cycle has been used
in a face-to-face environment with students
building their knowledge of the genre through
dialogue and interaction with tutors, students
and academic texts. These interactions are
harder to replicate in an online environment,
where students are physically separated from
their tutors and peers.

An online learning model which can
promote interaction and allows learners to
critically question genres is the Community
of Inquiry (CoI) framework (Garrison,
Anderson & Archer, 2000). The CoI
framework views meaningful online learning
as occurring at the intersection of three

supporting presences (social, cognitive and teaching). At its core, the CoI framework has the active presence of an online teacher, working towards active cognitive and social presence of all the participants. The focus is on the teacher and students collaboratively designing, facilitating and directing the educational experience in an online course (see Figure 2).

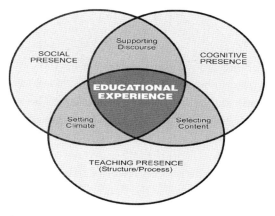

Communication Medium

Figure 2 Community of Inquiry model (Garrison et al., 2000)

[Source: Reproduced with permission of D. Randy Garrison, Professor Emeritus, University of Calgary]

Teaching presence consists of two general functions. First, the design of the educational experience, which is how the curriculum is designed to meet the needs of the students. Second, facilitation, which includes both webinar and forum moderation. Both of these functions may help to keep Bangladeshi students engaged in the course. Cognitive presence is defined as providing meaning, and making learning materials that are challenging and meaningful so students engage and learn. The students on the Legal English course are primarily studying Law; the challenge is to ensure all the materials are embedded within the context of Law, but

focused on the language the students need to help them succeed. Another challenge online is being able to predict these in advance, since materials cannot be adapted at short notice to meet students' needs, as they can in a face-to-face environment. The third core element of the model, social presence, has a pivotal role, which is not only setting the educational climate, but also supporting discourse and creating the educational experience. This presence may involve responding in asynchronous forums and building a community through live webinars.

COURSE DESIGN

The English for Legal Studies course aims to develop reading and writing skills of LLB students in Bangladesh, focusing on two key legal genres – the essay and the problem question. The problem question is a defining feature of legal academic writing (Bruce, 2002; Bhatia, 2009). This type of writing tests students' knowledge of a particular area of the law and their ability to apply the law to the facts of a fictitious case. The legal essay covers a broad range of writing sub-genres, such as discursive, cause-effect and comparative essay types. To make it easier for the non-specialist EAP tutor, Bruce (2002) recommends limiting the context to one area of substantive law. All materials were therefore developed in the context of Contract Law, which students also study in their first two terms of the LLB.

The course is made up of asynchronous self-study materials and forum tasks, and synchronous weekly webinars. Self-study materials were created using the e-learning software Articulate Storyline, and the webinars are delivered through Adobe Connect. All content sits within Moodle, an open source (freely available) Learning

Management System (LMS). The course development team consisted of three EAP specialists and a learning technologist.

The structure of the course and how it followed the Teaching and Learning Cycle can be found in Appendix 1. The field and context were built in the forum and in the workshop materials. A video presentation of the new genre was provided in the workshop, where the genre was broken down (deconstruction), and further self-directed learning activities were used to work on the joint construction phase, with the final stage (independent construction) being mainly self-study.

METHOD OF EVALUATION

In order to evaluate the ELS course, this study applied a mixed-methodology approach (May, 2001). At the end of their second and final term, students were asked to complete an online questionnaire consisting of both quantitative and qualitative questions (see Appendix 2). The questions focused on three specific areas: (1) online technology, (2) online content and (3) synchronous and asynchronous communication. To ensure that the questionnaire was appropriately graded, we first ran a pilot study with learners of an equivalent language level. Feedback from this pilot study was used to make revisions to the questionnaire.

The questionnaire was followed by a focus group, where students were given the opportunity to expand on their comments. This focus group was conducted face-to-face in Dhaka by the online Programme Manager, who had developed a good rapport with the students and who had a good understanding of the project, but had no direct involvement in developing the materials or teaching the course. The focus

group followed a semi-structured format (see Appendix 3 for list of questions). This allowed for a degree of flexibility so that the facilitator could probe, where necessary, in more depth and pursue other potentially rewarding lines of enquiry (ibid.).

PARTICIPANTS

Twenty students from a cohort of 25 completed the questionnaire (11 male, 9 female). Of these students, only two had any previous experience of online learning, although 75% of respondents either agreed or strongly agreed that they were comfortable using online technology. The focus group included ten students – six of whom had demonstrated a high level of engagement with the self-study materials and four who had accessed the materials less than five times over the two terms. All focus-group participants had over 80% attendance at the webinars. It was hoped that selecting students with different levels of engagement would provide a wider range of feedback.

RESULTS AND DISCUSSION

In this section, the results and feedback from the questionnaire and focus group are discussed and evaluated in respect of the two pedagogical models: the CoI framework and the Teaching-Learning cycle. The section has been divided into three specific areas: online technology, online content and synchronous/asynchronous communication.

ONLINE TECHNOLOGY

In the focus group, all of the students reported that they would have preferred face-to-face teaching, but that online learning had been a positive experience. This can be summarised in the following student comment, 'Studying online is great, mainly because it's new to us and pretty interesting. However, nothing beats face-to-face teaching. Still, I enjoy online classes as it's [sic] flexible and allows us to learn a lot in a very interesting manner'.

Students also valued the social aspect of studying on campus, with 85% of participants in the focus group reporting that they regularly travelled to the partner centre to attend the webinars. In the questionnaire, one student commented, 'Studying from home can be lonely. I like to be around my friends'. We had not anticipated that students would want to come together to study the webinars in one room, with the tutor as the main deliverer of knowledge via a webcam. This approach reflected the traditional teacher-centred pedagogies often found in Bangladeshi classrooms (Hamid, 2010). Over the course of term one, we achieved a shift in the students' approach to the webinars with learners increasingly logging in on their own devices, either at home or in the physical classroom. By the end of term two, 15% of students regularly logged in from home, and 65% logged in individually from computers

on campus. This allowed students to benefit from the social aspects of campus-based education, whilst receiving a more student-centred, interactive online learning experience. Results from the questionnaire suggest that students enjoyed this new approach, with 80% finding the webinars interactive and 90% reporting that they were interesting.

In terms of areas for improvement, the majority of students commented that the internet speed on campus was not fast enough; as one student in the questionnaire stated, 'Around campus we need faster internet service so that students with personal laptops/tabs can have better access'. This is an important consideration, as Hampel & de los Arcos (2013) note that technical difficulties can seriously hamper the teaching/learning experience when using audiographic conferencing tools.

ONLINE CONTENT

The majority of respondents (85%) reported that the self-study materials were relevant to their studies and 75% stated that the materials were useful (see Table 1). In the focus group, students reported that the

Table 1 Questionnaire responses to online content

	Strongly disagree	Disagree	Neither agree nor disagree	Agree	Strongly agree
I found the self-study materials useful.	0	2	3	11	4
I found the self-study materials relevant to my studies.	0	0	3	12	5
I found the self-study materials too easy.	1	5	10	4	0

course had helped them with their legal writing, with one student commenting, 'This module has helped me a lot to develop my writing and break down essay questions'. Another student noted 'The feedback I received helped me a lot and gave me confidence for my law assignments'.

This positive feedback suggests that using the Teaching-Learning cycle may improve learner engagement in online in-sessional ESAP courses. From a teaching perspective, developing materials within the context of Contract Law also meant that it was quicker and easier to build the field for learners. However, as this was the first iteration of the course, it is too early to assess the impact of the Teaching-Learning cycle on student performance.

Despite the positive feedback on content, students did not view the self-study materials as often as we had expected. Only 45% of students viewed the materials every week, with 35% viewing them less than five times over the 20 weeks. The data demonstrates differences in learning styles and preferences, with some learners regularly accessing the materials as prescribed, but others preferring to access the materials on an ad hoc basis. Online in-sessional EAP courses may therefore benefit from allowing flexibility in how learners use the materials. Twenty per cent of students did not view the self-study materials at all over the two terms. In the focus group, three students stated that they had found the materials too easy. This data highlights the challenges of meeting the needs of a range of students with different language abilities through asynchronous self-study materials alone. In this regard, synchronous webinars can add an important level of flexibility to fully online courses.

Feedback was provided in the self-study activities in order to support the cognitive presence, but it seems that this was not enough for students. In the focus group, one student commented, 'I want the self-study materials to be explained by the teachers, so that we can discuss our problems whilst studying. This will be more interactive and useful and also easy to catch up with the topics'. Such higher levels of learning are facilitated by cognitive and social presence and are only achieved if a facilitator or teacher is present to guide the learners (Kanuka & Garrison, 2004). In this respect, the live webinars had a key role to play in supporting learners and explaining any difficult areas of understanding.

SYNCHRONOUS/ASYNCHRONOUS COMMUNICATION

Students responded very positively to the synchronous element of the course, with 95% reporting that the webinars were useful and interesting (see Table 2). This indicates that live tutor contact was important for supporting learners and building cognitive presence. All students also reported that they valued having the same tutor every week for the two terms, suggesting that synchronous course elements can be effective at building social presence. This sense of community online is difficult to achieve through asynchronous elements alone (Wang & Chen, 2009).

Asynchronous communication in the discussion forum was less successful. Although 75% of students said that they enjoyed posting in the forum, only 25% reported actually using the forum regularly either to communicate with classmates or to check their understanding of topics (see Table 3). In fully online courses, the discussion forum acts as an important tool for building social presence (Thompson &

Table 2 Questionnaire responses to synchronous communication

	Strongly disagree	Disagree	Neither agree nor disagree	Agree	Strongly agree
I found the webinar sessions useful.	0	0	1	15	4
I found the webinar sessions interesting.	0	0	1	13	6
The webinar activities were interactive.	0	0	4	11	5
The pace of the webinar sessions was appropriate.	0	0	4	15	0
I liked having the same tutor every week.	0	0	0	12	8

Table 3 Questionnaire responses to asynchronous communication

	Strongly disagree	Disagree	Neither agree nor disagree	Agree	Strongly agree
I used the forum to communicate with classmates.	1	4	10	3	2
I enjoyed posting ideas in the discussion forum.	0	1	5	12	2
I used the forum to ask questions and check my understanding of topics.	3	10	5	2	0

Ku, 2005), but in this particular context, social presence was provided through the academic support centre in Dhaka, creating less of a need for a social forum.

Another role of the forum is to build cognitive presence. The data indicates that this was not achieved successfully, partly because the tutor did not spend enough time encouraging students to participate. Time was a factor, as this was a new course and the tutor spent time developing their own expertise in other aspects of online delivery. In future cohorts, tutors will be allocated more time for forum administration (two hours per week), and detailed guidelines on forum moderation will be added to the teacher-training materials.

LIMITATIONS

This study draws on the evaluation of a small-scale study in the first iteration of an online legal English course. There are two limitations to the study which should be considered in future investigations. First, the study draws on a small sample of students, and it would benefit from a larger cohort and sample size. Second, this is the first iteration of the programme, and it would provide a richer data set if several iterations could be compared, with a focus on variables such as grade averages.

CONCLUSION

This study has attempted to show that the combination of the CoI model and the Teaching and Learning Cycle could be an effective way to offer an online in-sessional academic writing course. The webinars facilitated the students' learning and may be seen as a '… significant determinant of student satisfaction, perceived learning, and sense of community' (Garrison & Arbaugh, 2007, p. 163). Further work is required to encourage learners to participate more in discussion forums to help promote deeper learning.

REFERENCES

Bhatia, V. K. (2009). Intertextual patterns in legal English discourse. In D. Belcher (Ed.), *English for specific purposes in theory and practice* (pp. 186–204). Ann Arbor, MI: University of Michigan Press.

Bruce, N. (2002). Dovetailing language and content: Teaching balanced argument in legal problem answer writing. *English for Specific Purposes, 21*(4), 321–345.

Flowerdew, J. & Peacock, M. (2001). Issues in EAP: A preliminary perspective. In J. Flowerdew & M. Peacock (Eds.), *Research perspectives on English for academic purposes* (pp. 8–24). Cambridge, England: Cambridge University Press.

Garrison, D. R., Anderson, T., & Archer, W. (2000). Critical inquiry in a text-based environment: Computer conferencing in higher education. *The Internet and Higher Education, 2*(2/3), 87–105.

Garrison, D. R., & Arbaugh, J. B. (2007). Researching the community of inquiry framework. *The Internet and Higher Education, 10*(3), 157–172. doi:10.1016/j.iheduc.2007.04.001

Gilbert, J. (2013). English for Academic Purposes. In G. Motteram (Ed.), *Innovations in learning technologies for English language teaching* (pp. 117–144). London: British Council.

Hamid, M. (2010). Globalisation, English for everyone and English teacher capacity: Language policy discourses and realities in Bangladesh. *Current Issues in Language Planning, 11*(4), 289–310. doi: 10.1080/14664208.2011.532621

Hampel, R., & de los Arcos, B. (2013). Interacting at a distance: A critical review of the role of ICT in developing the learner–context interface in a university language programme. *Innovation in Language Learning and Teaching, 7*(2), 158–178. doi: 10.1080/17501229.2013.776051

Hyland, K. (2004). *Genre and second language writing.* Ann Arbor, MI: University of Michigan Press.

Hyland, K. (2007). Genre pedagogy: Language, literacy and L2 writing instruction. *Journal of Second Language Writing, 16*, 148–164. doi:10.1016/j.jslw.2007.07.005

Ivanič, R. (2004). Discourse of writing and learning to write. *Language and Education, 18*(3), 220–245.

Kanuka, H., & Garrison, D. R. (2004). Cognitive presence in online learning. *Journal of Computing in Higher Education, 15*(2), 30–49.

Kiely, R., & Rae-Dickins, P. (2005). *Program evaluation in language education.* Basingstoke: Palgrave McMillan.

May, T. (2001). *Social research. Issues, methods, and process.* Buckingham: Open University Press.

Murray, D., & McPherson, P. (2004). *Using the web to support language learning.* Sydney: National Centre for English Language Teaching and Research.

Rose, D. (2008). Writing as linguistic mastery: The development of genre-based literacy pedagogy. In D. Beard, D. Myhill, J. Riley, & M. Nystrand (Eds.), *The SAGE handbook of writing development* (pp. 151–166). London: Sage.

Rothery, J. (1994). *Exploring literacy in school English* (Write it right resources for literacy and learning). Sydney: Metropolitan East Disadvantaged Schools Program.

Sun, S. (2014). Learner perspective on fully online language learning, *Distance Education, 35*(1), 18–42. doi: 10.1080/01587919.2014.891428

Thompson, L., & Ku, H.-Y. (2005). Chinese graduate students' experiences and attitudes towards online learning. *Educational Media International, 42*(1), 33–47.

Wang, Y., & Chen, N.-S. (2009). Criteria for evaluating synchronous learning management systems: Arguments from the distance language classroom. *Computer Assisted Language Learning, 22*(1), 1–18. doi: 10.1080/09588220802613773

APPENDIX 1

THE STRUCTURE OF THE ELS COURSE

Term 1

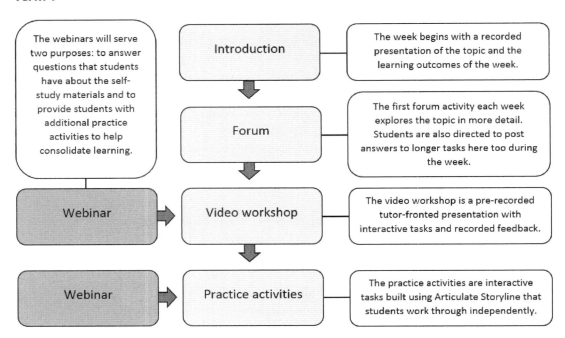

Term 2

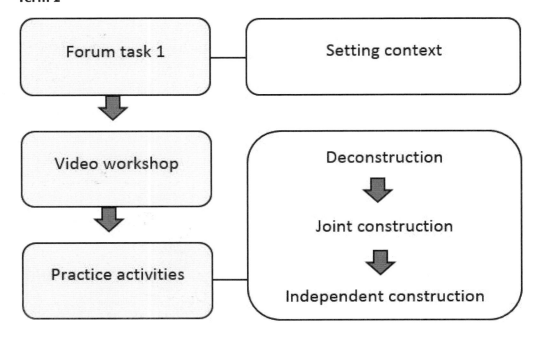

APPENDIX 2

SAMPLE QUESTIONNAIRE

ENGLISH FOR LEGAL STUDIES

We would be very grateful if you could complete this short survey about your experience of the online English for Legal Studies module. All completed questionnaires are anonymous and your participation is voluntary. Many thanks for your help!

1. Sex

○ male

○ female

2. What is your previous education experience?

☐ state secondary school (taught in first language)

☐ private secondary school (taught in first language)

☐ international school (taught in English)

☐ university (taught in first language)

☐ university (taught in English)

☐ home study

Please provide any additional information

[   ]

3. Before this course had you ever studied an educational or professional course online? (If yes, please provide more information in the box below)

○ Yes

○ No

Additional information

[   ]

4. I am comfortable using online technology

Strongly disagree	Disagree	Neither agree nor disagree	Agree	Strongly agree
○	○	○	○	○

Other (please specify)

[   ]

5. Approximately how often did you view or access the English for Legal Studies module on Moodle? (e.g. Once a week, 5-6 times, never)

[   ]

6. Overall I would say the level of the material is...

○ Too easy

○ Easy

○ About right

○ Difficult

○ Too difficult

7. What is your opinion of the **technology?**

	Strongly disagree	Disagree	Neither agree nor disagree	Agree	Strongly agree
I found the webinars easy to use	○	○	○	○	○
I found the online self-study materials easy to use	○	○	○	○	○
I found the discussion forum easy to use	○	○	○	○	○
My internet connection is fast enough	○	○	○	○	○

8. Please state how the technology can be improved

```


```

9. What is your opinion of the **Webinar** sessions? (tick as many as you find appropriate)

	Strongly disagree	Disagree	Neither agree nor disagree	Agree	Strongly agree
I found the Webinar sessions useful	○	○	○	○	○
I found the Webinar sessions interesting	○	○	○	○	○
The technology was easy to use	○	○	○	○	○
The Webinar activities were interactive	○	○	○	○	○
The pace of the Webinar sessions was appropriate	○	○	○	○	○
I liked having the same tutor every week	○	○	○	○	○
I would like to see a different tutor from week to week	○	○	○	○	○

* 10. What improvements would you make to the Webinar sessions?

```


```

11. What is your opinion of the self study material in Moodle?

	Strongly disagree	Disagree	Neither agree nor disagree	Agree	Strongly agree
I found the self-study materials useful	○	○	○	○	○
I understood how to use the self-study materials	○	○	○	○	○
I found the self-study materials relevant to my studies	○	○	○	○	○
I found the self-study materials too easy	○	○	○	○	○
I found the self-study materials too difficult	○	○	○	○	○

* 12. What improvements would you make to the self-study materials?

13. What is your opinion of the discussion forum?

	Strongly disagree	Disagree	Neither agree nor disagree	Agree	Strongly agree
I used the forum to communicate with classmates	○	○	○	○	○
I enjoyed posting ideas in the discussion forum	○	○	○	○	○
I used the forum to ask questions and check my understanding of topics	○	○	○	○	○
I would like the forum to be more social e.g. like facebook	○	○	○	○	○

* 14. What improvements would you make to the discussion forum?

* 15. Overall, how would you rate your experience of the online English course?

1 (Very poor)	2	3	4	5	6	7	8	9	10 (Excellent)
○	○	○	○	○	○	○	○	○	○

Additional comments

APPENDIX 3

FOCUS GROUP QUESTIONS

Online experience

Most of you have had little experience in studying online, what did you like about this course? What else would you like? Would you have preferred face-to-face study?

Materials

What were the materials like? Were they useful? Have they been useful in your own legal studies?

Tools

Would you have liked to use more online tools? How often did you engage in the forums? What would you like to do in the forums? How about the webinars? What did you like about these?

Technology

How did you find the technology? Did you have any tech problems accessing the materials/participating in webinars/forums?

Anne Heaton, Andrew Preshous and Simon Smith

Joined-up ESAP: Drawing on in-sessional provision to establish an ESAP pre-sessional programme

Introduction

While it is generally agreed that some level of specificity is beneficial for students of Academic English preparing for UK university courses, this is not consistently reflected in pre-sessional course design. Although Hyland (2006a) stresses the importance of subject-specific content in contextualising EAP and making it relevant to learners, others, including Kuzborska (2011), Anderson (2014) and de Chazal (2012), have noted the difficulties its inclusion can present for teachers and course designers. Incorporating subject-specific content necessitates collaboration with subject specialists, but it can be difficult to engage subject lecturers with pre-sessional courses. The positioning of pre-sessional departments within wider institutional contexts can be a significant factor; EAP is often marginalised within universities (as noted by Turner, 2011 and Jackson, 2009), and many pre-sessional departments have been privatised in recent years. Additionally, pre-sessional students may be destined for a huge number of courses distributed across all faculties and departments in an institution, and all levels of study. This paper details the approach we took to setting up an ESAP component within an otherwise EGAP pre-sessional course, and how we were able to meet some of the challenges by working closely with in-sessional lecturers.

The context

In our institutional setting at Coventry University, there is a large pre-sessional provision, with over 1,000 student enrolments across eight intakes annually. Some of the destination courses incorporate English study, and, in these cases, credit-bearing, in-sessional EAP modules are an obligatory part of the course. Because these modules support a specific academic discipline, there is an opportunity to tailor EAP content to subject modules in an ESAP model. The only constraints on the degree of collaboration are time and the willingness of all involved, and, on several in-sessional offerings, the institution has been fairly successful in this regard. The joint work of EAP and subject tutors goes beyond the level of 'cooperation' in Dudley-Evans & St John's (1998, p. 44) account of EAP engagement with the disciplines; it constitutes 'collaboration', whereby the two tutors work together 'to prepare students for particular tasks or courses'.

One of the most closely integrated degree courses at Coventry is International Business. On this course, EAP represents a significant portion (20%) of the overall course credit. Credits for Semester 1 of the course are distributed as follows:

- Global Business (ten credits European Credit Transfer System (ECTS))
- Principles of Strategy (ten ECTS)
- Advanced Business English (EAP) (five ECTS)

This course attracts approximately 180 students per year. It is a Year 3 direct-entry course, which means that students have taken their first two undergraduate years at partner institutions in their home countries, and, on completion, will graduate with a UK degree. Their English proficiency on entry is around CEFR Level B2, and 90% of the cohort originates from China, although there are also students from other parts of Asia, Africa, the Middle East and continental Europe.

The pre-sessional provision is institution-generic and therefore mainly follows an EGAP model. There are a number of reasons for this; some are administrative and logistical, but pedagogical and pastoral principles do also play a role. For many of our students, attendance on the pre-sessional accompanies a period of cultural adjustment in both their personal and academic lives, and a transition from an academic experience that centres mainly on content delivery by lecturers to one in which participation, discussion and reflection have an equally important role. The opportunity to interact with colleagues from a variety of cultural and disciplinary backgrounds, and to discuss both academic and general topics in a relatively informal small-class setting, is, in our opinion, invaluable in helping students make the transition to formal classes in their own specialist area, and the benefits of mixed disciplinary groups have also been noted by Charles and Pecorari (2016).

We do, however, recognise the need for students to work with text genres and topics that are relevant to their destination courses and will prepare them for the academic conventions of their own discipline. For this reason, we offer pre-sessional students a weekly breakout session. On one morning per week, students leave their normal pre-sessional groups, and work with other students who will be joining the same degree course on materials and activities that have been tailored to their subject area. These breakout sessions are known as EIMS (English In My Subject). Materials were typically developed in such a way that the same task type (for example, paraphrasing) was presented across all EIMS groups, yet was tailored to different subject contexts.

OUR APPROACH TO **ESAP**

Hyland has suggested (2006b, p. 10) that 'Language teachers are said to lack the training, expertise and confidence to teach subject-specific conventions'. From this, one might infer that the responsibility to deliver subject knowledge to students rests with teachers alone. De Chazal, on the other hand, believes students have responsibility for their own learning, and sees them 'as chief investigator in their discipline' (2012, p. 141); our approach, following de Chazal, is to treat the students as experts in their field. The Year 3 direct-entry students have generally studied two years of a degree or HND course in their home country, so bring a wide range of knowledge and expertise to the subject. In related subjects, such as Human Resource Management, students often come from a background in professional practice, which gives them a wealth of experience to draw upon. The first lesson on the EIMS syllabus requires students to create a 'word tree', where each branch is a term or area of their academic subject. As well as generating vocabulary, the task requires students to consider different ways in which the elements of their subject relate to one another, and to negotiate and justify their thoughts.

The timetable in Figure 1 illustrates the positioning of the ESAP strand within the wider pre-sessional course. The EIMS lessons occur at the end of the week to allow recycling of skills and language from earlier sessions in the week; the session devoted to EIMS is twice the length of the EGAP lessons to allow students the opportunity to discover paths of interest within their field. Digressions which generate discussion, or suggestions for reading, self-study and future class focus are encouraged.

In this way, the ESAP component of the course can be seen as moving away from a 'deficit model' (Turner, 2011; Coffin & Donahue, 2012) and towards an academic literacies approach, where students and teacher co-construct elements of the syllabus. As well as sharing prior experience of their subject, students are encouraged to research their future course – for example, by identifying key texts from the reading list, and to suggest texts for study in class.

	MONDAY	TUESDAY	WEDNESDAY	THURSDAY	FRIDAY
09:00–10:30	Reading & Writing	Reading & Writing	Reading & Writing	Reading & Writing	English in my Subject *ESAP Strand*
10:30–11:00					
11:00–12:30	Speaking & Listening	Speaking & Listening	Study & Research Skills *ESAP Strand*	Speaking & Listening	English in my Subject *ESAP Strand*
12:30–13:30					
13:30–15:00	Self Study	Self Study	Lecture	Tutorials/ Self Study	Tutorials/ Self Study
15:00–16:30			Self Study		

Figure 1 The positioning of the ESAP component within the pre-sessional course

The EIMS classes are intended to facilitate students' learning about the language and genre features of their subject and experimenting to see how far the 'rules' they have learnt in EGAP apply in their own discipline.

Joined-up ESAP: Parallels between the pre- and in-sessional courses

Links with department

As the in-sessional modules are credit-bearing and form an integral and concurrent part of the International Business degree, relationships between in-sessional lecturers and subject specialists were already in place at the beginning of the present study. We capitalised on this when designing the new pre-sessional course, and used the in-sessional links to mitigate the difficulty identified above of persuading subject lecturers to become actively involved. Among the many insights afforded by this collaboration, principal benefits lay in providing a source of module reading lists, as well as texts and copies of assignment briefs. Because similarly profitable collaborations have not yet been identified on all degree courses, especially those which do not include credit-bearing modules in EAP, International Business was used as the starting point from which to design the syllabus and materials for the EIMS lessons, before adapting them for other subjects.

Reading lists and target texts

As Hyland (2006a) identifies, one of the primary goals of ESAP is to help students to become more familiar with the text-types they will encounter on their degree course.

The course book (Johnson, Whittington & Scholes, 2012) used by International Business students in their core modules highlighted to us the importance of the case study, also identified by Nesi and Gardner (2012) as a key genre in Social Science subjects, including Business.

In the pre-sessional EIMS classes, case studies were used as texts to recycle language and skills from previous EGAP sessions. A case study about a social networking website *Myspace* (Johnson et al., 2012) was exploited for its use of summarising, reporting verbs and in-text referencing. Students were asked to identify in-text citations within the case study, along with any reporting verbs used to introduce the citations; they then compared the list to one they had compiled in an earlier EGAP session to see how texts in their subject might differ from generic academic texts, e.g., in the ratio of integral to non-integral references or the tense used for reporting verbs. Students then wrote a short summary of the case study using an appropriate in-text referencing style for their subject.

The use of a similar case study in a typical in-sessional lesson would take a slightly different approach, and might begin with a lead-in task to draw on students' existing knowledge of their subject. For example, a lesson looking at brand awareness asked students to guess the world's top five global brands, and engage in a discussion justifying their choices before accessing a relevant website to check (Best Global Brands, 2015). Text analysis tasks were devised to check understanding of key elements of the case study, including a particular focus on subject-specific vocabulary. Students were asked to complete an exercise on collocation such as the one in Figure 2 (page 201). Finally, students

The words below all collocate (go together) with *market*. Without looking back at the case study, decide if they go **before** or **after** *market* and add them to the correct column of the table. Then look back at the case study and write a definition of each term.

target	leader	niche	core
labour	share	segment	penetration
		market	
		market	
		market	
		market	
		market	
		market	
		market	
		market	

Figure 2 An exercise on collocations with 'market'

were asked to relate the case study back to their core module, by identifying which business frameworks (e.g., Porter's Five Forces, SWOT, Four Ps) would be useful for evaluating the company's performance.

This demonstrates the move from language- and skills-focused tasks on the pre-sessional course to a more integrated language and content-based instruction (Melles, Millar, Morton & Fegan, 2005) in the in-sessional modules.

ASSIGNMENTS AND ASSESSMENT

In the second semester, 50% of the in-sessional module is assessed by a group presentation, and there is greater emphasis on seminar discussion skills. Subject lecturers fed back that international students found it difficult to engage in group work and seminars, and often relied upon pre-rehearsed mini-speeches that bore little relation to the contributions of others. Because group, as opposed to individual, speaking tasks constituted both a key feature of the

assessment of students' future course and a notable area of difficulty, it was decided to address this within the pre-sessional EIMS classes. A rubric for seminar discussion tasks was devised, which could be adapted for every academic subject and reused for various topics; an example of a discussion task from International Business, intended as a lead-in to the lesson on the MySpace case study (Johnson et al., 2012), is given below:

Discuss and try to agree on the statements below:

- In order to be competitive, a social network must be innovative and offer something unique.
- The most successful social networks are run by users.
- The only way for a social network to make money is through advertising.

The final speaking assessment on the pre-sessional course was also adapted to include a group discussion and, thus, to encourage a positive washback effect in the classroom (Alderson & Wall, 1993). The new assessment consisted of two parts: a seminar discussion, conducted in groups of four students and marked on interactive competence as well as grammar, vocabulary and pronunciation; and an individual presentation as used more typically on pre-sessional EAP courses. Feedback from lecturers and students in International

Business indicated that the change of approach enabled students to participate more actively in class discussions. The same impact was not noted in all departments, however, and we have observed that students in some subjects continue to have difficulty interacting with their peers in seminars. We suspect this is due to the demographics of

Table 1 A comparison of assignments on the core International Business and in-sessional modules and the pre-sessional course

Global Business (content module)	In-sessional	Pre-sessional
Assignment: *Write a 1,750-word essay critically evaluating General Electric/ Kodak using the Key frameworks of Global Business.* **Case Study:** General Electric or Kodak **Word Limit:** 1,750 max **Frameworks:** International business trade theories (Legal, political, cultural, economic); FDI (Greenfield, JVs, Franchising); Marketing (4Ps); Strategy (SWOT, Value Chain, 5 Forces) **Guidelines:** Use the theories and frameworks of International Business as an analytic lens to explain the policies of the organisation.	**Assignment:** Write an essay on the title below: ***Discuss the challenges of operating globally confronting Facebook and one other social media business. Examine how these two companies can address these challenges.*** **Case Study:** Facebook **Word Limit:** 1,200–1,500 You must cite the three recommended texts: The case study, the article from the *Guardian* newspaper and the chapter from your business textbook. You can cite up to five additional sources, i.e., a <u>maximum</u> of eight sources in total.	For your next portfolio task, you are going to write an academic essay **related to your subject.** You must refer to **at least three** appropriate academic sources, and your essay should be approximately **1,000 words** long. ***Discuss the expansion of IKEA in China and the challenges the company encountered when setting up their stores in this new market. To what extent did IKEA deal successfully with these challenges and what potential problems remain?*** You should structure your answer according to the SPRE [situation, problem, response, evaluation] model you have studied. Remember you will need to <u>evaluate</u> how successful IKEA's response to the problems was.

different courses: the International Business course is, like the pre-sessional, exclusively made up of international students. Having been through the pre-sessional course, students are well prepared for interacting with other non-native speakers. Courses where we have noted that students struggle in seminars (e.g., Graphic Design and Communication, Culture and Media) often have higher numbers of native-speaker students, and pre-sessional graduates may find that their discussion skills are not yet sufficient to cope comfortably in this context.

We also used written assignments from the in-sessional course to inform the teaching and assessment of writing in EIMS. Three sample assignment briefs are reproduced in Table 1.

Lecturers on the in-sessional module designed their assignment to reflect the skills and language needed on the content module, and this, in turn, fed into the design of the pre-sessional assignment. In both the pre- and in-sessional assignments, students were expected to demonstrate the ability to evaluate the subject (an important task outcome, according to Nesi and Gardner, 2012). On the pre-sessional course, students experimented with applying a situation–problem–response–evaluation model, which they had encountered in their EGAP sessions, to a topic within their own field of study. In the in-sessional assignment, by which stage, students are more familiar with both the subject matter and the assignment type, they are expected to apply the Business frameworks that they are simultaneously studying on their core degree modules.

Figure 3 shows how students' learning trajectory proceeds not only from general to specific, but also from familiar to less familiar material, with each stage of their studies consolidating the previous one, yet

adding something new. Students are able to trace a direct link from their pre-sessional classes to the modules of their degree course, and they are thus supported in their core studies from the earliest possible opportunity.

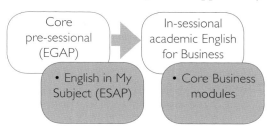

Figure 3 The progression from language to content focus

CONCLUSION

In the present study, our approach was to draw on existing, credit-bearing modules on the International Business degree programme as a source of meaningful and authentic content in the form of business texts and tasks. In addition, we benefited greatly from the expertise of departmental staff, and were able to exploit all these resources to establish a subject-specific component within an otherwise EGAP pre-sessional course. Feedback from lecturers and students in International Business indicated that the approach was effective.

Because ESAP provision for students joining courses other than International Business is currently less effective, our aim now is to extend the approach across all disciplines. Establishing strong relationships with the various departments remains the biggest obstacle to this, but we are prioritising this kind of cross-faculty outreach; it is hoped that sharing the outcomes of the present study will provide encouragement to other departments in our own institution, as well as to colleagues in BALEAP. Closer collaboration between EAP departments and subject specialists is necessary, and we agree with Melles et al. (2005) that greater awareness and closer integration of language and content benefits not only students, but also the subject departments, and can help to assert the vital role of EAP in universities.

REFERENCES

Alderson, J. C., & Wall, D. (1993). Does washback exist? *Applied Linguistics, 14*(2), 115–129. doi: 10.1093/applin/14.2.115

Anderson, R. (2014). A parallel approach to ESAP teaching. *Procedia – Social and Behavioral Sciences, 136,* 194–202.

Best Global Brands. (2015). Retrieved April 16, 2015, from Interbrand Best Global Brands 2015 http://www.bestglobalbrands.com/2015/ranking/

Charles, M., & Pecorari, D. (2016). *Introducing English for academic purposes.* London: Routledge.

Coffin, C., & Donahue, J. P. (2012). Academic literacies and systemic functional linguistics: How do they relate? *Journal of English for Academic Purposes, 11,* 64–75. doi:10.1016/j.jeap.2011.11.004

de Chazal, E. (2012). The general–specific debate in EAP: Which case is the most convincing for most contexts? *Journal of Second Language Teaching and Research, 2*(1), 135–148.

Dudley-Evans, T., & St. John, M. (1998). *Developments in English for specific purposes: A multi-disciplinary approach.* Cambridge: Cambridge University Press.

Hyland, K. (2006a). Specificity revisited: How far should we go now? *English for Specific Purposes, 21,* 385–395.

Hyland, K. (2006b). *English for academic purposes: An advanced resource book.* Abingdon: Routledge.

Jackson, F. (2009). EAP course design within a context of institutional change and cross-disciplinary collaboration: Factors shaping the creating of 'writing for commerce'. *Per Linguam, 25*(2), 61–81. http://dx.doi.org/10.5785/25-2-35

Johnson, G., Whittington, R., & Scholes, K. (2012). *Fundamentals of strategy* (2nd ed.). Harlow: Pearson.

Kuzborska, I. (2011). Teachers' decision-making processes when designing EAP reading materials in a Lithuanian university setting. *Journal of English for Academic Purposes, 10,* 223–237. doi:10.1016/j.jeap.2011.07.003

Melles, G., Millar, G., Morton, J., & Fegan, S. (2005). Credit-based discipline specific English for academic purposes programmes in higher education. *Arts & Humanities in Higher Education, 4*(3), 283–303. doi:10.1177/1474022205055617

Nesi, H., & Gardner, S. (2012). *Genres across the disciplines: Student writing in higher education.* Cambridge: Cambridge University Press.

Turner, J. (2011). Academic literacies: Providing a space for the socio-political dynamics of EAP. *Journal of English for Academic Purposes, 11,* 17–25. doi:10.1016/j.jeap.2011.11.007

Andrew Preshous and Jenny Kemp

Exploiting corpora to address the subject-specific vocabulary needs of students

Introduction

Teaching English for Specific Academic Purposes (ESAP) can be both an exciting and a daunting prospect. Students are often highly motivated because they are working within their own discipline and, yet, the uncertainties of teachers can increase as they have to deal with language from disciplines with which they may be unfamiliar. Further challenges include assessing student needs, as well as selecting appropriate language to teach. Taking a corpus-based approach can help teachers address these areas, as it can be an effective way to assess the lexical needs of students, raise awareness of the particular vocabulary they require and develop learner independence. This paper describes corpus-based approaches to assessing subject-specific language needs and creating materials for two different disciplines and contexts: postgraduate Law students at Leicester University and undergraduate Business students at Coventry University.

Previous research into how corpora can be exploited in the EAP context has focused on a range of aspects, including studies that draw on discipline-specific data (Mudraya, 2006; Chang, 2014), use learner corpora (Cotos, 2014) or promote corpus building (Charles, 2012). Despite these and many other useful projects, it seems fair to say that corpus-based approaches are still not common practice in the EAP classroom, and there exists great potential for further practical application. Firstly, corpora can help teachers decide what lexis to teach (e.g., Hyland & Tse, 2007), as a corpus gives quantitative information about word frequency and the most common words in a particular field or compared to other fields. Secondly, corpus software provides clear visual information in the form of concordance lines, which enable both teachers and students to look at multiword units as well as single words and see qualitative features, such as patterns of use.

It is important to focus on students' subject-specific needs. In some contexts, there has tended to be a reliance instead on general academic vocabulary and on word lists derived from corpora, such as the Academic Word List (AWL) (Coxhead, 2000) and, more recently, the Academic Vocabulary List (Gardner & Davies, 2014). Such lists continue to be useful for pre-sessional courses with mixed-discipline classes, when a common-core approach is more appropriate. However, Hyland (2008), Hyland and Tse (2007) and Durrant (2014) have all argued that it is not enough to target general academic language, as there is too much variation between disciplines and discipline groups or 'clusters'. For example, Durrant (ibid. p. 341) noted that discipline-specific words had a mean coverage of 18% in the essays he examined from the British Academic Written English (BAWE) corpus (Nesi & Gardner, 2012). In other words, 18% of the total word count was discipline-specific, technical vocabulary. Furthermore, most of this lexis is not usually explicitly taught by content experts; that is, it is not glossed in lectures or seminars (Flowerdew, 1993, p. 236; Durrant, op. cit.). Students also indicate that they have difficulties with this specialist vocabulary, as highlighted in a study of undergraduates' perceptions conducted by Evans and Morrison (2011, p. 395), which suggested that they need 'particular assistance' in this area.

ASSESSING STUDENT NEEDS AND IDENTIFYING TARGET VOCABULARY

There are various ways to use corpora to assess learner needs and help EAP teachers identify key subject-specific lexical items. Firstly, existing corpora and corpus-informed word lists can be used; for example, the discipline-specific word lists developed by Durrant (2014) drawn from the BAWE corpus. These lists cover a range of disciplines at four levels: levels 1–3 are undergraduate and level 4 postgraduate. One quick way of assessing student needs is to use items from the list in a self-assessment task based on Paribakht and Wesche's (1983) Vocabulary Knowledge Scale at the start of a course or class. This checklist test was designed to test vocabulary depth, but can be used for diagnostics:

precedent

- I have never seen this word.
- I have seen this word before, but I don't know what it means.
- I have seen this word before, and I think it means _____.
- I know this word. It means _____. (give synonym or translation)
- I can use this word in a sentence:

_____.

Another way to use these lists is to ask the content specialists which words they gloss; those words that are not explained need to be covered in language classes (Flowerdew, op. cit.). Whichever method is used, the teacher can use the results to design appropriate tasks.

Sometimes, the questions that we have about students' lexical needs are more specific. Moreover, they may concern multiword units, rather than single words. The Law students at Leicester were having difficulty reading reports of legal cases. In order to see what the vocabulary issues were, students were asked to send the tutor links to the cases they were reading. Twelve cases comprising approximately 130,000 words were downloaded, converted into .txt files, and then combined into a single file. This simple corpus was then uploaded to the N-gram Phrase Extractor (Cobb, n.d.). The output listed 5-, 4-, 3- and 2-word multiword units (or 'n-grams') with their raw frequency (in squared brackets). Figure 1 shows the output for the 3-word strings. Rather than making assumptions about which were unknown, these were then shown to the students. It transpired that the ones they had problems with were not phrases such as *judicial review proceedings* or *the applicant*, but *in accordance with*, *in the light of* and *by reason of*. Although these terms seem quite generic, in legal texts, they have more specific usage and patterning (see highlight section in Figure 1).

A further approach to identifying key vocabulary – that draws on the BAWE word lists – uses Durrant's (2014) analytical framework, which incorporates the Deviation of Proportions (D.P.) mechanism developed by Gries (2008). For instance, this measurement can be used to indicate words that are statistically more frequent in assignments for Business than for other disciplines. The higher the D.P. statistic, the more specialised the item is in a particular subject (see Table 1). An investigation found that the 20 Business vocabulary items with the highest D.P. scores were identified as *customer, corporate,*

```
3-wd strings: 114,689
Repeated: 2998 (2.61%)
TTR: 2998:7790 (1:2.59)
Words: 8994 (7.84% of tot)

001.[22]   CITED ABOVE PARA
002.[19]   THE COURT HAS
003.[18]   AS TO THE
004.[16]   THE APPLICANT WAS
005.[16]   IN ORDER TO
006.[15]   ACCORDING TO THE
007.[12]   IN RESPECT OF
008.[12]   THERE IS NO
009.[12]   OF THE APPLICANT'S
010.[12]   WOULD NOT BE
011.[11]   IN WHICH THE
012.[11]   OF THE JUDGMENT
013.[11]   SO AS TO
014.[11]   THE TRIAL JUDGE
015.[11]   IT IS NOT
016.[11]   THE PAROLE BOARD
017.[11]   TO THE APPLICANT
018.[11]   THERE WAS NO
019.[10]   AS REGARDS THE
020.[10]   IT WOULD BE
021.[10]   THAT IT WAS
022.[10]   SEE FOR EXAMPLE
023.[10]   THAT THE COURT
024.[10]   THE FIRST APPLICANT
025.[10]   IT WAS NOT
026.[10]   THE APPLICANT HAD
027.[10]   JUDICIAL REVIEW PROCEEDINGS
028.[9]    THE HIGH COURT
029.[9]    BY REASON OF
030.[9]    AS WELL AS
```

Figure 1 N-Gram Phrase Extractor output: Top 30 3-strings in law reports

Table 1 D.P. scores for frequent Business words

Word	Frequency per million words	Percentage of texts	Percentage of subcorpora	D.P.
1. *customer*	2069.548078	54.83871	19.76744	0.746869
2. *corporate*	1182.598902	25.80645	10.46512	0.735326
3. *customers*	2674.926088	61.29032	22.09302	0.728641

customers, manager, employees, sales, team, budget, staff, company, project, strategy, management, service, market, performance, training, cost, product, costs.

Having identified these target items, lexical data in the BAWE corpus can be accessed using the corpus query tool SketchEngine (Kilgarriff, Rychly, Smrz & Tugwell, 2004), which allows the user to search for the items and locate key information and patterns. For example, collocations with *customer* that appear in BAWE with some frequency can be compared with statistical data from a learner corpus of your students' own work (using freeware such as AntConc, Anthony, 2015) to identify items that might be less familiar for your cohort and, therefore, worthy of attention – for example, *customer margins, expectations* or *base* (see Figure 2 below). Once lexical needs have been identified, appropriate materials and activities can be developed to introduce vocabulary items systematically over the duration of a course.

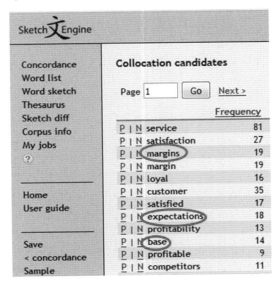

Figure 2 Collocations with *customer* from BAWE using Sketch Engine (Kilgarriff et al., 2004)
[Source: Reproduced with permission from SketchEngine, www.sketchengine.co.uk]

PRACTICAL WAYS TO EXPLOIT CORPORA IN THE ESAP CLASSROOM

The most common format for corpus output is in the form of concordances, that is, extracted lines of text all containing a target word or phrase (see Figure 3). The target item is often placed in the centre of the line in what is known as 'KWIC' (Key Word In Context) format, which provides a clear visual representation. Thus, concordance lines offer many opportunities for noticing (Tribble, 2002, p. 133). It is known that a word needs to be encountered multiple times before it is learnt (see e.g., Nation, 1990), and, as Cobb (1997) argues, concordance outputs allow learners to see a target item in a variety of authentic contexts in an 'escalated' manner. Such consciousness-raising (Schmidt, 1990) can also lead to increased language awareness – a conscious knowledge of language which aids learning (Svalberg, 2007, p. 288). It allows time for the cognitive processing of key elements such as the form/meaning distinction (Batstone, 1996) and is particularly appropriate for learning lexical features such as collocation and connotation, as well as syntactic and lexicogrammatical patterns (examples of which will be given below). However, students need to learn how to interpret key features and identify patterns, and therefore, some learner training is essential. In the methodology used here, there are, broadly speaking, four stages: *observe, highlight, extract* and *use.*

STAGES OF LEARNER TRAINING: OBSERVE, HIGHLIGHT, EXTRACT AND USE

Observe
Learners are given concordance lines, for example, from a purpose-built corpus like the

law report corpus mentioned above, or from an online concordancer such as the Brigham-Young interface for the British National Corpus (Davies, 2004–). The corpus does not need to be a variety of texts: a single text which is also being used in class for other purposes, such as generic moves or other discourse features, can be further exploited by turning it into a mini-corpus using freeware like AntConc (Anthony, 2015). The lines can be presented to students as they are, or selected and grouped by the teacher beforehand. Students are asked to act as 'detective' (Johns, 2002, p. 108), i.e., to study the examples, find patterns and work out the meanings of the keywords. For example, the Law students are given a handout with concordance output (an unmarked version of Figure 3) with the following instruction:

The following concordance lines are all taken from a small purpose-built corpus of Law Reports from your reading lists. Study the examples and work out the meaning(s) of the central phrase.

Another task can be seen in Table 2. It asks students to distinguish sentences from Business assignments from a range of samples from other disciplines, all containing the keyword *performance*. Such an activity can act as a springboard for more focused analysis of subject-specific collocations.

Highlight

Highlighting is an important part of the process as it reinforces the target item. When learners do an activity together on screen, then the 'highlighting' is done by drawing each others' attention to patterns, by pointing, reading out and discussing. Thus, although not physical highlighting with a pen, it is nevertheless a form of reinforcement.

14	which the jury would have had to have assessed in the light of all the evidence in the case. 146. Secondly, although
28	al lack of support there would not be accepted. In the light of the evidence provided by the applicant, it could neith
30	s of Afghanistan should each be assessed carefully, in light of the evidence presented by the applicant and other curr
19	he CACD did not itself assess all the evidence, in the light of the new evidence, in order to decide whether guilt had
11	ure in view of the state of health of an applicant. In light of the medical evidence in the instant case, there was a
22	s of the length of proceedings must be assessed in the light of the circumstances of the case and with reference to th
33	t contrary to art 3 of the Convention, particularly in light of the fact that the applicant had family in Afghanistan.
31	n Rights Practices – Afghanistan at para 49 above). In light of those facts, he argued that there were serious grounds
26	case 123. It remains to be considered whether, in the light of the foregoing observations, the present applicants' wh
4	46. In the light of all the foregoing considerations, the answer to the fi
15	d this concession inevitable and right in principle in light of observations made by the Lord Chief Justice in the cas
17	nocent of the crime of which he had been convicted. In light of his conclusion that no compensation was payable, it wa
6	ake a formal declaration, the judge concluded: 'In the light of my conclusion that his case does not give rise to any
7	r argued that any appeal would have been futile in the light of the fact that the court would not be able to compel th
20	of Appeal to evaluate the judgment of the CACD in the light of the section 133 criteria. 131. Turning to the judgment
3	e sitting as Deputy High Court Judge held that, in the light of the principles laid down in Group Josi, it was not ope
24	ty of the 2003 Act with art 3 of the Convention in the light of Kafkaris v Cyprus [2008] ECHR 21906/04 Having observed
34	. He argued that the Court should consider his case in light of M.S.S. v Belgium and Greece, cited above, and his inab

Figure 3 Highlighted concordance lines for *in (the) light of*

Table 2 Collocations with *performance* from BAWE

Employee satisfaction does not necessarily lead to high employee	*performance.*	
Formula-1 car engines have excellent	*performance*	as they are about ten times more powerful.
Management are seeking greater job	*performance*	and job satisfaction.
A-grade in A-levels should increase the exam	*performance*	by 2.92 percentage points.
This outcome is due to the poor company	*performance*	in the last few quarters.
by mainly focusing on theatre as the live	*performance*	of drama.
Adopting such an approach would lead to improved financial	*performance.*	

Table 3 Collocations with *product* from BAWE

competitors will react and **launch a** similar	*product*	in the future
then will they **launch a** more innovative	*product*	based on Powermop
having products at different stages in the	*product*	**life cycle** is essential for the long-term
that is at the mature end of the	*product*	**life cycle**
IKEA's goods are standard, flat packed and share components across	*product*	**lines**
Companies are trying to differentiate themselves by extending	*product*	**lines** away from traditional lines

Figure 3 on page 209 shows the patterns associated with *in (the) light of*, which Law students would be guided towards and encouraged to highlight. As can be seen here, the phrase is associated with particular patterns in law reports which are not represented in general or general academic usage. The phrase is often preceded by verbs meaning 'appraise' (*assess, consider, evaluate*), and is usually followed by a noun phrase with *evidence, fact(s), observations, conclusion*, relating to 'the applicant' or 'case' in question. In the last four examples,

it is followed by a reference to a specific legal authority. Learners are encouraged to highlight patterns to both the left and right of the keyword in this way.

In the activity below, which uses sample sentences from BAWE (see Table 3), students identify and highlight the three different collocations with the keyword *product*: *launch a* (+ optional adj) _____, _____ *life cycle*, _____ *lines*. They can then work out the essential meaning of the terms.

Extract

Students then extract key information from the concordance lines, recording it on a worksheet or in a notebook. This can be done on the whiteboard first, as feedback on the highlighting stage. An alternative is to provide guided tasks as shown below:

1) Find two words which describe different types of budgets. Write down an example sentence for each one.

2) Identify a collocation with budget that means the following:

   a) A budget that can be changed:

      _____ *budget*

      [answer: *revisable budget*]

   b) Budget limitations: *budget*

      _____

      [answer: *budget constraints*]

At this stage, activities based on definitions (*Cambridge Dictionaries Online*, 2015) will consolidate the focus on particular collocations:

- a group of employees whose job is to sell their company's products or services: *sales* _____ [answer: *force*]

Further gap-fill tasks adapted from concordance lines can be designed to reinforce understanding:

- The company currently has a _____ of 101 spread across the three outlets. [answer: *sales force*]

Once students have been introduced to the techniques, they can combine the *observe*, *highlight* and *extract* stages in hands-on workshops using online concordancers. Workshops are ideal because concordancers are a valuable self-study tool enabling learners to prepare a presentation, respond to tutor feedback, or answer their own questions when writing. For such workshop

activities, step-by-step guidance for using corpus tools is vital, either as a screencast or as written guidelines (see Appendix).

Use

Whether the initial exploration has been carried out with handouts or on screen, it is important that the learners have the opportunity to *use* the language afterwards and to experiment with it: it is this *manipulation* of language that reinforces learning. This stage should include both guided or scaffolded receptive tasks and more productive output. An example of a highly scaffolded task can be seen in Figure 4, which uses the idea of a 'miniature concordance' discussed in Johns (2002). Here a guided gap-fill task has been created using extracts from Law essays in BAWE, which contain the multiword units identified from law reports. By doing such a task, learners begin to see how they can use the lexis in their own writing.

Another idea is to find errors in the students' own essays or from a learner corpus and to use these in an editing task. Here is a task using sample sentences from BAWE:

- Nestle adopted a non-stop *competition strategy*. [answer: *competitive*]
- Last but not least, McDonald's *costumer service* is another important process. [answer: *customer*]
- The *superior staffs* are a good prospect for the corporation. [answer: *senior staff*]

Interactive software such as the Triptico software designed by Riley (Triptico Ltd., n.d.) can be used to create a variety of tasks which engage learners. The items in the 'word magnets' activity (Figure 5) can be moved around to form different collocations. Collocations crosswords (Figure 5) can be designed with different types of clue:

Use phrases from the box (right) to complete these concordance lines from the BAWE corpus. There are two extra.

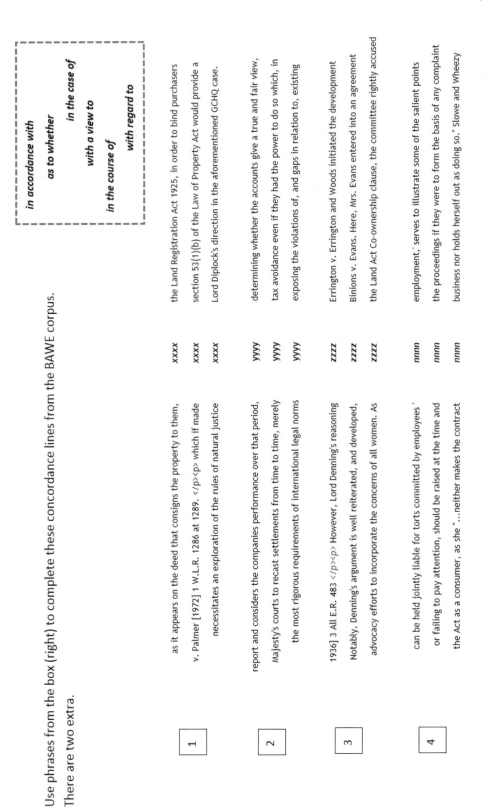

in accordance with

as to whether

in the case of

with a view to

in the course of

with regard to

1	as it appears on the deed that consigns the property to them,	xxxx	the Land Registration Act 1925, in order to bind purchasers
	v. Palmer [1972] 1 W.L.R. 1286 at 1289. \</p\>\<p\> which if made	xxxx	section 53(1)(b) of the Law of Property Act would provide a
	necessitates an exploration of the rules of natural justice	xxxx	Lord Diplock's direction in the aforementioned GCHQ case.
2	report and considers the companies performance over that period,	yyyy	determining whether the accounts give a true and fair view,
	Majesty's courts to recast settlements from time to time, merely	yyyy	tax avoidance even if they had the power to do so which, in
	the most rigorous requirements of international legal norms	yyyy	exposing the violations of, and gaps in relation to, existing
3	1936] 3 All E.R. 483 \</p\>\<p\> However, Lord Denning's reasoning	zzzz	Errington v. Errington and Woods initiated the development
	Notably, Denning's argument is well reiterated, and developed,	zzzz	Binions v. Evans. Here, Mrs. Evans entered into an agreement
	advocacy efforts to incorporate the concerns of all women. As	zzzz	the Land Act Co-ownership clause, the committee rightly accused
4	can be held jointly liable for torts committed by employees'	nnnn	employment,' serves to illustrate some of the salient points
	or failing to pay attention, should be raised at the time and	nnnn	the proceedings if they were to form the basis of any complaint
	the Act as a consumer, as she "…neither makes the contract	nnnn	business nor holds herself out as doing so." Slowe and Wheezy

Figure 4 Law gap-fill task

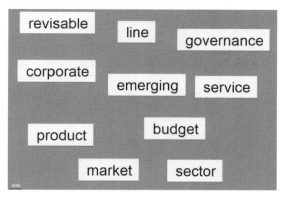
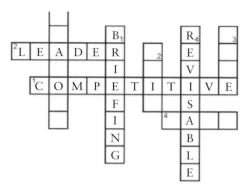

Figure 5 Word magnets created with Triptico software and collocations crossword extract

Leader, briefing, multi-purpose, members, spirit _____ [answer: **team**]
The company that sells most of a product or service. **Market** _____ [answer: **leader**]

From the system, we can find out lots of useful business vocabulary.
It can help me to work out the meaning of collocations.

Whatever activities are set up, it is always important to check meaning as well as form and to include less controlled tasks and, ultimately, free written and oral productive output, allowing for monitoring of appropriate and authentic usage in an appropriately discipline-specific context. It is also important to remind and encourage students to use concordancers – for instance, when correcting an essay, by underlining a lexicogrammatical error and writing 'check concordance'.

Just over 80% of the cohort said they would use the BAWE corpus to check vocabulary again in their future studies. A recent cohort of Law students gave a hands-on concordancing session 5/5 for usefulness, and several said it was the highlight of the course. A few students on the courses described did state that corpus-based approaches were 'a little difficult', reinforcing the need for carefully scaffolded tasks in short, regular vocabulary slots that foster independent study.

POSITIVE FEEDBACK

There was clear evidence of positive impact on learning from student feedback. Comments made in informal class surveys completed by 50 of the Business students indicated that 90% of this cohort considered the approaches to have been useful in raising awareness of Business vocabulary:

CONCLUSION

It is essential that EAP professionals use an evidence-based approach to teaching and learning. Corpora and corpus software such as concordancers enable us to do this, whether we are using an existing corpus or creating our own. They offer an effective means of identifying appropriate lexis from authentic, subject-specific language, and provide a rich variety of opportunities to raise awareness of key vocabulary. A corpus-based approach can also ensure that vocabulary teaching is relevant and engaging, and, importantly, meets students' needs. Moreover, it gives them a tool with which they can independently continue their vocabulary learning beyond the classroom.

REFERENCES

Anthony, L. (2015). AntConc (Version 3.4.4) [Computer software]. Tokyo, Japan: Waseda University. Retrieved September 12, 2015, from http://www.laurenceanthony.net/

Batstone, R. (1996). Key concepts in ELT: Noticing. *ELT Journal, 50*(3), 273.

Cambridge Dictionaries Online. (2015). Retrieved February 24, 2015, from http://dictionary. cambridge.org/dictionary/english/business

Chang, J.-Y. (2014). The use of general and specialized corpora as reference sources for academic English writing: A case study. *Recall, 26*(2), 243–259.

Charles, M. (2012). 'Proper vocabulary and juicy collocations': EAP students evaluate do-it-yourself corpus-building. *English for Specific Purposes, 31*, 93–102.

Cobb, T. (1997). Is there any measurable learning from hands-on concordancing? *System, 25*(3), 301–15.

Cobb, T. (n.d.). Corpus concordance English [Computer program]. Retrieved September 13, 2015, from http://www.lextutor.ca/conc/eng/

Cotos, E. (2014). Enhancing writing pedagogy with learner corpus data. *Recall, 26*(2), 202–224.

Coventry University (n.d.). British academic written English corpus (BAWE). Retrieved September 12, 2015, from http://www.coventry.ac.uk/research/research-directories/current-projects/2015/british-academic-written-english-corpus-bawe/

Coxhead, A. (2000). A new academic word list. *TESOL Quarterly, 34*(2), 213–238.

Davies, M. (2004–). BYU-BNC. (Based on the British National Corpus from Oxford University Press). Retrieved September 12, 2015, from http://corpus.byu.edu/bnc/

Durrant, P. (2014). Discipline and level specificity in university students' written vocabulary. *Applied Linguistics, 35*(3), 328–356.

Evans, S., & Morrison, B. (2011). The first term at university: Implications for EAP. *ELT Journal, 65*(4), 387–397

Flowerdew, J. (1993). Concordancing as a tool in course design. *System, 21*(2), 231–244.

Gardner, D., & Davies, M. (2014). A new academic vocabulary list. *Applied Linguistics, 35*(3), 305–327.

Gries, S.T. (2008). Dispersions and adjusted frequencies in corpora. *International Journal of Corpus Linguistics, 13*(4), 403–437.

Hyland, K. (2008). As can be seen: Lexical bundles and disciplinary variation. *English for Specific Purposes, 27*, 4–21.

Hyland, K., & Tse, P. (2007). Is there an "Academic Vocabulary"? *TESOL Quarterly, 41*(2), 235–253.

Johns, T. (2002). Data-driven learning: The perpetual challenge. In B. Ketteman, & G. Marko (Eds.), *Teaching and learning by doing corpus analysis* (pp. 107–117). Amsterdam: Rodopi.

Kilgarriff, A., Rychly, P., Smrz, P., & Tugwell, D. *The Sketch Engine*. Proc EURALEX 2004, Lorient, France; pp. 105–116. Retrieved December 1, 2016 from http://www.sketchengine.co.uk

Mudraya, O. (2006). Engineering English: A lexical frequency instructional model. *English for Specific Purposes, 25*, 235–256.

Nation, I. S. P. (1990). *Teaching and learning vocabulary*. New York: Newbury House.

Nesi, H., & Gardner, S. (2012). *Genres across the disciplines: Student writing in higher education*. Cambridge: Cambridge University Press.

Paribakht, T. S., & Wesche, M. B. (1993). Reading comprehension and second language development in a comprehension-based ESL programme. *TESL Canada Journal, 11*(1), 9–27.

Schmidt, R. (1990). The role of consciousness in second language learning. *Applied Linguistics, 11*, 129–158.

Svalberg, A. (2007). Language awareness and language teaching. *Language Teaching, 40*, 287–308.

Tribble, C. (2002). Corpora and corpus analysis: New windows on academic writing. In Flowerdew, J. (Ed.), *Academic discourse* (pp. 131–149). Harlow: Addison Wesley Longman.

Triptico Ltd. (n.d.) *Triptico* [Computer software]. Retrieved January 30, 2015, from https://www.tripticoplus.com/

APPENDIX

A. INSTRUCTIONS FOR BUSINESS STUDENTS USING *SKETCH ENGINE*

- Go to *Sketch Engine* open access: https://the.sketchengine.co.uk/open/
- Click on the link *British Academic Written English Corpus (BAWE)*.
- In the *Simple query* box, type *budget*.
- Click on *Text types*.
- In the *TEXT. DISCIPLINE* box type 'Business'. Press return.

How many times does the word *budget* appear in the corpus? _____

- In the left-hand column, click on *Collocations*.
- The new screen appears, click *Make Candidate List*.
- Focus on the 30 words at the top of the list and answer these questions:
  1. Which collocations are the most frequent and appear more than ten times?
  2. Identify a collocation with *budget* that means the following:
     A *budget* that can't be changed: _____ *budget*
     Example sentence: _____

B. INSTRUCTIONS FOR LAW STUDENTS USING LEXTUTOR (COBB, N.D.) AND BYU-BNC (DAVIES, 2004–)

1. What noun phrases tend to follow *in accordance with*?
   Type **in accordance with** *(with spaces) into the* **keyword** *box, then select corpus* **bnc Law***. Choose 'sort by one to the right of the keyword', '*150*' for width and '*100*' for number of lines. Then click* **get concordance***. Make a note of the main patterns. Include one or two useful examples.*

2. Can I say *the English Law*? What prepositions are often used before *English Law*?
   Use the concordancer to check, and note the patterns.

3. In British Law Reports, which is more common: *in light of* or *in the light of*? Can you see any useful patterns? Where does it tend to come in the sentence (start/mid/end)? Is it associated with any particular structures or punctuation?
   Select the **BLaRC** *Law Reports corpus. Search for* **light of***. Sort left, and then right. If you click on the keyword in any one line, you will get the full context.*

   When they have done a number of similarly scaffolded tasks then more open questions are possible:

4. *Regard* is used in many different ways. What are the differences?
   Use the byu-bnc. Ask it to sort left then right: SORT - - 2 | 3 - - . Remember to look both to the left and to the right of the keyword, and don't forget to notice punctuation as well as grammar and vocabulary. Note the main patterns.

NOTES ON THE CONTRIBUTORS

DINA AWAD is an experienced EAP lecturer. She has a BA in English Literature (Baghdad), a Masters in English Language Teaching and Applied Linguistics (Kings College London), Diploma in Public Service Interpretation (Middlesex University) and a PhD in Linguistics (Lancaster University).
Email: dinafirasawad@gmail.com

BEE BOND is a Senior Teaching Fellow at the University of Leeds. She is a TEAP Senior Fellow, Mentor and Assessor. Her main areas of interest lie in EAP practitioner knowledge and understanding development, specifically through scholarship embedded within and threaded through practice.
Email: b.bond@leeds.ac.uk

EMMA BLYTH manages the English for Legal Purposes modules at BPP University. She has a background in Law and has been designing and delivering EAP courses in higher education for over eight years. Her research interests are online learning and legal academic writing.
Email: emmablyth@bpp.com

OLGA BURAKOV is an EAP tutor at the Centre for English Language Education (CELE) at the University of Nottingham. She is currently teaching on CELE's Foundation programme and is responsible for delivering academic skills and English language modules. She holds an MA (2004) and a PhD (2008) in English from New York University (USA), and is a Fellow of the Higher Education Academy. Her main research interests include performativity and language, discourse and ideology, and discipline writing.
Email: olga.burakov@nottingham.ac.uk

DAVID CAULTON started his ESP career in Italy and is now Deputy Section Head of ESP at ELE, University of Edinburgh. He teaches on a range of pre- and in-sessional ESAP courses. His interests include Business English and ESAP course design and materials development in both face-to-face and online learning.
Email: david.caulton@ed.ac.uk

KATRIEN DEROEY Katrien Deroey (PhD) is a Senior Lecturer in Applied Linguistics and Language Teaching. She is an EAP practitioner and corpus linguist. She is Head of English at the recently established University of Luxembourg Language Centre.
Email: katrien.deroey@uni.lu

DAVID DONNARUMMA is Head of English for BPP University. He has been involved in English Language Teaching for over 15 years as a

manager, academic, teacher educator, test developer and materials developer. He has designed and delivered English programmes both in print and online. His areas of research lie in language assessment and online learning.
Email: daviddonnarumma@bpp.com

SHEENA GARDNER is Professor of Applied Linguistics in the School of Humanities, Coventry University, where she teaches on the Coventry PGCert/PGDip/MA in TEAP. Her research and supervision centre on academic genres and registers in the BAWE corpus of university student writing, and the transfer of learning from EAP to disciplinary contexts.
Email: sheena.gardner@coventry.ac.uk

ZOE GAZELEY-EKE has taught English in Mexico, Russia, Japan, China and Saudi Arabia. She is currently a lecturer in Academic English at Coventry University, where her main teaching is on Academic English courses and the MA in English Language Teaching. Her research interests are in digital materials development and teacher training.
Email: ab2931@coventry.ac.uk

PAULINE GILLIES is an ESP Teaching Fellow at the University of Edinburgh. Her main area of work and interest involves teaching on and designing materials for a wide range of English for Medicine courses, both face-to-face and online. She started her ESP career in Saudi Arabia and Oman.
Email: pauline.gillies@ed.ac.uk

SIMON GOOCH works as an EAP tutor, course coordinator and developer in CELE at the University of Nottingham. His interests include the development of EAP tasks and materials, the learning processes relating to EAP concepts and the different ways language is used between academic disciplines.
Email: simon.gooch@nottingham.ac.uk

ANNE HEATON is Associate Director of Pre-sessional Courses at Coventry University. Her interests include assessment, materials and syllabus design and the role of EAP within institutional contexts. Before joining Coventry in 2013, she worked in FE and HE institutions in the UK and has taught abroad in France and China.
Email: anne.heaton@coventry.ac.uk

MAGGIE HEENEY teaches EAP reading and writing in the Department of Culture and Language Studies, and is coordinator of the TESOL teacher-training program at Renison University College, University of Waterloo, Ontario, Canada. Her research interest is the relationship between teaching and learning in second language writing development.
Email: mheeney@uwaterloo.ca

REBECCA HUGHES is Director of Education at the British Council. She gained a personal chair in Applied Linguistics at the University of Nottingham in 2007, and was Pro-Vice-Chancellor (International) at The University of Sheffield 2010–2013. She has published widely on spoken language and continues to work at the interface between Applied Linguistics, international education analysis and policy.
Email: rebecca.hughes@britishcouncil.org

KEN HYLAND is Professor of Applied Linguistics and Director of the Centre for Applied English Studies at the University of Hong Kong. He is best known for his research into writing and academic discourse, having published over 200 articles and 25 books and received over 23,500 citations on Google Scholar.
Email: khyland@hku.hk

JENNY KEMP is a lecturer in EAP at Leicester University, where her current roles include directing a pre-sessional, providing in-sessional Law support and encouraging professional

development. She is a Senior Fellow of BALEAP and of the Higher Education Academy, and a Mentor and Assessor for the TEAP Scheme. Her main research interests lie in discipline-specific vocabulary and the use of corpora in teaching and learning.
Email: jenny.kemp@le.ac.uk

STEVE KIRK is a Senior Teaching Fellow and Director of summer pre-sessional programmes at Durham University. He also leads modules in Teaching EAP and SLA for teachers on an MA in Applied Linguistics. His ongoing doctoral research uses Legitimation Code Theory to explore classroom enactment of the EAP curriculum.
Email: s.e.kirk@durham.ac.uk

MEHTAP KOCATEPE holds a PhD in TESOL from James Cook University in Australia. She has been teaching EAP for 18 years and, since 2010, has been working at Zayed University, United Arab Emirates. Her research interests include learner autonomy, motivation, sociocultural theories of learning and qualitative research methods.
Email: mehtap.kocatepe@zu.ac.ae

BLAIR MATTHEWS is an EAP teacher at the University of Bristol and helps coordinate the pre-sessional EAP courses at Bristol during the summer. He has experience designing online materials for English as a Foreign Language (EFL) and English for Academic Purposes (EAP).
Email: blair.matthews@bristol.ac.uk

JILL NORTHCOTT is Head of ESP at ELE, University of Edinburgh. Her research and publication interests include legal English and ethnographic exploration of academic learning contexts for teacher development, and ESAP course design. She is a member of the JEAP Editorial Board. Her ESP teaching career began in Malaysia.
Email: jill.northcott@ed.ac.uk

ANDREW PRESHOUS is Senior Lecturer in Academic English at Coventry University. He specializes in EAP, teacher training and Business English. His current interests include subject-specific materials development and online international learning projects. He has taught English in Greece, Poland and Malaysia, and is co-author of *IELTS Foundation*.
Email: ab3258@coventry.ac.uk

CHRISTOPHER SMITH is an engineer at Glasgow Caledonian University. He is interested in interdisciplinary collaboration that has an impact on educational experience and practice. He has a passion for work-based education, and in UK and transnational delivery patterns that have a personal, organizational and societal impact. His research interest is in product and service innovation around education and within organizations.
Email: chrismacbsmith@gmail.com

ELAINE SMITH teaches EAP at CELE, University of Nottingham, and is currently involved in the ongoing development, teaching and coordinating of the 'new look' Presessional EAP courses that they have been running since 2012.
Email: elaine.smith@nottingham.ac.uk

SIMON SMITH is a corpus linguist and EAP practitioner at Coventry University. His research is on the use of corpora in English and Chinese learning, in particular, data-driven learning, learner-constructed corpora and vocabulary portfolios. He works on collaborative EAP-disciplines projects, including integrated course design, assessments and feedback. He also teaches Applied Linguistics and Chinese.
Email: smithsgj@gmail.com

IRINA VELEANU taught A-level EFL and History through English in Romania for approximately 14 years, after which she undertook postgraduate studies in the UK on L2

Mediated Learning (TESOL and CLIL), and on Research in Social Sciences. Since 2009, she has mostly been involved in teaching and developing EAP syllabuses and materials on pre-sessional and postgraduate programmes for the School of Education and CELE at the University of Nottingham.

Email: irina.hawker@nottingham.ac.uk

JULIE WATSON is an Emeritus Fellow of the University of Southampton. She was formerly Principal Teaching Fellow and Head of eLearning in Modern Languages, where she taught and supervised postgraduate students. She led the eLanguages research and development team and designed online courses and resources such as the EAP Toolkit, LOC Tool and the Prepare for Success website for international students. She retired in July 2016.

Email: juliewatson487@gmail.com